LEARNING AND VOLUNTEERING ABROAD FOR DEVELOPMENT

Learning/volunteer abroad programmes provide opportunities for cross-cultural understanding, partnership-building, and cooperative development, but there are also significant structural challenges and inequality of opportunity issues that result from these partnerships between host organizations in the Global South and learning/volunteer abroad for development (LVA4D) participants from the Global North. *Learning and Volunteering Abroad for Development* aims to unpack the complex benefits and disadvantages of learning/volunteer abroad programmes, using insights from the volunteers who travel abroad and the communities who host them.

Based on empirical research within both volunteer and host communities, this book provides students and scholars with an alternative framework for a more careful and nuanced analysis of international volunteering programmes, highlighting ways to improve critical reflection, development outcomes, and intercultural competence.

Supported by a website with additional learning resources, this book is an integral resource for senior undergraduate and graduate students interested in going abroad, as well as for scholars or development professionals who are leading or researching such programmes.

Rebecca Tiessen is Associate Professor, School of International Development and Global Studies, University of Ottawa, Canada.

Rethinking Development

Rethinking Development offers accessible and thought-provoking overviews of contemporary topics in international development and aid. Providing original empirical and analytical insights, the books in this series push thinking in new directions by challenging current conceptualizations and developing new ones.

This is a dynamic and inspiring series for all those engaged with today's debates surrounding development issues, whether they be students, scholars, policy makers and practitioners internationally. These interdisciplinary books provide an invaluable resource for discussion in advanced undergraduate and postgraduate courses in development studies as well as in anthropology, economics, politics, geography, media studies and sociology.

Celebrity Humanitarianism and North–South Relations
Politics, place and power
Edited by Lisa-Ann Richey

Education, Learning and the Transformation of Development
Edited by Amy Skinner, Matt Baillie Smith, Eleanor Brown and Tobias Troll

Learning and Volunteering Abroad for Development
Unpacking Host Organisation and Volunteer Rationales
Rebecca Tiessen

Communicating Development with Communities
Linje Manyozo

Multipolar Globalization
Emerging Economies and Development
Jan Nederveen Pieterse

LEARNING AND VOLUNTEERING ABROAD FOR DEVELOPMENT

Unpacking Host Organization and Volunteer Rationales

Rebecca Tiessen

Routledge
Taylor & Francis Group

LONDON AND NEW YORK

First published 2018
by Routledge
2 Park Square, Milton Park, Abingdon, Oxon OX14 4RN

and by Routledge
711 Third Avenue, New York, NY 10017

Routledge is an imprint of the Taylor & Francis Group, an informa business

British Library Cataloguing-in-Publication Data
A catalogue record for this book is available from the British Library

Library of Congress Cataloging-in-Publication Data
Names: Tiessen, Rebecca, 1970– author.
Title: Learning and volunteering abroad for development : unpacking host
    organisation and volunteer rationales / Rebecca Tiessen.
Description: Abingdon, Oxon ; New York, NY : Routledge, 2017. |
Series: Rethinking development | Includes bibliographical references.
Identifiers: LCCN 2016057291| ISBN 9781138746961 (hbk) |
    ISBN 9781138746978 (pbk)
Subjects: LCSH: Voluntarism—Developing countries. | Volunteer workers in
    community development—Developing countries. | Volunteer workers in
    education—Developing countries. | International education. |
    Experiential learning.
Classification: LCC HN981.V64 T54 2017 | DDC 361.3/7091724—dc23
LC record available at https://lccn.loc.gov/2016057291

ISBN: 978-1-138-74696-1 (hbk)
ISBN: 978-1-138-74697-8 (pbk)
ISBN: 978-1-351-70941-5 (ebk)

Typeset in Bembo
by Apex CoVantage, LLC

The book is supported by a website with additional learning resources, available at
http://globalcitizenshipedu.weebly.com

For Philip, Jonah, and Adrienne

"International youth volunteering is often portrayed as bad or good for development. This book sheds light on how it can be valued and improved, taking into account the structural inequalities at the root of global injustice. It highlights the crucial importance of solidarity, deeper global citizenship, and most importantly doing what local hosts need and want."

—*Peter Devereux, Curtin University Sustainability Policy Institute, Western Australia*

"This important and timely book is essential reading for anyone designing, facilitating, or participating in student learning/volunteer abroad programs. It tackles the complexity of the pedagogical and ethical tensions involved in cross-cultural teaching and learning, through critical insight into the experiences of volunteers and their host partners in developing countries."

—*Nichole Georgeou, Director of the Humanitarian and Development Studies Research Initiative (HADRI), Western Sydney University, Australia*

CONTENTS

ACKNOWLEDGEMENTS

My sincerest thanks to the many people who contributed to this book in some way, including 165 host organization staff and the 138 Canadian learners/volunteers who took part in interviews for this study. Many research assistants have contributed to data collection and analysis, and to the development of this book, including the locally based researchers who conducted interviews in the seven host countries. I would especially like to thank Katie Fizzell and Katie MacDonald and many other research assistants for their help over the past ten years. I also want to thank Dr Barbara Heron, who began this research journey with me in 2006 (ten years prior to the completion of this book). Barbara Heron's academic writing has been a source of great inspiration to me and working with her during the data-collection phase was immensely rewarding. I also wish to thank the International Development Research Centre for providing funding so that the research could be carried out and this book could be produced.

1

LEARNING/VOLUNTEER ABROAD FOR DEVELOPMENT (LVA4D) STARTS WITH UNPACKING

Introduction

Volunteer abroad programmes provide opportunities for cross-cultural exchange and knowledge-sharing for all individuals involved. For sojourners who take part in learning/volunteer abroad programmes, these placements also offer occasions for education, adventure, travel, personal growth, and skills/career-building. Furthermore, in the context of international development and global studies, volunteer programmes may be designed such that volunteers facilitate development partnerships and are able to contribute to development assistance. Host partners (the individuals who receive the volunteers and facilitate their volunteer placements in the partner countries) may see value in receiving international volunteers for personal, professional, and/or cooperative development reasons. This book explores in greater detail the rationales for participation in learning/volunteer abroad programmes from the perspectives of the individuals who go abroad and also the people who receive them. In addition to the individual roles and perspectives of the host organization staff and volunteers, this book examines those insights in the corresponding contexts of structural inequalities and desires for cooperative development, cross-cultural understanding, and international solidarity.

Throughout the book, I 'unpack' the rationales for participation in LVA4D programmes with examples emerging from interviews conducted in Canada and in seven countries in the Global South.[1] I situate the desires and aspirations of these study participants within the broader international development debates concerning partnership-building, cooperative development, international solidarity, and global citizenship. In this introductory chapter I outline some of the academic contributions to understanding development cooperation and return to these debates and frames of analysis throughout the chapters of the book to situate the empirical findings within the broader question: How do host organizations and international volunteers make sense of (unpack) and rationalize their participation in learning/volunteer abroad for development (LVA4D) programmes?

The development debates explored throughout the book include post-colonial critiques that question the role of North–South volunteerism in perpetuating inequality and reinforcing 'Othering', and more normative analyses of the value of international volunteering in support of international development priorities such as the Sustainable Development Goals (SDGs) or in the promotion of human capabilities (Nussbaum, 2011; Sen, 1999). Palacios (2010) argues that the success of volunteer abroad programmes depends on a distancing from development aid discourse and calls instead for the careful use of a volunteering language. However, international volunteering can foster international development outcomes through the dedication of committed volunteers. Host organizations and international volunteers alike see important development cooperation outcomes emerging from LVA4D programmes. However, ongoing challenges stemming from structural inequalities, expectations, as well as practical limitations of these programmes highlight important areas for improvement. For example, tackling negative or problematic attitudes of volunteers, charity-oriented approaches of development delivery (including helping imperatives and paternalistic approaches), and broader systemic issues (such as neo-colonialism and/or neo-imperialism) are central to improving learning/volunteer abroad programmes for both international volunteers and the host organization staff. Conducting interviews with volunteers and volunteer-receiving staff provides important insights into overlapping and distinct rationales for participation in these programmes. Some of these rationales must be examined in light of the critical scholarship on neo-colonial practice and/or neo-imperial motivations. However, other findings from the interviews point to goals of solidarity and mutual benefits, including commitments to cross-cultural understanding and international development outcomes. In particular, these rationales highlight a deep desire for intercultural engagement and interpersonal connections. There are also many practical reasons identified for participating in these programmes that highlight structural inequalities such as the perceived benefits of having a foreign volunteer working in a host organization for donor and/or community credibility for the organization's work. These diverse rationales are often overlapping in nature and need to be examined in relation to the active agency of the individuals involved in these programmes as they make carefully constructed decisions about the kind of participation they wish to have and how they negotiate structural inequalities in doing so. Heron (2015), furthermore, concludes that "it is also our responsibility to not impose these frames of interpretation [post-colonialism] on peoples in the global South, but rather to recognize that alternative views are operating" (p. 90). There is a need, then, for careful listening to what our host country partners have to tell us and how they themselves frame and interpret these experiences with international learners/volunteers.

Unpacking privilege as a starting point

Answering questions pertaining to why people participate in learning/volunteer abroad programmes necessitates an analysis of *who* can participate and in what capacity (by travelling abroad to volunteer or by hosting international volunteers). An important starting point for understanding why individuals participate, therefore, is an understanding of the privilege(s) accorded to those in the Global North. Deeper analysis of privilege is given below. The 'invisible knapsack' and 'unpacking' metaphors are useful in the deconstruction of volunteer privilege and to explore inequality of opportunity in the context of international development debates.

In 1989, Peggy McIntosh's article "White Privilege: Unpacking the Invisible Knapsack" offered an important critique of privilege focusing on both male privilege and white privilege. Her analysis sheds light on the privilege accorded to some groups – a privilege that often determines and maintains the disadvantage of others. McIntosh (1989) employed the metaphor of the invisible knapsack to convey the idea that those who hold privilege carry around that privilege wherever they go, even if they are not conscious of it. For volunteer abroad programmes, the knapsack – or backpack – is a fitting image given the nature of mobility associated with those who are able to volunteer abroad. It can also be symbolic of the heavy load – or burden – of host communities who work tirelessly to support and accommodate international volunteers. Throughout the book, white privilege is examined alongside other privileges accorded to those who can take time off from work or school to travel (time); the freedom to travel and cross national borders often without the need for visas (mobility); relative wealth enabling a select group of individuals to purchase passports, airline tickets, and often expensive volunteer abroad excursions or travel packages (affluence); and a particular status resulting in a combination of the above privileges as well as access to post-secondary education and/or work experience that enables young Northerners to travel abroad as 'development experts' (position). Thus, privileges are rooted in individual opportunities stemming from one's positionality that are not shared equally within and across countries. These privileges are often mirrored in the structural inequalities at the global level and they reinforce social, political, and economic capital, which facilitate the opportunities available to some, but not most, people in this world. Thus, while individual privilege is enacted on the personal level, it is also reflected in the structures that facilitate those privileges. Examples of the factors that facilitate this include the nature of aid funding allocated to LVA4D placements, access to travel visas, and access to student loans, travel bursaries, and other financial awards. The volunteer abroad opportunities for those who already have individual privileges further build their capital, thus conferring even greater privilege and opportunity to international volunteers.

The analysis of gender- and race-related privileges articulated by McIntosh are examined alongside the privileges accorded through other forms of opportunity and advantage, such as the privilege of striving for global citizenship status as well as those privileges corresponding to time, mobility, affluence, and position (noted above). Such privileges are intimately connected to the broad range of rationales for participation in volunteer abroad programmes, and can be understood through an analysis of important theoretical contributions within the field of International Development Studies.

McIntosh's employment of the invisible knapsack remains important now, more than 25 years later, in the context of LVA4D programmes, particularly for understanding privilege in relation to how participation in LVA4D is rationalized by international volunteers from the Global North. However, the rationales for participation in volunteer abroad (by hosting international volunteers) are less well understood. Throughout this book, I examine the rationales for participation in LVA4D as expressed through the transcripts of host country participants, and in connection with the Canadian volunteer interview responses.

Throughout this book, Peggy McIntosh's work is extended to unpacking additional forms of privilege, perceptions of privilege, access to privileges, and how such inequalities arising from privilege may be rationalized to ourselves and to others. The 'invisible backpack' is thus a physically and metaphorically significant aspect of what we carry with us in our communities and around the world, including the rationales we use to make sense of privilege in relation to our decisions and our rationalizations to take part in LVA4D programmes. An exercise in unpacking rationales enables a deconstruction of assumptions and taken-for-granted notions of why we do what we do, what we perceive to be the benefits of our contributions as volunteers and partners in LVA4D, and how our actions can reinforce or diminish outcomes that perpetuate inequality.

However, the analysis of privilege(s), motivations, and rationales has limited value if: (1) it does not lead to a thoughtful reflection and evaluation of LVA4D programmes that can ultimately contribute to improved programming; and (2) it offers little more than naval-gazing for those who engage in the reflection process. Critical reflection or hyper-reflexivity can therefore be of great value but must also coincide with carefully coordinated action for social change (Langdon and Agyeyomah, 2014). Similarly, critical analysis of volunteer abroad programmes must take into consideration the motivations and deeper rationales for participation as expressed by host country staff and community partners for the purpose of transforming LVA4D programmes such that positive outcomes are maximized and negative impacts are eliminated. The concluding chapter returns to these points with some insights into effective practices drawing on the experiences of LVA4D participants.

Making sense of North–South volunteering as one component of international volunteering practice

North–South volunteering takes many different forms and comprises diverse time frames, which are examined in greater detail in Chapter 2. In this book, the focus of analysis is medium-term (3–6 months) volunteer placements as part of broader international development initiatives (or LVA4D). Studies documenting the contributions of national and international volunteering offer a much more expansive frame for examining the impacts of volunteers. For example, the Voluntary Services Overseas (VSO) report *Valuing Volunteering*, in collaboration with the Institute of Development Studies in the United Kingdom, documents the diverse and significant ways that volunteering can contribute to poverty reduction and sustainable development (VSO, 2015). The United Nations Volunteers (UNV) Programme calls for increased volunteer participation to realize the SDGs, which are designed to facilitate development programming between 2015 and 2030. These studies remind us that there is immense potential for – and existing practise of – international (South–South) volunteering for sustainable development (a new vision that is distinct from old-school colonial practices centred on North–South relations). There are volunteer cooperation organizations – of the not-for-profit variety, in particular – that have made a focus on the SDGs a priority. Such organizations situate these commitments in the context of a new paradigm of 'everyone's development' and mutual learning and in terms of a global commitment rather than a donor imperative to offer solutions to development 'problems' elsewhere. Yet there is a large and growing sector of for-profit volunteer-sending organizations that continue to position the often privileged international volunteer as the 'helper' or 'solution-provider' in relation to those characterized as needing help, charity, and/ or development. While the for-profit sector providing international volunteering opportunities is a substantial part of the volunteer abroad community, it is not the focus of this book.

Situating the contributions of this book in the larger literatures

A vast collection of reflections and analyses on international volunteering and voluntourism is now available. Newspaper articles, op-eds, blog posts, documentaries, stories, and academic scholarship cover a range of perspectives and diverse analyses of the rationales for – and (to a lesser extent) impacts of – volunteer abroad programmes. Such discussions and debates are elaborated throughout this book and serve as reminders of the importance of careful empirical research. What sets this book apart from other reflections on volunteer abroad programmes is the focus on the rationales for participation in relation to critical and normative development scholarship. The analysis is specific to a particular sub-sector of volunteer abroad programmes which I term medium-term (3–6 months) LVA4D, particularly those programmes aimed at preparing students and recent graduates for careers in international development contexts. The participants in LVA4D programmes from the Global North may be trained in International Development Studies and/or are preparing to work in international development in some capacity (perhaps as aid workers, engineers, or nurses) whether as a temporary or life-long career goal. Study participants from the Global South (host organization staff and host community members) are directly involved in international development work through aid programming initiatives to address poverty and inequality in their own country.

The contribution of an analysis of rationales to the literature

In this book, a range of rationales for participation in LVA4D programmes are examined from the perspectives of the participants from the Global North, as well as the recipients of these volunteers in the volunteer-receiving organizations and communities in the Global South. More specifically, I examine the rationales and experiences of LVA4D participants in the context of broader international development debates. These rationales are the basis for Chapters 3 through 6 and enable a deeper reflection on core motivations such as cross-cultural understanding, skills development and career training, personal growth, travel and adventure, and helping obligations. By situating the rationales for participation in LVA4D programmes in the broader debates within International Development Studies and the volunteer abroad literature, this book underscores the value of unpacking rationales for improved practice in LVA4D programmes. These debates highlight volunteer privilege and inequality of opportunity, as well as the significance of learning and mutual understanding for 'global citizenship' and global competence.

To set the stage for a deeper and more nuanced analysis of the rationales for participation in LVA4D, this book begins by examining several motivations for LVA4D identified by the study participants. In Chapter 2, a comprehensive and quantitative assessment of motivations identified by the study participants is provided. The most prevalent motivations for participation in LVA4D as identified by the Canadian participants include: cross-cultural understanding, skills development and career preparation, personal growth, travel and adventure, and helping obligations. The host country participants provided a number of their own motivations for participation in these programmes, including: interpersonal connections and cross-cultural exposure, helping hands and small contributions, fresh perspectives, sharing of specific skills, and real or perceived credibility (to donors and the broader community) brought by the presence of foreign staff. These motivations can be analysed in a number of ways reflecting both positive and negative outcomes as identified by both the Canadian participants and the host organization staff. Yet, the expression of rationales attached to these motivations provides a deeper analysis of the justifications for taking part in these LVA4D programmes. The rationales include cross-cultural desires that can contribute to solidaristic values and connections; human capabilities-oriented claims expressed in terms of carefully calculated decisions to host or not host international volunteers; capital gains – whether cultural, political, economic, or social capital; helping desires that are expressed in both individualistic and community-oriented ways; and global citizenship identities that encapsulate many of the previous rationales in distinct and overlapping ways. As such, the rationales provide a more complex and nuanced consideration of the motivations expressed by the participants by highlighting agency, power, and structural inequalities. The study participants are discussed in greater depth in Chapter 2. The qualitative and open-ended interviews with Canadian youth and host country participants enabled the participants to elaborate and provide nuance in their reflections and thereby to explore a deeper set of perspectives, beyond what quantitative surveys can normally provide.

Throughout this book the research study on LVA4D is situated within the broader literature and debates on volunteering abroad and development. One of the major sets of debates and analyses begins with reflection on motivations for participation in international volunteerism. While many of the motivations for participation from participants in the Global North stem from well-meaning individuals with good intentions, the motivations are often articulated as egoistic or self-oriented, with many references to the extrinsic rewards obtained by the Northern participants (Tiessen, 2012).

The reasons for participation in volunteer abroad programmes, from the perspective of volunteer-receiving organization staff, is less well known as fewer studies have documented their experiences and rationales for participation. Scholarship by Perold *et al.* (2012) offers one example of the small body of literature exploring host country perspectives. Other studies include a collection edited by Marianne Larsen titled *International Service Learning: Engaging Host Communities* (2015). In this collection, a selection of authors examine the impact of international service learning (ISL) in the Global South. Studies focusing more exclusively on the experience of international volunteering include work by Benjamin Lough, such as: *Global Partners for Sustainable Development: The Added Value of Singapore International Foundation Volunteers* (2016), *Participatory Research on the Contributions of International Volunteerism in Kenya: Provisional Results* (2012b), and *Measuring and Conveying the Added Value of International Volunteering* (2013). This contemporary scholarship builds on a small but growing sample of literature offering insights into the host community and host organization perspectives of the impacts of learning/volunteer abroad programmes (see Illich, 1968; Crabtree, 2008; Grusky, 2000; Ogden, 2008). For much of the scholarship on learning/volunteer abroad or ISL, the focus has been divided between the research and literature on student/volunteer experiences and host country evaluations. A particular limitation of this literature is the lack of connections between these experiences between students/volunteers and the hosts/partners.

An important contribution of this book is therefore the bridging of these bodies of literature by bringing together and simultaneously reflecting on host country and Canadian volunteer perspectives on motivations and rationales for participation in volunteer abroad programmes. The analysis of the rationales from the perspectives of the participants themselves provides a richer agency-oriented framework for evaluating the successes and challenges of volunteer abroad programmes (see Tiessen, Lough and Cheung, forthcoming). Throughout the book, I attach significant value to the voices and views of the participants in this study. To ignore their perspectives on participation in volunteer abroad programmes denies them their agency and perpetuates the colonial continuities of paternalism and marginalization. It is also a limited approach to representing the experiences of host and Canadian youth participants as my own biases, expectations, and understandings will, no doubt, influence how I interpret the empirical findings. In fact, this methodological challenge has been a central focus of the analysis in this book, where a more balanced and open-minded approach to the potential positive contributions of LVA4D has emerged as a result of the careful attention to these voices. There is immense analytical value in understanding the larger context of international development: the gendered, historical, political, social, economic, and environmental context in which volunteer for development programmes are designed (the framework that generally guides my examination of LVA4D and has been challenged through the interpretation of agency-oriented reflections in the interview transcripts). This context includes neo-colonial practices, inequality of opportunity, and other injustices. Participants in volunteer abroad programmes navigate this complex context, and rationalize their participation in it in diverse ways that are captured in this book. They also attempt to mitigate some of the inequalities that emerge in the context of structural inequalities, and these strategies are important to the nuanced analysis of international volunteer impacts.

In the process of 'unpacking' rationales for participation in LVA4D, diverse motivations ranging from personal incentives or egoistic rationales to broader global citizenship or solidarity interests are uncovered. The findings emerging from this analysis of motivations is the broader structural context in which participants rationalize their participation in LVA4D. A post-colonial analysis, for example, can portray that context as problematic in so far as inequality can be reinforced, privileged positions can be entrenched, and social injustice may prevail through LVA4D initiatives. The post-colonial critique is used throughout this book to explore a range of factors that perpetuate inequality between the Global North and Global South. A post-colonial analysis rejects the assumption that colonial and empirical practices have ended. Rather, in a post-colonial context, colonial continuities remain powerful forces that reinforce inequality through structural relations. As a critical theory, post-colonial analyses provide insights into the nature of the language and practices used to entrench power in the hands of those who already experience comparative advantage and privilege. A critical lens through post-colonialism offers insights into some of the discursive ways that power and inequality are maintained through the images, norms, practices, and language used in the articulation of international volunteer experiences. The language and images of the 'white, privileged saviour' helping the 'Other' in former colonies of the Global South are problematized and analysed in the context of continuities and change. In so doing, the discursive analysis speaks to the rationales underlying the North–South volunteer abroad milieu.

However, other rationales for participation in LVA4D are not fully explained through a post-colonial analysis and another lens is needed to examine desires for global citizenship, deep cross-cultural engagement, aspirations of social justice and solidarity, and ultimately the agency of individuals to choose to participate in LVA4D programmes. The Capability Approach (building on the works of Amartya Sen and Martha Nussbaum), for example, facilitates an alternative perspective on the potential of LVA4D in terms of expanding capabilities of all participants in relation to development outcomes and relationship formation in intercultural contexts. International development volunteers *may* be integral to global development (Korten, 1990); and they *may* also constitute new spaces of development partnerships (Schech et al., 2015). As such, international volunteers *may* indeed serve as highly valuable partners working towards community development (UNDP, 2003). The word 'may' is put in italics here to reinforce the point that there is great variation within and between programmes. There are also diverse experiences from the volunteers and hosts alike that need to be situated in broader contexts of inequality.

Nonetheless, there are prospects for important social change vis-à-vis volunteer abroad programmes as this book outlines. Volunteer abroad programmes promoting development outcomes are therefore attractive options for those who aspire to work in international development contexts, and the volunteers who take part in these programmes may offer valuable contributions to development programmes and projects. Host communities may see benefit in their participation in volunteer abroad placements for a variety of reasons, including development outcomes, cross-cultural understanding, and a desire for international collaboration, as well as more instrumentalist rationales such as perceived value in the presence of a foreigner working in an organization's office or assistance with attracting donor funding.

Critical theoretical frameworks

Several bodies of literature and theoretical frameworks have been employed to understand international development trends and structural inequality in International Development Studies. For example, a post-colonialism framework offers important insights for making sense of the relationships, ethical issues, and cross-cultural experiences (as a continuation – though under different circumstances and with different practices – of colonialism) and North–South relations. Thus, post-colonial analysis and other critical development scholarship are employed throughout the book to situate the rationales presented by host country participants and Canadian volunteers. A post-colonial lens combined with additional critical theoretical perspectives (such as critical race theory) have been the central focus of important scholarly contributions by scholars such as Barbara Heron in her analysis of the 'helping imperatives' in her book *Desire for Development* (Heron, 2007). In other international development scholarship, Maria Erikson-Baaz (2005) examines the paternalistic attitudes of Northern donor agencies and their development workers who represent themselves as knowing what is best for 'others' (in this case, Tanzanians). Similar critiques are employed in relation to analyses of neoliberalism and individualism in Nancy Cook's analysis of the desire on the part of white Western women to serve as 'role models' and to guide the actions and behaviours of people encountered in Pakistan (2007). In this critical scholarship, the motivations that are expressed by the Northern volunteers and development workers are rooted in race-based attitudes and the studies document how racism can shape the impacts of international development work and the nature of relationships formed in the host country. These analyses provide important cautionary frameworks for understanding the often negative or problematic impacts of volunteering for development. The analysis presented in this book draws on these critical studies of 'othering', including an analysis of the 'subaltern' by including the voices of the participants from the Global South. The value of these critical insights can be found in the reflection on deeper structural issues and how personal attitudes and approaches can be reflected in – and also strive to defy – broader colonial challenges including colonial continuities. These analytical frameworks are useful for understanding helping imperatives or ways of seeing the world in terms of 'problems' in the Global South requiring solutions from the 'Global North', examined in greater depth in Chapter 7, or the quest for an 'authentic' experience (examined in Chapter 5) reflecting perceptions held by some international volunteers in relation to the communities they expect to find when volunteering abroad.

Understanding rationales and motivations for participation in LVA4D involves analysing notions of global citizenship and the perceived value of this construct for the Canadian volunteers and the host community participants alike. An examination of the literature on global citizenship and cosmopolitanism exposes the employment of both dichotomies and overlaps in terms of individualism/solidarity, thin/thick cosmopolitanism (Cameron, 2014), and soft/critical global citizenship education (Andreotti, 2006). Other studies have fostered an improved understanding around motivations for LVA4D in the context of egoistic versus altruistic motivations (Tiessen, 2014; Otoo, 2013).

An important contribution of this book builds on the analysis of motivations (as egoistic or solidaristic) to a more complex analysis of how rationales for participation are articulated in multilayered and non-binary terms whereby problematic structural inequalities are navigated in highly strategic ways by informed participants who enact their power and agency in complex ways.

Interviews with host communities demonstrate how the experience of hosting international volunteers is structurally problematic but the host participants do not see themselves as 'victims' of the effects of neo-colonialism and neoliberalism. The international volunteers do not consider themselves fully implicated in the systemic processes that perpetuate inequality and may actively pursue social justice models to enact change. Normative theoretical lenses have value, then, for making sense of thematic and conceptual notions that inform LVA4D programmes. Commitments to reciprocity, mutuality, global and intercultural competencies, ethics, and social justice point to human capabilities and human development theories characterized by people-centred, participatory, and partnership-oriented strategies of international development, all of which are explored in the analysis throughout the chapters of this book, along specific thematic lines.

In Martha Nussbaum's (2011) evaluation of a capability theory of justice, she provides a list of fundamental capabilities including life, bodily health, and bodily integrity, as well as imagination and thought, emotions, practical reason, and affiliation, among several other fundamental capabilities such as other species, play, and control over one's environment. The focus on respecting human dignity is apparent in this list and several capabilities can clearly be linked to the potential benefit of international volunteering, particularly in relation to affiliation: living and working with others, showing concern for others, and imagining the situation of others (empathy). In order to ensure these attributes, Nussbaum argues that we must protect the institutions that enable improved affiliation and relationships. Employing the normative frame of justice through a capabilities approach underscores the potential for improved quality of life across the globe (Nussbaum, 2011). This analysis of capabilities draws from, and builds on, Amartya Sen's (1999) analysis of development as opportunities for capabilities expansion beyond the expansion of material goods. This normative framework allows for the consideration of other human capabilities and improvements stemming from good health or meaningful or loving relationships, for example. International volunteering can play an important role in facilitating friendships and meaningful cross-cultural relationships forged in a spirit of solidarity, and with a commitment to addressing inequality.

However, the capabilities approach must also be understood in the context of the broader structural inequalities that reinforce injustices. As such, the focus on agency and capacity of individuals and organizations to effect change must also coincide with the deconstruction of systems of oppression, neo-colonialism, and neo-imperialism. The imperial continuities can be understood in relation to the power exerted through volunteer-sending countries in the Global North in relation to Global South recipients. As an extension of foreign relations and public diplomacy, international volunteers play a role in projecting the donor country values abroad (Tiessen, 2010). The extension of colonial-like power enables the transmission of a particular set of values, approaches, and acceptable practices. Volunteer nations, thus, play a significant role in determining the rules of such international interactions. Critical development scholarship addressing volunteer abroad programmes within the lenses of post-colonialism or critical race theory thus offers immense value for reflection on the structural and discursive constraints to the promotion of equality and human capabilities, and must be part of the transformative thinking in international development scholarship. Nonetheless, critical development scholarship focusing on post-colonialism is often juxtaposed against the more normative scholarship on global citizenship or cosmopolitanism, such that these two frames of analysis are often considered completely incompatible with each other.

Situating the research findings for this book in these two distinct sets of scholarship offers a more balanced, comprehensive, and nuanced analysis of the findings, as well as insights for improving volunteer abroad programmes by establishing effective practices that include solidarity imperatives and global justice.

Summary

A commitment to learning and critical reflexivity enables thoughtful reflection on the impact of our assumptions, values, and actions (in international development) as the central goal of learning from and with each other in cross-cultural and global contexts. Nonetheless, post-colonialism serves as an important starting point for reflection on the broader structural limitations of global interactions in the context of widespread inequality within and between countries. The research presented in this book contributes to our understanding of *why* host country staff members and international volunteers in LVA4D participate in this initiative; however, much of what arises from the reflections on rationales points to broader implications of how volunteering abroad can be simultaneously harmful and helpful.

This introductory chapter has unpacked some of the core issues required to make sense of inequality of opportunity and inequitable power structures reinforcing benefits and challenges. The scholarly literature on LVA4D offers a range of analytical frameworks from post-colonialism to global citizenship and human capabilities. Both sets of scholarship offer insights into the rationales for participation in LVA4D and are examined in greater detail and in reference to the study findings throughout the chapters of this book. Post-colonial development scholarship and global citizenship literature provide insights into privileges that are divided within and across borders. These privileges are part of the invisible backpack. Beyond privileges accorded along gender and racial lines are other privileges that need to be examined, including the privilege of time, mobility, affluence, and position. The rationales for participation in LVA4D programmes are the central focus of this book. However, understanding these rationales requires careful attention to the changing landscape of international volunteering opportunities, and the trends and development outcomes arising from them. Many of the motivations and desires are overlapping and difficult to articulate. I disentangle the diverse perspectives by examining the common themes that emerged in the interview responses while also presenting the complexity of the rationales by providing a range of voices and quotes from the participants who took part in this study. Desires for global citizenship identity, intercultural understanding, and/or social justice are important rationales for participation in LVA4D, as articulated by the study participants. These rationales are situated within the broader scholarly debates throughout the chapters of this book. Before turning to these rationales, however, information about the study – including the research methods, the study participants, and an overview of the motivations for participation – is presented in Chapter 2.

Note

1 The term Global South is used to recognize the wide-scale poverty and inequality faced by people around the globe. The Global South includes those who live in poverty in North America, Europe, and other more developed countries. The majority of the people living in what is defined as the Global South, however, are in nations in Africa, Central and Latin America, and large parts of Asia where poverty and inequality are widespread, resources are often limited, health conditions may be poor, poverty can be endemic, and inequality between rich and poor may be extreme. The countries listed as less developed by the United Nations Human Development Index comprise approximately 157 of the total of 184 countries of the world. While there are pockets of immense wealth and also middle-class communities in the less developed countries of the world, there is also a very high percentage of poverty, and often of extreme poverty (people living on less than $1.25 per day). The Global South is thus defined here as the pockets of poverty that exist around the world resulting from historical and contemporary global policies and practices that deepen inequalities between and within regions. The participants from the Global South for this study are residents of seven countries: Zambia, Malawi, South Africa, India, Guatemala, Peru, and Jamaica. From an international development perspective, the North–South dimension is an important part of the analysis throughout this book as reflections from both host country participants and Canadian youth who travel abroad for LVA4D programmes are examined.

2

AN OVERVIEW OF THE DIVERSE VOLUNTEER ABROAD OPTIONS, TRENDS, AND MOTIVATIONS

In this chapter, the diverse definitions and approaches to learning/volunteer abroad for development (LVA4D) programmes are examined. Several characteristics and trends in international volunteering are important to consider in order to navigate a large and growing number of options available to those who wish to engage in development cooperation through volunteerism. This chapter situates the sample from the empirical research presented in this book within the broader forms and experiences of volunteer abroad programmes. A survey of the literature and data on diverse volunteering abroad options underscores many important themes and delineations pertaining to *how* and *why* volunteers and host organizations participate in volunteer abroad programmes. This chapter begins with an examination of how volunteers participate in programmes abroad and the kinds of programmes available to prospective volunteers. To make sense of the vast array of volunteer abroad options, a typology is presented specific to length of time abroad combined with other important overlapping features for short-, medium-, and long-term volunteer abroad placements. The focus of the study presented here – LVA4D – is defined as medium-term volunteer abroad programmes with expectations of high levels of development cooperation and partnership-building. In particular, the Canadian participants in this sample went abroad on medium-term (approximately 3–6-month placements) and were specifically interested in development-related outcomes as well as personal-oriented benefits. Here, medium-term LVA4D placements are considered a form of volunteerism but distinct from other options for volunteer abroad such as voluntourism (very short stays and limited connections between volunteers and hosts) or long-term volunteering (of one year or longer, in which deep intercultural relations are expected to emerge).

Related to this typology is an important consideration of the trends that are associated with length of time abroad as well as the nature of the programmes that correspond with these diverse time frames. The categorization of programmes enables a positioning of the research participants in this study. Details of the study sample are therefore included in the characterization of programmes.

Following the delineation of programmes and related trends, this chapter turns to an analysis of why volunteering abroad programmes have gained popularity, and why the volunteers and hosts choose to participate in them. Many of these motivations for participation are linked to broader trends. However, the introduction to motivations serves as an overarching guide to some of the broader rationales for participation in learning/volunteer abroad programmes as they relate to (or not) development cooperation and partnership-building in the Global North/Global South contexts. The core motivations – as an initial and 'unpacked' summary of several core themes emerging in the research as the reasons why LVA4D volunteers and host partners participate in these programmes – are presented at the end of this chapter to provide an overview of themes that are the focus of the chapters that follow. These core motivations are then elaborated and complicated by employing a careful analysis of the voices of the study participants and the structural context that helps us make sense of rationales for participation.

Diverse time frames: short-, medium-, and long-term options

In this section I highlight important differences between short-, medium-, and long-term volunteer abroad programmes, particularly in the context of North–South international volunteering. However, this is but one form of international volunteering around the world. Opportunities for international volunteering may also involve South–South interactions. For example, Tanzanian volunteers may be posted to rural Zimbabwe for skills-sharing and mutual learning in agricultural practices or nutrition awareness. The United Nations Volunteers (UNV), which was formed in 1970 by a United Nations General Assembly Resolution (2659), recognized the role of volunteer service in international development work. The UNV programme currently hosts approximately 8,000 volunteers working in development assistance, humanitarian aid, and peacekeeping operations around the world, with an expectation that the UN volunteer will serve for a minimum of one year (or long term). While the UNV programme offers a range of volunteer abroad placements, in 2012, 81 per cent of the UN volunteers were from the South, working in the areas of capacity-building and delivery of basic services, among other environment, security, and development goals (UNV, 2014). Thus, the larger number of volunteer opportunities through the South–South Cooperation programme within the UNV is an important component of international volunteering.

Nonetheless, the focus of this book is on the particular dynamic of volunteers from the Global North (in this case Canada) travelling to the Global South (a sample of seven countries: Malawi, Zambia, South Africa, India, Peru, Guatemala, and Jamaica) for learning/volunteer abroad (LVA) programmes. When research for this study first began in 2007, short-term was defined as a 3–6-month placement abroad. This definition of short-term volunteerism, however, did not resonate with the Canadian study participants who considered their placements of 3–6 months to be 'long' relative to other experiences they had had or had observed of their peers. Short-term programmes were defined by the Canadian youth participants as 1–2 weeks in duration. Given the difference in understanding of 'short' versus 'long' programmes between the researcher and the Canadian research participants, the need for a new category to describe 3–6-month placements became increasingly clear and therefore I introduce the concept of medium-term volunteer abroad programmes. As such, three frames are used in this section to distinguish three different kinds of programmes, both in terms of the amount of time the volunteers spent abroad: short (1–2 weeks), medium (3–6 months), and long (one year or longer). There are important gaps between these divisions, and some variation within them, but these three frameworks are nonetheless useful because they represent fairly common durations for the distinct types of programmes abroad.

Medium-term LVA programmes for development

LVA4D is examined, through the empirical research for – and the writing of – this book, as a distinct volunteer abroad option characterized by a particular period of time abroad (3–6 months); an emphasis on learning while volunteering; and a focus on college and university students or recent graduates who are motivated by a *desire* to work in international development contexts (whether as aid workers, nurses, engineers, or a variety of other professions) and to contribute to development cooperation. In the section that follows, I distinguish LVA4D from other forms of volunteer abroad programmes: namely voluntourism (short-term) and long-term international volunteerism. The kinds of programmes examined for this book have been narrowed down to provide a richness and depth of analysis for those specific to Canadian-based youth who volunteered in the Global South on 3–6-month placements. Nonetheless, there may be parallels between LVA4D as defined here and other forms of volunteer abroad programmes.

LVA4D is thus defined as medium-term placements in international development contexts, primarily in the Global South, where participants from the Global North participate in internship programmes in collaboration with international development host partners. These unpaid 'internships' (as the participants in my study preferred to call them) often last between three and six months. As internships or volunteer abroad programmes, they are distinct from traditional study abroad programmes as there is a practical work component. LVA4D is generally characterized by some pre-departure orientation and, at times, a post-placement de-briefing. Many of the participants in my sample are studying – or have been trained in – International Development Studies (IDS) (or related programmes such as Global Studies) and therefore have as much as three or four years (or more) of pre-departure preparation through their academic studies. Other participants in this study have an interest in international development issues and are often actively engaged in activities and events related to international issues. The placements themselves are frequently carried out with international development organizations, including government agencies, non-governmental organizations (NGOs), or community groups where pre-departure preparation is normally a core part of the training. In these medium-placements, LVA4D participants are expected to act as development professionals and to work as colleagues with host country partners. As such, there is a significant emphasis on completing 'development work' through these medium-term learning/ volunteer placements. A further defining feature of LVA4D is the emphasis on education, cross-cultural learning, and development outcomes. Many of the participants from the Global North are students or recent graduates who have used their experiences abroad as part of their formative training in preparation for working in international development careers – or careers that may involve global development work in Canada or abroad. Some of the participants in LVA4D may receive academic credit for their practicum placements abroad while others may complete such internships during their studies (in some cases mandatory co-op programmes) or after graduation as part of their skills development and training considered necessary for finding full-time employment, or to test a career choice. LVA4D is distinguished from short-term and long-term volunteer abroad programmes for several reasons that are outlined in the sections that follow.

Very short-term placements: voluntourism

One of the most popular options for going abroad to learn about international development work is through voluntourism initiatives. While voluntourism is distinct from volunteer abroad programmes, a short discussion about these programmes and their popularity is warranted. Voluntourism programmes of 1–2 weeks can be described as a short-term travel abroad practical experience, often combined with a travel holiday. There are specific studies dedicated to voluntourism and these studies are often found in journals specific to studies of tourism. Volunteer tourism is explained by Lyons and Wearing (2008) as a form of alternative tourism. It is a highly contested term because it is used to describe "a wide range of tourist behaviours and tourism products and services" (Lyons and Wearing, 2008: 6). Voluntourism is popular among all age groups because it is something that can take place during study breaks, annual leave, or other holiday time. It generally consists of travel and adventure combined with a volunteer experience. For some, the short trip to volunteer is the adventure or holiday in and of itself. Some cruise lines now offer volunteer abroad cruise packages. The cruise ship model allows consumers to pay standard fare for a basic cruise and for a day of training on cross-cultural and/or development education. Those who do these cruises are then given an opportunity to volunteer for one or two days in schools on a Caribbean island. This alternative form of tourism raises a number of questions that cannot yet be answered (due to lack of research to date), such as the nature of the training, the kinds of volunteer experiences, as well as the environmental impacts and sustainability implications. There are also important questions to be raised about the quality of cross-cultural understanding and development outcomes that are possible from very short programmes of 1–2 days or 1–2 weeks, and also as a result of the nature of the programmes whereby foreigners travel in large groups or 'bubbles' with minimal contact with the local cultures, communities, and people.

Other scholarship has addressed what are perceived to be positive impacts of volunteer tourism (see: Lyons and Wearing, 2008; Stebbins and Graham, 2004). Voluntourism may include a particular focus on '*development* work'. Wearing (2001) argued that this alternative form of tourism has the potential to lead to changed lifestyles for the voluntourists and to contribute to *community development* in the voluntourist destinations. The terms 'development' and 'community development' are in italics here because these aspirations and perceived outcomes are scrutinized widely in the literature (see McGloin and Georgeou, 2015; Vodopivec and Jaffe, 2012). Some of the common 'development outcomes' of voluntourism include building schools, painting facilities, and/or caring for orphaned children. The contributions to 'development' in such programmes is advertised in relation to having an impact on local communities, providing short-term services, and bringing resources and volunteer labour through charitable programmes. Many important critiques of the 'development failures' resulting from voluntourism programmes are now widely publicized in scholarly literature and popular media. Campaigns to end orphan tourism (a popular form of voluntourism) have highlighted the harm that such programmes cause to communities and to individuals (see Reas, 2013; Guiney and Mostafanezhad, 2014). Other problematic development outcomes of voluntourism are examined in the paragraphs that follow. Voluntourism or volunteer tourism, in spite of a large number of important development critiques, is one of the fastest-growing forms of tourism (Lyons and Wearing, 2008) and is often wrongly conflated with international volunteering.

Returning to the metaphor of 'unpacking' examined earlier in the previous chapter, the short-term, voluntourism option presents interesting questions around the ability of participants to make sense of their own privilege in relation to what they have observed in their short time abroad. Short programmes run by for-profit companies are less likely to invest in substantive pre-departure training for their participants. Thus, the ability to unpack and consider the role of the voluntourist in relation to structures of global inequality limits their capacity to reflect on their own privilege and positioning in the world. A more literal employment of the idea of 'unpacking' is of interest to this analysis too, as voluntourists may never really unpack their backpacks in such short time frames, often rushing off for excursions on weekends or, in the case of 1–2-day volunteer projects, would find no need to unpack in the first place.

Voluntourism can be distinguished from other forms of short-term volunteering programmes such as professional volunteer placements of short time frames as well as from medium- and long-term international development volunteering for several reasons, not the least of which is the amount of time dedicated to living and volunteering overseas and the broader connections and partnerships that may exist before and after the placements. McGloin and Georgeou (2015) offer a comprehensive analysis and distinction between voluntourism and development volunteering. The distinctions between these programmes include (but are not limited to) an emphasis placed on individual experiences of the voluntourist through tourism and adventure, at the expense of development work. Furthermore, voluntourism programmes may be coordinated by for-profit companies, so it is therefore "an economic activity driven by profit occurring within an unregulated industry and operating without any accreditation process" (McGloin and Georgeou, 2015: 3). Voluntourism may also be facilitated by charity-oriented groups such as religious institutions and corporate tourism operators with little or no development cooperation mandate or training.

Voluntourism must be examined, then, as a contrast to development volunteering or LVA, and to international development volunteer programmes that are frequently organized by NGOs or governmental agencies as an extension of the services or official development assistance they deliver to developing countries where some volunteers have, throughout history, joined social – or solidarity – movements to end inequality and poverty (Vodopivec and Jaffe, 2012). As such, medium- and long-term international development volunteering programmes include programmes offered by organizations such as WUSC (World University Service of Canada) and CUSO (formerly Canadian University Services Overseas) in the Canadian context, or the Peace Corps in the United States. These programmes are often partially funded through government funding and the funds may be re-directed through volunteer-sending organizations, with a portion of the funds raised by the participants themselves.[1] The volunteer-sending organizations involved in international development volunteer placements may therefore receive large sums of money to support their programmes. Unstead-Joss' (2008) study of Voluntary Service Overseas funding from the United Kingdom's Department for International Development (DfID) found that DfID has channelled approximately 30 million British pounds in just a three-year period to fund volunteer-sending organizations. The growth in the number of programmes and participants is also reflected in the dividends; volunteering abroad is now a multi-billion-dollar industry around the world (CBC, 2015).

Voluntourism, on the other hand, is largely managed by for-profit companies and the programmes are paid for wholly by the participants themselves, therefore precluding individuals who may not have the means to pay the full cost of such a package. Costs of voluntourism programmes vary, but it is not uncommon for voluntourist participants to pay more than $5,000 for one week of volunteer/tourism/ adventure in a developing country.

Long-term volunteerism

In the United States, the Peace Corps programme has offered, for more than seven decades, two-year and longer placements abroad. Many countries offer long-term volunteer abroad positions lasting one year or longer. In Canada, these opportunities can be found in programmes offered by WUSC and CUSO, among other programmes. Participants in long-term volunteer abroad programmes may prefer job titles such as Development Worker or Cooperant to reflect an advanced skill-set and/or the nature of their roles abroad. Long-term volunteer abroad programmes are thus characterized by professional development-related work of one year or longer abroad. Participants on long-term volunteer abroad programmes may receive monthly stipends and cost-recovery or other benefits comparable to paid or partially paid employment. Long-term volunteer abroad programmes are considered opportunities for deeper cultural engagement and more intensive personal and professional relationship formation with host partners and communities. Host country participants may also see long-term volunteering as an opportunity for building partnerships for sustainable or long-lasting development programmes. The Peace Corps, for example, advertises its two-year abroad programmes as opportunities to work directly with communities for the purpose of capacity-building in the areas of education, health, youth in development, environment, community economic development, and agriculture. While other volunteer-sending organizations like WUSC, CUSO, or VSO offer a range of programmes based on various lengths of time abroad, they also provide long-term volunteer options such as VSO's trained professionals programme for those with some experience in related development fields. In addition, VSO lists several criteria for long-term volunteers, such as: between 3–5 years of experience as a professional, a university degree, aged between 24 and 75, and availability of upwards of 24 months of work abroad. CUSO, a volunteer-sending programme that began offering placements for international volunteers (particularly for university students and recent graduates) in 1961, advertises its current mission in relation to skills-building and knowledge transfer for the purpose of bringing positive and lasting change in developing communities. Long-term volunteer abroad programmes frequently stress the importance of learning local languages as part of the professional experience abroad. Some of the programmes will offer intensive language training before work placements begin. Long-term international development volunteering gained popularity in the 1960s but we are witnessing an overall reduction in the number of participants engaged in these programmes relative to other short-term options (Heron, 2005a).

A critical analysis of long-term international volunteering comprising placements that are one year or longer can be found in the works of several influential authors, such as Ruth Unstead-Joss (2008), Barbara Heron (2007), Nancy Cook (2007), and Maria Eriksson-Baaz (2005), among others. Their assessments of long-term volunteer programmes include critical insights into privilege, depth of cross-cultural engagement, long-term impacts, and neo-colonial attitudes that may or may not change as a result of these experiences abroad. I return to these debates later in this chapter and throughout this book as they have implications for the study of all volunteer abroad programmes, regardless of the length of time abroad.

The characteristics of (medium-term) LVA4D may overlap with long-term international volunteering opportunities of two years and/or very short-term voluntourism options in terms of rationales for participation, including the quest for personal growth, adventure, cross-cultural engagement, and/or development and social justice. Some of these similarities, as well as differences, across the range of programmes will be addressed throughout this book. A growing interest in – and demand for – short-term volunteering programmes of approximately one week in duration has meant that there have been fewer discussions of other volunteer abroad options, such as their strengths and limitations. Thus, a segment of the volunteer abroad population that often gets overlooked in these assessments, yet one that is of particular interest to the field of IDS, is medium-term LVA options for those individuals who wish to pursue careers in international development contexts, whether as aid workers, community development experts, doctors, or engineers, among other areas of expertise.

The significance of the learning component in LVA4D

Beyond period of time spent abroad, LVA4D includes the notion of 'learning' as a central feature and is therefore an important educational experience and training opportunity for students or recent graduates. LVA4D participants may wish to combine practical work, applied research, learning, and/or studying, or some combination thereof in the context of international development work located in the Global South. Participants taking part in LVA4D may combine their volunteer or practicum work with their academic studies. Furthermore, the LVA4D experience has been, in the past few decades, a popular option for university and college students and recent graduates, and especially for those students and graduates of IDS programmes. The reason for the popularity of LVA4D time frames for university students and recent graduates may reflect what Foroughi, Langdon, and Abdou (2014) refer to as a stage in the "scaffolding of experiences" whereby young people may begin with a voluntourism programme in high school or early in their undergraduate programmes, but feel unsure of a commitment of one year or more abroad, yet keen to get development work experience that may propel them in their careers or prepare them better for the work they wish to pursue post-graduation. Thus, the period of 3–6 months is attractive to students and recent graduates, given their stage of life. Furthermore, the medium-term placements serve as a commonly perceived minimum requirement for accessing desired positions in their chosen field.

LVA4D may indeed assist in the development of a particular skill-set that Global North participants identify as valuable when applying for jobs, as discussed in greater detail in Chapter 4. Some of these skills, at times, link to broader development outcomes of mutuality, solidarity, and cross-cultural understanding. For example, cross-cultural – or mutual – learning can facilitate "critical literacy [and] involves relinquishing the development driver seat" (Cook, 2008: 24), thereby demonstrating the valuable partnership-building and mutuality that can emerge through carefully designed LVA4D placements, a point to which I return in Chapter 7.

Examples of LVA4D programmes

There are many opportunities for medium-term North–South volunteering. DfID in the United Kingdom announced in 2010 the launch of a programme called 'International Citizen Service', which focuses mainly on youth 18–22 years old who will work on projects aimed at improving the lives of some of the poorest people in the world. The international development volunteering programmes offered by DfID generally last three months or longer (DfID, 2011), and DfID provides some funds to the volunteers to cover the costs of international placements. Examples of government-subsidized, medium-term international development volunteering opportunities for Canadians have, in the past, included the NetCorps programme that enabled Canadian youth to volunteer in a developing country for a period of six months to teach technical skills. The Canadian government provided approximately $17,000 per volunteer to participate in the NetCorps programme. The total contribution of funds from Industry Canada to the NetCorps programme alone was $29,471,064 for the years 1999 to 2006. This amount of money paid for 1,713 volunteers to volunteer in a developing country (CIDA, 2007b). Thus, the financial investment provided by countries like the United Kingdom and Canada to support medium-term international development volunteer programmes is significant. Other popular programmes in the medium-term LVA4D category include semester abroad programmes and practicum placements for students who take an academic term to gain practical work experience in development. Some programmes have requirements for such international experiential learning options, while most universities and many colleges provide these programmes as options for students. Volunteer-sending organizations and NGOs also facilitate LVA4D programmes. The organization Engineers Without Borders (EWB) offers a four-month practical programme for its constituency, called the Junior Fellowship Program in International Development. Other examples include the Students for Development programme offered between 2005 and 2015 to more than 1,000 Canadian students who participated in internships in host communities in developing and emerging countries. The Uniterra programme (offered jointly by two NGOs: WUSC and CECI) provides opportunities to volunteer abroad for three to eight months through the Students Without Borders (SWB) initiative, among a larger number of programmes offered through this initiative. Other Canadian initiatives providing medium-term volunteer abroad practicum placements or internships were offered through the government of Canada, the former Department of Foreign Affairs, Trade and Development (DFATD) under the International Youth Internship Program (IYIP). IYIP placements were administered by partner organizations such as CUSO, where placements range from a few months to over one year.

LVA4D opportunities through university programmes

LVA programmes also include a wide range of practicum placements offered by universities and colleges. These options often involve a combination of practical work experience and an educational component (course work) or a focus on mutual learning in the Global South. Many LVA4D programmes offered by Canadian universities are administered by programmes or departments of IDS or Global Studies, among other departments, or through central administrative units that are popular with students in IDS/Global Studies programmes. There are more than 25 such undergraduate programmes in IDS/Global Studies available within Canada. Most universities within Canada offer courses on international development and/ or poverty in the developing world as part of other disciplines such as sociology or political science. Canadian universities are witnessing a burgeoning interest in programmes in IDS and international exchanges at all levels. Canadian youth are increasingly interested in addressing the challenges of global poverty and inequality and they see the means to do so as partly through an enhanced knowledge of the development enterprise. As the White Paper on IDS in Canada states: "The steady increase in IDS programs and graduates testifies to the fact that young people are eager to become engaged in this enterprise." (CASID and NSI, 2003: 16). The White Paper reflects on the nature of global citizenship in Canada by noting that:

> An informed, engaged public is vital if we are to sustain our internationalism in a country – and a world – where lives are becoming ever more interdependent … the need for a globally-engaged citizenry has never been greater, particularly at a time when Canada's role in a fast-integrating world faces mounting critical scrutiny.
>
> *(CASID and NSI, 2003: 16)*

What the above study in the White Paper on IDS in Canada does not fully account for is the growing number of students who desire opportunities to learn abroad through other disciplines. Students from diverse fields of medicine, nursing, social work, and engineering, among others, are demanding opportunities to learn and volunteer abroad and there are many such opportunities available to students across these and other fields of study.

There are numerous other opportunities offered through universities, and these options may change from year to year depending on the expertise or availability of the course facilitator, or perceived risks associated with travel in the host country, among other variables. Examples of Canadian university options for learning and volunteering abroad include the 'Trent in Ghana' and 'Trent in Ecuador' programmes, which entail four months in a classroom in Ghana or Ecuador followed by four months doing applied community work in those countries. Dalhousie University's term abroad in Cuba also combines classroom learning and practical, community-based learning. Some universities have adopted the language of international student mobility, (international) experiential learning, or international service learning to describe these programmes. Universities may offer academic courses in preparation for field courses tailored to the specific cultural, political, economic, and social conditions of the country or region to which they are travelling. Courses are also offered, in some programmes at some universities, to students upon their return to allow them to reflect on these experiences academically and personally. Students who participate in these specialized practicum courses or field schools generally must also attend preparatory meetings, prepare a work-study proposal, write a research paper on the placement, and maintain a journal on a continuing basis while on their placement. The investment in the learning and educational component of LVA4D can lay the groundwork for cooperative development and effective partnerships.

The growing number of options for LVA4D for college and university students is in part a response to the demands of the students themselves, but also a component of college- and university-wide strategies to increase student mobility options as part of internationalization efforts. Thus, some universities and organizations are pushing for pre-determined numbers or percentages of students to go abroad (CBIE, 2012). For example, some universities have made commitments to see 30 per cent or more of their students take part in some form of learning abroad programme; other departments and programmes have talked about or instituted requirements of travelling abroad. When concerns about the cost of going abroad are articulated, several programmes and organizations have suggested the countries in the Global South as a more cost-effective location for LVA, thereby creating a growing market for future study abroad programmes. In addition, many universities offer scholarships that can cover part of the costs of international placements.

While there is a growing recognition of the increasing popularity of LVA programmes, the impacts of these programmes – both on the participants and the recipients – is not well understood (Epprecht, 2004; Lough *et al.*, 2009; Tiessen and Heron, 2012a). However, a wealth of recent scholarship has begun to document, in greater detail, the impacts and implications of LVA programmes.

Anecdotal reflections on volunteer abroad programmes and individual experiences are presented as general trends in newspapers, magazines, blog sites, etc. While we may be increasingly fascinated by the phenomenon of volunteering abroad, we know less and less about this industry as it grows and transforms over time, particularly in terms of how host country partners make sense of these placements and the challenges and opportunities they experience.

To conclude the discussion on length of programme and delineating these diverse programme options in relation to short, medium, and long terms, it is necessary to consider the ongoing debates about the significance of the length of time abroad. Kauffmann, Martin, and Weaver (1992) suggest that an optimal length of stay is 6–12 months. Furthermore, research with volunteer-receiving organizations in seven developing countries found that the majority of host organization staff considered six months to be the minimum amount of time for an effective engagement with Northern volunteers (Heron, 2011). However, medium-term placements of 3–6 months have a wide appeal for those who want to have a more substantial work experience than that which is offered in a 1–2-week short-term (voluntourism) package and still want to fit these experiences into a summer term break, a semester abroad, or a short internship between studies and finding full-time employment. The distinction made between short-, medium-, and long-term abroad programmes is one of several ways of making sense of the range of opportunities for volunteering abroad and helps us begin to shed light on the trends and implications of these diverse options. Some of the literature on volunteer abroad programmes has made explicit reference to certain kinds of programmes, while other analyses have conflated volunteer abroad programmes into one category, providing sweeping conclusions about the broad range of volunteer abroad options.

Exploring trends and implications of the broad range of volunteer abroad options

In addition to the considerations around length of time, there are also important variations across the diverse programmes as they pertain to broader trends and perceived benefits between them. Aspiring development workers may choose long-term volunteering as the avenue for skills development, testing an academic career choice, and/or 'solving' development 'problems', among other rationales. And these motivations can share some similarities with voluntourism programmes, but also point to differences in terms of those who may wish to have an adventure combined with some form of 'helping'. It is important to highlight that there are also individuals who wish to make a career in international development work but have also made a conscious decision not to participate in any volunteer or internship abroad programmes for fear that they may do more harm than good. Nevertheless, several trends in volunteer abroad programmes correspond with specific time frames abroad and are worth noting as they help explain the broader context of the suite of volunteer abroad options.

A review of the contemporary scholarship on volunteer abroad programmes highlights several trends that help serve as additional contextual information for examining rationales for participation in volunteer abroad programmes. I summarize these trends in terms of: the growing numbers of volunteer abroad options; the surging number of people going abroad, particularly among participants as young as 14 years of age; the lucrative nature of the volunteer abroad industry with the growth of for-profit volunteer abroad options; and the focus on global citizenship and 'helping' discourses used to promote and justify volunteer abroad placements. Searching for volunteer abroad programmes has never been easier in the sense that there are so many options; nor more difficult in relation to the challenge of deciding between the diverse options. There are now thousands of organizations that offer volunteer abroad services. GoAbroad.com bills itself as a comprehensive Volunteer Abroad directory of 5,545 *verified* volunteer programmes and projects in 156 countries (goabroad.com, 2015). The use of the term 'verified' is significant here as it underscores the fact that there are numerous volunteer placement organizations that may not be reputable and/or reliable. It also raises questions about the standards required to be labelled as volunteer abroad beyond the legitimacy of an actual organization. With such a large number of organizations from which to choose, advertising approaches must respond to the selection of services available. To be effective in their advertising campaigns, volunteer placement organizations use a particular set of images and discourses that appeal to as wide an audience as possible. I return to these common images and discourses throughout the chapters of this book because they too provide the broader context within which decisions and rationales to volunteer abroad are made and for which motivations are shaped.

The ability to shop for an experience abroad means that prospective participants are able to choose the length of time they want to go abroad; the country they will travel to; and the perceived values of the organization as presented to the 'consumer'. The process of selecting a country and programme must be examined in relation to other approaches to recruitment, such as demand-driven placements whereby host organizations prepare requests for assistance based on needs they have in their organization and/or communities. The experience of shopping for such an experience is on full display at the Go Global Expo. The Go Global Expo is a travel, study, work, and volunteer abroad trade show put on by *Verge Magazine* every September in Toronto and Montreal. It is geared towards young people, namely students and recent grads between the ages of 18 and 30, who are looking to go outside of North America to gain experience in another country. Booths at the expo range from government-sponsored student travel, work, and study abroad options, to travel magazines (such as *Verge Magazine*). Overall, the event underscores the broad range of options for alternative travel opportunities and/or volunteer experiences abroad.

Another important – and related – trend involves a younger constituency of participants going on volunteer abroad programmes and particularly the growth in the number of young people travelling abroad to the Global South (Mostafanezhad, 2013). The exposure to such opportunities for volunteer abroad in the Global South begins, for many youth, in junior high and high school (Fizzell and Epprecht, 2014), with participants as young as 14 years old. These trends are important because they shape the nature of volunteer abroad programmes, as well as the discourse and norms of what international volunteering is about and for whom, particularly in relation to development outcomes and benefits to the host communities. Such trends are critically examined in the scholarship on international volunteering in relation to persistent inequalities and the perpetuation of individualistic goals of the sojourners. It is important to note that the nature of these trends emerge from demands from the volunteers themselves but also from the growing industry of for-profit volunteer-sending organizations shaping the discourse in a way that perpetuates the myth that inexperienced youth as young as 14 or 15 years old are able to provide substantive development assistance that can have benefits beyond the youth's personal growth. Short-term, volunteer abroad (often more aptly categorized as voluntourism) programmes for high school students may be offered by individual secondary school teachers (Fizzell and Epprecht, 2014), as well as a large and growing number of volunteer-sending organizations or companies such as 'Projects Abroad' or Me to We's volunteer trips and other independently organized high school-targeted volunteer abroad programmes for youth as young as 14–17 years old.

In *Verge Magazine*, author Jessica Lockhart underscores the growth area of volunteer abroad opportunities and highlights some of the 'growing pains'. In her article "International Volunteering: State of the Nation" (2012), Lockhart documents the changing landscape of international volunteering in which volunteers can choose the length of time they spend abroad, the country, the project focus and dates of travel. What was once a "call to action has been institutionalized into a rite of passage". Lockhart goes on to note: "In fact, international volunteerism has become … mainstream." As Lockhart argued, there are countless non-profits, social entrepreneurs, and tour operators; she cites: "A 2008 study by Tourism and Research Marketing, which surveyed 300 organisations, estimated the market size to be 1.6 million volunteer tourists per year and put the value of the market at around £1.3 billion" (travelmole as cited by Lockhart, 2012). In 2012, 35 per cent of adults said they would like to try a holiday involving a voluntourism component, in addition to the 6 per cent who had already done so (Volunteertourism-views, 2013). A 2008 survey by the Brookings Institute's Initiative on International Volunteering and Services of 29 volunteer organizations noted an increase by 55 per cent of volunteers going abroad, from 55,000 volunteers in 2007 to 85,000 in 2010. In the United States alone, it is projected that more than one million individuals volunteer abroad each year (Lough, 2013a). In Canada, more than 100,000 Canadians were estimated to volunteer abroad in 2015 (CBC, 2015). NBCnews.com reported a tripling of volunteers going abroad between 2007 and 2014 (NBCnews.com, 2014). Furthermore, Lough's (2008: 1) research found that 39 per cent of the volunteers said they spent less than one week abroad. Other trends arising from the Volunteering Solutions study showed that 18 per cent of international volunteers were in the 15–18 age category, 41 per cent were in the 18–25 age category, and 26 per cent were in the 26–30 age category (Volunteering Solutions, 2014).

Thus, participation in voluntourism and LVA in the twenty-first century has grown exponentially and has involved a larger number of volunteers as well as recipient organizations and communities (Sherraden *et al.*, 2008) – a growth that is unprecedented (McBride and Sherraden, 2007; Peace Corps, 2007; Plewes and Stuart, 2007). Despite their prevalence, forms of civic service worldwide remain one of the least understood practices (McBride *et al.*, 2007). McBride *et al.* (2007) categorize international service learning as: technical (expert assistance), nontechnical (doing good work), or learning-oriented (connected to course work). The desire for volunteer abroad – or international experiential learning opportunities – among youth must also be understood in the context of a changing global society whereby "skills needed for success in today's world differ from those needed even 15 years ago" (Rundstrom Williams, 2005: 357). The current job market facing college and university graduates is competitive and youth are preparing themselves for careers requiring global competency as well as careers that may change several times in their lives. Thus, employers are increasingly looking for employees with a skill-set that is adaptable, as well as those who have strong communication skills (Rundstrom Williams, 2005).

Volunteer abroad trends also include positive affirmations that the work completed during placements contributes to positive change. Common themes in the promotion of volunteer abroad options include opportunities for 'helping', 'making a difference', and becoming 'global citizens'. Several organizations and volunteer abroad programmes are presented as opportunities for youth to become global citizens. VSO and Transitions Abroad (two organizations sending large numbers of volunteers abroad annually) employ the language of 'making a difference' in the communities abroad as a core mission. There are numerous references to these key terms of helping, making a difference, and becoming a global citizen, a topic to which I will return later in this book. Some of the promotional material uses images that depict these notions of helping, including pictures of white volunteers holding babies, medical practitioners saving lives, and other images of adventure-seeking youth engaged in exploration and globetrotting – also important themes in the chapter that follows. A growing literature offers critical reflections of the negative impacts of these images (see Clost, 2014). A deeper analysis of the critiques, implications, and prospects for positive change arising from these trends is employed throughout this book in relation to the comments provided by the study participants and the broader scholarly contributions to this literature.

About the research for this study

The impetus for this book was a desire to better understand how LVA4D programmes are rationalized by the participants (volunteers and hosts) in relation to development outcomes, social justice imperatives, and global citizenship identity formation. To answer these questions, research funded by the International Development Research Centre (IDRC) was conducted between 2007 and 2012 with 138 Canadian youth and 165 volunteer-receiving staff and overview informants from the country who had knowledge about volunteer abroad programmes.[2]

The Canadian youth participants all participated in an LVA programme for a period ranging from approximately three to six months in a country in the Global South. These LVA4D placements included university practicum options, NGO-supported volunteer abroad initiatives, and government-subsidized internships. While there were diverse programmes included in this sample, the programmes all had a focus on LVA4D at the heart of their mandate with an emphasis on training and preparing Canadians for careers in fields involving international or global development priorities.

Research methods

Research with Global North participants

The interviews with Global North participants consisted of a sample of Canadian youth who were interviewed via telephone or Skype. The interviews involved semi-structured questions. Of the 138 participants in the Canadian youth sample, 30 were interviewed before going abroad. These same participants were interviewed upon their return to Canada and they were again contacted 2–3 years later for a longitudinal interview. A larger sample of 108 participants were interviewed only one time and the interviews took place a few months after they returned to Canada from their LVA programmes. The results presented in this book are based on the 138 responses of the returned volunteers. The interviews were approximately 1.5 hours

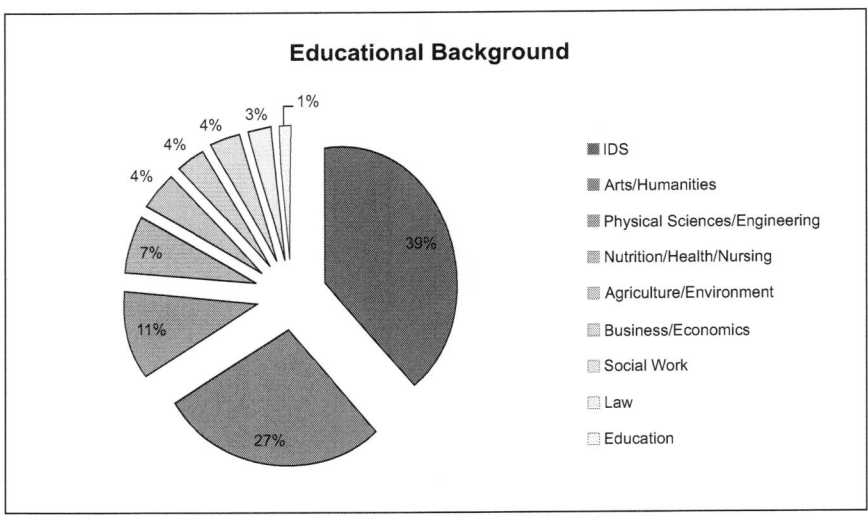

FIGURE 2.1 Educational backgrounds of participants.

in length (though sometimes much longer) and provided rich and thoughtful reflection on the motivations for participation and their perceived impacts abroad and at home. There were many Canadian participants who offered critical and highly analytical reflections of LVA programmes and the development industry more broadly. The interviews with Canadian youth were transcribed and analysed using Nvivo software.

While the Canadian study participants interviewed had been abroad for 3–6 months in duration, many had also been abroad on shorter-term placements prior to the LVA4D programme and may well remain influenced by these initial very short-term or voluntourism experiences. In fact, most of the Canadian youth participants in this study sample had been abroad previously and some were making plans to go abroad again or had decided to stay abroad for an extended period of time. There is a need, therefore, to reflect on the layering of experiences that arise from multiple exposures to international development through LVA programmes (Foroughi *et al.*, 2014).

The definition of youth used here is those young people between the ages of 18 and 30 years. This definition was chosen in line with the definition of youth provided by the former Canadian International Development Agency (CIDA) – now part of Global Affairs Canada (GAC). The Canadian participants came from a broad range of academic backgrounds, though the largest representation in this sample comes from those with IDS backgrounds. In Figure 2.1 I provide a break-down of the educational backgrounds of the participants. In total, 39 per cent of the participants had an educational specialization in international development. The second largest category in this sample included those in Arts and Humanities programmes more broadly, with a general interest in international development and global issues.

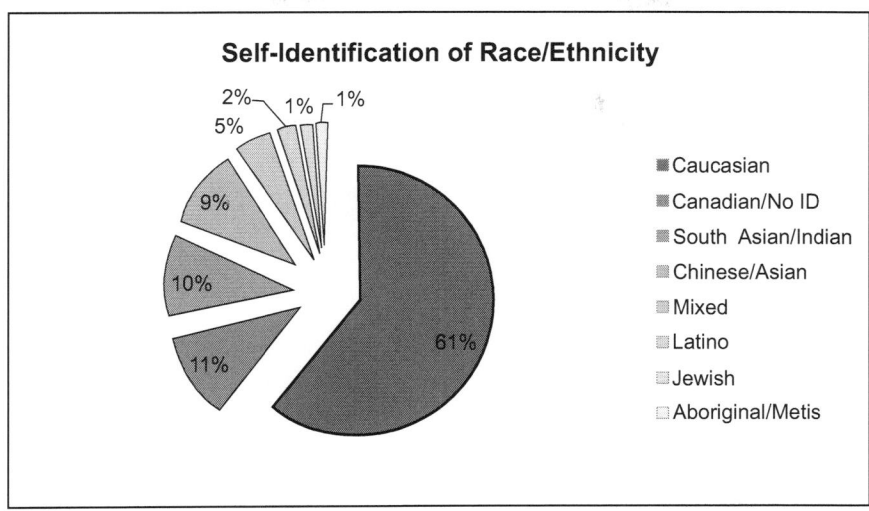

FIGURE 2.2 Self-identification of race/ethnicity among participants.

Participants also came from academic backgrounds including physical sciences and engineering, health studies, environmental/food studies, business and economics, social work, law, and education.

The Canadian participants also provided information about their level of study, with the largest number of participants indicating they had completed a Master's degree or postgraduate diploma. Approximately 10 per cent of the participants were currently enrolled in graduate school; the rest of the participants indicated they had completed a Bachelor's degree or were in the process of doing so, with participants ranging from second year to fourth year undergraduate programmes.

The participants also came from diverse geographic locations across Canada, though 50 per cent of the participants identified Ontario as their home province; the other 50 per cent were split across the Western provinces, Atlantic Canada, Quebec, and, to a very small extent, Northern Canada.

In the interviews we also asked the participants to self-identify along race/ethnicity lines. The majority of the participants self-identified as white or Caucasian, some (11 per cent) responded that they identify as Canadians and do not self-identify along any race/ethnicity lines. Figure 2.2 provides additional information about the self-identification of the Canadian participants.

Training and preparation of Canadian LVA participants

For this study, the Canadian youth were asked to consider whether they were sufficiently prepared for their LVA experience prior to departure. While information about the nature of pre-departure training was not collected, a series of questions was asked to better understand whether pre-departure training contributed meaningfully to their perceptions of preparedness. Keeping in mind that nearly 40 per cent of the participants had a background in IDS and therefore some measure of understanding of the ethically and critically informed debates surrounding international development issues, it was interesting to learn that nearly half of the Canadian participants did not feel they were sufficiently prepared. In terms of being informed about the country where the participants were volunteering, only one-quarter of the Canadian youth said they received this information in pre-departure training sessions. The Canadian youth were more likely to learn about the host country through independent readings or research: 69 out of 108 indicated they became prepared for their placement in this manner, compared to 27 of 108 youth who said they learned about the host country from pre-departure training. For those who indicated they did know enough about the country before departure, many indicated that they were able to learn things efficiently 'on the ground' and credited their ability to learn quickly to their open-minded nature.

This study did not focus extensively on pre-departure training; it is a topic requiring further exploration. There is indeed a large range in the training and preparation that Canadian youth may receive prior to travelling abroad. Most students will have access to pre-departure training through the International Office at the home university or college. Some post-secondary institutions require pre-departure training of students travelling abroad. These trainings range from intensive, theoretical, and ethical debates in the format of an entire course offering prior to and upon return from the international internships, such as the programme offered in Development and Global Studies at Queen's University or the several weeks of intensive readings, reflections, and discussions at University of Ottawa's Faculty of Social Science International Internship Program. These models of structured and comprehensive pre-departure and return orientation sessions, however, reach a small number of the post-secondary students travelling on LVA programmes (approximately 20–25 students in each of these two intensive models). Many other students get access to pre-departure training programmes through International Offices at the respective college or university. Several pre-departure training packages at different universities in Canada were examined, and the primary focus of the majority of the content in these trainings was consideration of the risks of travel, including information about different levels of risk for different countries, the medical-related requirements for preparing to go abroad, the nature of activities that may not be covered by health insurance companies while abroad, and information about 'culture shock' which I explore in greater depth in Chapter 3. For some post-secondary institutions, the pre-departure training might entail an online video followed by a five-question quiz on the above topics. Other programmes offer day-long events covering similar information pertaining to risk and country-specific danger, health considerations, and 'culture shock'. And there are also a range of field-study course options offered by individual professors that may include substantial training, including an intensive academic course on the region or country of focus and/or pre-departure seminars and training activities. As such, there is a great deal of diversity in pre-departure preparation and the participants in this study experienced this broad range of pre-departure (and sometimes return orientation) sessions. Pre-departure training is also part of the requirements for participation in programmes offered by many volunteer-sending organizations. There is also a great deal of variation across different volunteer-sending organizations and the material covered in their pre-departure modules. Despite there being immense variation, nearly half of the participants did not consider themselves to be adequately prepared or sufficiently knowledgeable about the country to which they were travelling. Some of the host organizations also indicated that they provide in-country training to youth upon their arrival; this is examined more closely in the sections that follow.

Interviews with host partners in the Global South

In addition to the interviews conducted with Canadian youth, 165 interviews were conducted with study participants who have experience hosting or working with international youth volunteers in seven countries in the Global South: India, Malawi, Zambia, South Africa, Guatemala, Peru, and Jamaica. Semi-structured interviews were employed to ensure that the participants were able to answer a consistent set of questions, but that there were also opportunities for expanding on points of interest, and flexibility in the amount of elaboration of discussion and responses taking place. In most cases, two staff members per organization were interviewed and ten organizations were included for a total of approximately 20 interviews per country. Key informants from the host countries – individuals who have a broad range of experience working with international volunteers and those who have knowledge about the national context of hosting international volunteers – were also interviewed in each of the seven countries.

The semi-structured interviews with host country participants lasted 1–3 hours and provided important insights into the experiences of LVA programmes from the perspective of host country staff. The interviews were conducted by locally based research consultants who could speak the language of operation in the country. For example, Spanish was the language of interviews in Peru and Guatemala. Transcribed interviews were then translated into English by a professional language translator. The locally based research consultants were selected by the research grant co-principal investigator – Dr Barbara Heron – and the host country research component was overseen primarily by Dr Heron. One of the perceived advantages of hiring locally based researchers – beyond language issues – was the reduction of polite bias. In other words, we anticipated more honest and critically informed responses to our questions when they were asked by someone from within the country rather than a foreign researcher. A similar challenge is identified in research conducted by O'Sullivan and Smaller (2015), who argue that host country participants are "reluctant to respond when asked specifically if they had any problems with the program or its visitors" (p. 50). The authors strove to overcome this challenge by assuring anonymity, as we also did in the collection of our data. The added strategy of hiring a locally based researcher further reduces some of the polite bias that might come from a researcher from Canada conducting research in host communities about the experiences of working with Canadian volunteers. There are few studies to date that examine the experiences of hosting volunteers from the Global North and the material collected from this part of the study was extremely valuable for making sense of the nature and impact of volunteer abroad programmes for development outcomes. Specifically, host country staff members were asked to reflect on what they considered to be some of the opportunities and challenges of hosting international volunteers, particularly medium-term volunteer placements of 3–6 months' duration. All of the interview material was analysed by reviewing the transcripts and looking for common themes and trends in the data using the software Nvivo. The empirical data and the corresponding quotations used in this book allow the voices of individuals – Canadians and our partners in the Global South – to be present.

Perceived age and experience of the volunteers they have hosted

Host country staff members were asked to reflect on the average age of the international volunteers they have hosted and if they considered there to be any significant differences across the range of ages. It is important to keep in mind that host organizations may facilitate placements for a range of volunteers, including long-term placements of one or two years or even longer, as well as short-term placements of 1–2 weeks. We asked the host partners to comment specifically on the medium-term placements of 3–6 months. However, given the large number of participants some host country partners have worked with over the years, it was difficult for the host staff to differentiate between the diverse participants. Overall, the host country participants noted a range of ages, with the majority of the partner organizations indicating that many of the volunteers they work with are in the age range of 20–30 years, with many being in their mid-20s. Their impressions of age of volunteers corresponded with the age of the Canadian youth who participated in this study.

There was also a range of perspectives on the effectiveness of recent graduates and students they have worked with over the years. Some host country interviewees noted that the younger, university-aged students were valuable because of their open-mindedness or flexibility. Others reflected on the stability of older participants who were, at times, perceived to manage their time better.

In-country orientation and training

Host country staff also commented on preparedness and the role that they play in preparing the participants once they have arrived in-country. More than half of the host country participants offered details of the intensive training and orientation that they provide to the participants once they arrive. A participant from Zambia noted that the orientation can be a formal process taking at least 3–5 days, but the amount of time spent on orientation depends on the length of the stay of the volunteer. A short-term volunteer gets a shorter orientation because of limited time in the country. Many topics were identified as part of the orientation, including an introduction to office facilities, staff members, or community participants as well as how to dress or how to communicate. The discussions of orientation and settling in included a number of extensive reflections on the challenges and time required for proper orientation and how to keep the volunteers safe in their communities. Many of the participants talked about imparting information about safety, muggings, appropriate transportation, etc. And many noted that the training provided to the newly arrived volunteers incorporated information about the country, the issues, and the challenges of delivering development programmes.

Understanding motivations

One of the initial questions asked in the interviews with the Canadian youth was to reflect on their motivations for participation in LVA4D. Motivations are defined here as the desires and aspirations for participation in LVA programmes. The motivations for participation in LVA4D that are expressed by the participants in this study reflect the reasons for taking part in these programmes. The motivations may indeed be a result of conscious and unconscious factors pertaining to needs, values, goals, and expectations. There is a range of ways that motivations are articulated or analysed, and making sense of motivations can be highly challenging. For example, we rarely articulate why we do things; when we do, we often find particular rationales for our actions that correspond with accepted norms and discourses. While many of the motivations for taking part in LVA programmes may indeed be self-serving, or egoistic in nature, to stop there does not reveal the complexity of motivations expressed, as well as the internal strife and struggle that many LVA4D participants (youth and receiving organization staff and communities alike) encounter as they try to make sense of their experiences in volunteer abroad programmes. Nonetheless, understanding the reasons for taking part in LVA4D can tell us a great deal about ourselves, our perceived contributions, and our expected impacts, as well as broader discourses and mantras shaping the landscape of – or broader rationales for – LVA4D. Motivations for participation must also be understood in the context of the social, political, and historical experiences of Global North participants and how Global North identities are shaped by the broader structural processes.

Rationales are defined, for the purpose of this book, as the underlying reasons or explanations for our beliefs, values, and practices. Making sense of the motivations by examining them in the context of rationales brings an additional dimension to this analysis by bringing in the broader social, cultural, and economic factors used to justify LVA4D participation. In other words, the motivations expressed by hosts of LVA4D participants provide insights into broader structural realities. Understanding motivations for participation in volunteer abroad programmes is also valuable for making sense of development outcomes arising from these programmes. For example, if volunteers expect their participation in LVA4D programmes to have international development or social justice outcomes, then the evaluation of motivations for participation plays a role in determining how and why these development outcomes are (or are not) achieved. Volunteers who are focused primarily on personal benefit may be less concerned with how volunteer-receiving organizations and communities benefit (Anheier and Salamon, 1999; Rehberg, 2005). But uncovering motivations is challenging and, as Unstead-Joss (2008) points out, there are layers of motivations that need to be examined, keeping in mind that some motivations are more prominent than others, at different times in our lives.

The nature of the volunteer abroad programmes will also play a role in determining development and social justice outcomes. Given the significant variation across volunteer abroad programmes from short-term (including some forms of voluntourism) to long-term (cooperant or development worker) volunteer options, it is important to reflect carefully on the motivations and broader rationales inherent to specific programmes. It is important to keep in mind, also, that motivations vary by race, age, gender, and ethnicity (Sherraden *et al.*, 2008). Consequently, there are several challenges to making sense of – and writing about – motivations for participation in LVA4D programmes. Throughout the chapters of this book I examine the motivations in relation to broader rationales and development debates, keeping in mind the complexity and nuances that affect the range of perspectives.

Before turning to the rationales for participation, I introduce some of the basic motivations as identified by the participants themselves. In isolating several of the most commonly identified motivations (cross-cultural communication, skills development, adventure and travel, and helping), I am able to elaborate on how these specific motivations are expressed by the Canadian and host country participants in overlapping and distinct ways. However, this initial reflection is insufficient, which is why the reflection on narratives, including quotes for the participants, plays an important role in a more in-depth analysis of rationales. In each chapter I provide quotes from study participants: the Canadian youth and the host country participants interviewed for this study.

In making sense of the motivations for participation in LVA4D and the broader rationales that contribute to these motivations, I situate the findings from the study in the context of two major frameworks employed in the literature to examine motivations in volunteer abroad programmes more broadly, namely: individualistic/egoistic versus solidaristic/global citizenship approaches to LVA4D programmes. The first frame is useful for understanding individual motivations pertaining to perceived personal benefit; the latter frame enables a deeper analysis of the perceived broader development outcomes and partnership-building that can emerge from these encounters. Employing these frequently overlapping lenses of analysis gives a better picture of the complexity of experiences in LVA4D for the sojourners and hosts alike. Examples of studies examining motivations for international volunteering can be found in literature in the fields of international social work, international development studies, and elsewhere. I begin by examining motivations and, later, in this chapter and the chapters that follow, turn to the broader rationales for participation in volunteer abroad programmes.

Overview of initial findings pertaining to motivations

In this section I provide an overview of the initial findings pertaining to motivations as self-identified by the participants in the study. It is important to note that these serve as merely initial findings because the ranking of motivations early in the interview (for the Canadian participants) does not provide a complete picture of the rationales for participation that are described throughout the entire interview. For example, while one motivation might be ranked low relative to other motivations listed, it might also be the motivation that surfaces the most frequently throughout the interview in complex and interesting ways.

At the start of the interview with the Canadian youth, the interview participants were asked to rank different motivations (as very important, somewhat important, or not very important). The ranking results are presented in Table 2.1.

The findings from this ranking exercise demonstrate that the Canadian youth considered personal growth to be among the most important motivations, followed by helping, testing an academic background or career choice, getting a job, language acquisition, and then by much less significant motivations stemming from personal reasons such as friends travelling or for religious reasons.

Participants were then asked to reflect back on their motivations for going abroad and to rank the motivation they considered the *most* important. Table 2.2 summarizes those motivations, ranked as most important (in hindsight) and divided by male and female respondents.

The findings from this second ranking exercise show a different ranking of motivations, beginning with cross-cultural understanding as the most important motivation identified by women, and testing an academic background or career choice as the most important motivation noted by men, with cross-cultural communication coming in as a close second for these men. This resonates with a study conducted

TABLE 2.1 Motivations as expressed in terms of *very important, somewhat important, not very important* (number of responses).

Motivation	Very important	Somewhat important	Not very important
Personal growth	55	12	1
Desire to help others	51	13	3
Cross-cultural understanding	51	13	2
Skills development	50	14	1
Test academic background/career choice	41	20	6
Get a job/start career	35	22	9
Adventure/travel	29	33	6
Language acquisition	14	24	27
Friends travelling	5	8	55
Religion	2	3	63

TABLE 2.2 Ranking of most important motivation by sex (number of responses).

Theme	Female	Male
(a) Cross-cultural understanding	38	7
(b) Test academic background and career choice	33	10
(c) Find a job/start a career	27	5
(d) Personal growth	26	4
(e) Skills development	21	4
(f) Adventure/travel	17	6
(g) Help others	12	5
(h) Other	11	4
(i) Language acquisition	9	3

by Japanese researchers on the Japan Overseas Cooperation Volunteers (JOCVs) programme that found that men ranked career advancement as a primary motive (Shiratori, 2015). The motivation of travel and adventure was also in the top three motivations for men, while this motivation ranked fairly low for women overall.

The ranking of most important motivation overall is used as a guide for the organization of the chapters of this book. While there are some important differences to be noted in relation to the motivations of personal growth, testing an academic background or career choice, and finding or starting a career, the importance attached to skills development in the narratives provided by the Canadian youth suggest that dealing with these motivations together under the broader heading of 'skills development' is useful in the analysis provided in subsequent chapters. Cross-cultural communication, while an important skill, is examined separate from 'skills development' because of the range of references to intercultural relationships, friendship formation, cultural understanding, and most importantly because of the significance attached to cross-cultural understanding as articulated by the host country participants. I turn now to an overview of the findings pertaining to motivations as expressed by the host country participants.

Motivations for participation as expressed by volunteer-receiving organization staff and communities (host country responses)

Interviews with volunteer-receiving organization staff and community members in the seven host countries in the Global South were not asked to rank their motivations for participation in the way the Canadian youth were. A different set of questions was employed to examine their motivations in relation to their perceived advantages and disadvantages of hosting international volunteers. The comments that were provided lend insights into the motivations for participation. Host country participants were motivated to participate in the hosting of international volunteers because of the perceived value of gaining new skills or information technology support, and cross-cultural exchange opportunities that would facilitate opportunities (for organization staff and community members) to get to know and understand people from other places. Other valuable contributions of international volunteers were summarized as capacity-building for the organization (institutional and staff capacity); new ideas or fresh perspectives; improved visibility of the organization to the communities and to donors; improved credibility from donors; increased funding and resources; international collaborations and linkages to other organizations in Global North countries; and improved understanding of work as a result of explaining it to the 'newcomers' (Tiessen and Heron, 2012b).

Several disadvantages were also identified. Understanding these disadvantages in relation to the advantages is important for considering how host organization staff rationalized their ongoing commitments to hosting international volunteers. The costs of hosting volunteers include adjustment and orientation issues experienced by volunteers; sexual harassment and security issues; translation and language issues; food sensitivities and illness; handling homesickness; volunteers imposing their own values; time, energy, and resources invested in logistical support; cultural insensitivity and cultural adaption challenges; problematic behaviour including arrogance or prioritization of personal activities at the expense of organizational needs; and inequality of benefits such that the volunteer benefits but less so the organization or the host staff (Tiessen and Heron, 2012b).

Neither the quantitative data for the Canadian youth noted above, nor the advantages and disadvantages noted by the host country participants, provide the full story. A great deal of information about motivations can be gathered through an analysis of responses to a broad range of questions that arise. A more thorough discussion of these rationales as they unfold throughout the interviews is offered in the chapters that follow. However, these motivations begin to unravel a story about the complexity – as well as similarities and differences – of motivations for Canadian and host country participants. These self-assessed motivations also offer some understanding of self-oriented rationales such as personal growth and adventure and travel, as well as broader goals of global competency through cross-cultural understanding and desires for human connection and shared understanding. The motivations also need to be understood in the broader context of gendered, historical, political, and social contexts in which Canadian youth consider their contributions important to international development goals, and how host country participants may view the symbolic presence of foreigners (who are often white and who represent favourable attributes and expertise), thus bringing (a perceived) credibility or legitimacy to an organization. Thus, rationales for participation must incorporate broader structure-oriented dynamics (systems of inequality) as well as agency (individual and organizational commitments to alter broader structural realities and to navigate problematic processes for their own benefit).

In the volunteer abroad literature there are several important debates reflecting diverse perspectives on the motivations for – and potential impacts of – LVA programmes. For example, post-colonialism and critical race theories (see Heron, 2007 for example) and neo-imperialism analyses (see Cook, 2007; Georgeou and

Engel, 2011) offer frameworks for many of the critiques, which shed light on the problematic nature of volunteering abroad, the 'Othering' that results from such programmes, as well as some important ethical questions about the impact of placements (Tiessen, 2012). What requires additional analysis is a thorough reflection on the reasons propelling the growth in options for LVA experience, particularly in relation to the motivations and expectations of the youth participants, the experiences of host partner staff (and their own motivations for continuing to work with international volunteers) combined with some reflection on the broader discourses surrounding the international development context of LVA in terms of discourses and images perpetuated through glossy advertisements and a specific rhetoric enticing young people to go abroad. An international development lens, employing post-colonial analysis and structural inequality, is important here because it exposes how capitalist notions and deeply held convictions along with post-colonial values affect how participants in LVA4D are shaped by – and articulate – their rationales for participation. The consumption of experience combined with a collection of places travelled translates into cultural capital for the traveller – a topic I return to in Chapter 5. In a study conducted by Brown (2005), he noted that "volunteer vacationers seem to be driven by a sense of adventure and desires for exploration and novelty, that are not as prominent with the more serious volunteer travellers" (p. 493). The use of the term 'driven' is interesting here, as it too speaks to a desire to understand motivations and the nature of some motivations in relation to others. What is interesting about Brown's study, as compared to the participant responses noted in this book, is that many of the responses reflect the elements and motivations that Brown associates with the vacation-minded volunteer tourist. This may indicate that the motivation to participate in volunteer abroad programmes, especially those related specifically to development work, are more closely aligned with the growing trends of mainstream tourism motivations than may be initially imagined. Understanding the motivations surrounding adventure and travel also require knowledge about the broader context in which participants are making decisions to go abroad. Media representations and imagery accompanying the advertising of volunteer abroad programmes will also influence why volunteers choose to go abroad. Recognizing this broader context helps make sense of potential expectations of LVA4D participants and those who host them. As this book is particularly concerned with the experiences of those students and youth interested in (potentially) pursuing careers in international development and organizations actively engaged in the delivery of development programming, a range of rationales are examined in the context of international development debates.

Brown's (2005) research examining motivations of those who participate in volunteer vacations found two different types of volunteer tourists that speak to distinct motivations – 'volunteer-minded' versus 'vacation-minded'. With respect to the relationship between travel and volunteering, Brown noted that his study adds a new dimension to the postmodern tourism phenomenon because his participants' responses highlight the increasingly popular relationship between the desire for travel that embarks on a "spiritual search" (2005: 493) to seek out opportunities that increase the sense of place, with an altruistic desire to "help others" (2005: 493). Similar motivations and corresponding rationales are examined in relation to the study findings in the chapters that follow.

Cross-cultural understanding stood out as the most important motivation for the Canadian study participants overall. Examples of value placed on cross-cultural understanding were also presented by the host country staff. I turn to this motivation and the underlying rationales of solidarity and global citizenship, as well as individualist or egoistic motivations, in the next chapter.

As demonstrated in Figure 2.1, skills development is also an important motivation for Canadian youth to take part in LVA4D. Volunteer-receiving organization staff also commented on the value of skills delivery as a motivation for – and benefit of – working with international volunteers. Chapter 4 pertains to motivations pertaining to skills development and career advancement rationales. Adventure and travel motivations are examined in Chapter 5. The motivation pertaining to personal growth must be understood in relation to other motivations. References to personal growth tended to overlap with several of the other motivations identified, such as skills development, cultural competency, and adventure and travel. A discussion of personal growth is therefore included in the chapters that deal with these other motivations.

Is a desire to give and receive 'help' in the Global South a key factor in the decision to participate in LVA4D programmes? Chapter 6 examines the helping imperative and situates the experiences of Canadian youth and host country staff members in the broader critiques and analyses of feminist theory, post-colonialism and critical race theory.

LVA programmes offer much potential for the promotion of global citizenship and global solidarity. Participation in international service learning (ISL) is believed to foster more engaged citizens, as Bringle and Hatcher (2011) explain in their examination of the pedagogical approach of ISL, which they compare to the discovery of a cure for cancer in terms of our need for celebration of its benefits. They note that "ISL holds the potential and may be a pedagogy that is best suited to prepare college graduates to be active global citizens in the 21st century" (Bringle and Hatcher, 2011: 3). Thus, promoting global citizenship identities while fostering cross-cultural skills and intercultural competency are central to the core rationales for LVA4D. Cross-cultural exposure and communication were also important motivations for participation in LVA4D programmes, as noted by both the Canadian and host country participants in this study. In the next chapter I examine this particular motivation in greater detail. The motivation for cross-cultural understanding must be understood in the context of broader structural rationales. For example, cross-cultural understanding or intercultural learning for what purpose? If, for example, cultural immersion or exposure to foreigners serves an important role in helping to indoctrinate or familiarize communities with Western values and practices, then the structural limitations of this exposure need to be examined more carefully. However, we cannot let these broader structural challenges completely overshadow the highly valuable interpersonal relationships that emerge through volunteer abroad programmes and the agency that is formed as a result of important professional relationships and friendships. As one host organization staff member noted, the value of hosting an international volunteer has less to do with the products or skills that the volunteer brings and more to do with 'getting to know the person' and improved understanding across cultures and between individuals. His comment reinforces the real and perceived value of cross-cultural engagement. The rationales surrounding cross-cultural engagement are examined in greater depth in Chapter 3.

Since the early 1990s, the language of global citizenship has been adopted to reflect the desire to learn about the world and to travel to far-off places. University students are increasingly familiar with the language of global citizenship, in part because many post-secondary institutions have employed the term as part of their internationalization mandates (Jorgenson and Shultz, 2012). Part of the growing desire for a cross-cultural experience in the developing world is arising out of rationales for global citizenship identity formation, which are also examined in Chapter 3. In the concluding chapter (Chapter 7) I return to the analysis of global citizenship identities and their prospects for enabling deep or 'thick' cosmopolitan values (Cameron, 2014), including aspirations of solidarity and social justice, or 'thin' global citizenship (Cameron, 2014), such as superficial, individualist, or egoistic rationales.

Summary

This chapter has mapped out a range of international volunteering options delineated by length of time abroad as well as some important trends and common practices within this sector. This information provides the broader context for introducing the research study, the methods employed, and the nature of the participants. A brief introduction to the diverse motivations for participation in LVA4D was also provided. Making sense of motivations for participation in volunteer abroad programmes is limited by some of the challenges highlighted earlier in this chapter, notably the challenges of expressing our true motivations and how our motivations may change depending on changing life circumstances. For example, students may be motivated more by learning-based motivations, while recent graduates may be motivated by finding a job and improving their skill-set. Furthermore, motivational analyses require a complex and nuanced analysis of a range of factors as expressed in response to direct questions and also throughout the interviews, necessitating a more elaborate discussion of rationales. These motivations can be shaped by broader discourses and images that facilitate perceived value associated with volunteer abroad participation. International structural realities defined by political, economic, social, environmental, and gendered dynamics also factor into these rationales and form an important part of the analysis. The subsequent chapters are designed to elaborate on these very brief summaries of motivations for participation to examine more carefully and in a more nuanced fashion the broader rationales; I do this by sharing the voices and experiences of the participants in this study and analysing how we can understand these in the context of broader structural realities.

The purpose of this book is to critically and constructively engage in an analysis of the rationales for participation in LVA4D so that we can better understand them and their implications in the context of international development debates and the prospects for improving development outcomes. This information can then help us consider existing practice, reflect on challenges and opportunities within existing LVA4D models and imagine new possibilities for engaged global citizens who are actively involved in social justice and partnership-building goals.

Notes

1 In 2013, the Canadian International Development Agency was folded into the Department of Foreign Affairs and Trade to form a new department, the Department of Foreign Affairs, Trade and Development (DFATD). This Canadian government department changed names in 2015 with the election of a new government and is now called Global Affairs Canada (GAC).
2 This research was conducted collaboratively by Rebecca Tiessen and Barbara Heron with the help of several very talented research assistants in Canada and research experts who conducted interviews in seven countries in the Global South. Barbara Heron oversaw the collection of data in the host countries and I have overall supervision of the Canadian interview data collection. The transcribed materials were shared with each other.

3

LVA4D AND CROSS-CULTURAL ENGAGEMENT

In an interconnected world, cross-cultural communication and global competency are imperative. I employ the term global competency to refer to a capacity for interactions with people from diverse places, facilitated by the ability to listen, learn, observe, analyse, interpret, and understand. Strong communication skills in intercultural contexts play an important role in facilitating the exchange of ideas, new friendships, and improved learning/volunteering opportunities. Volunteer-sending organizations engaged in development cooperation and global partnership-building place intercultural competence and global understanding at the heart of their mandates, practices, and outcomes.

The broad spectrum of international internships, experiential learning, and volunteering opportunities generally employ the language of cross-cultural engagement. Participants in these programmes may also justify their involvement in these programmes in relation to normative goals of intercultural activities.

Among the motivations identified by Canadian youth, cross-cultural understanding stood out as one of the most important. In this chapter, I reflect on the existing literature on cross-cultural engagement through international volunteering. I then turn to an examination of the nature of cross-cultural engagement as a core motivation for participation in learning/volunteering abroad (LVA) according to both the volunteer-receiving organization staff and the Canadian LVA participants who travelled abroad. Several themes are examined here pertaining to the exchange of ideas and building relationships as core elements of cross-cultural engagement. The analysis of cross-cultural motivations for participation in learning/volunteering abroad for development (LVA4D) highlights a number of rationales ranging from solidarity-oriented goals and global citizenship identities to self-oriented or egoistic expressions of individual-oriented benefits of cross-cultural skills development for career advancement, as discussed in this chapter.

Cross-cultural engagement in volunteer abroad programmes

A large body of literature is dedicated to making the link between volunteer abroad opportunities and cross-cultural enrichment. Lough (2011), for example, reflects on the widely-held view that international volunteering is associated with increased intercultural competence. International volunteer-sending organizations nearly universally "claim that volunteering will increase intercultural competence" (p. 452). Lough's 2011 study, however, found that perceptions of intercultural competence depend on multiple factors; namely, duration abroad, cultural immersion, guided reflection, and reciprocity as important factors in achieving intercultural competence. Research on motivations for participation in international volunteer programmes from the perspective of the host community and staff have been documented in studies such as that conducted by Erin Barnhart (2012). Barnhart discovered that the second most commonly expressed motivation for participation in volunteer abroad programmes (according to 31 per cent of her respondents) is the opportunity for "cross cultural connections, learning, and understanding" (p. 73). This was one of the important perceived benefits of hosting international volunteers, a sentiment echoed by Tiessen and Heron (2012a).

In a study of international placements for American social work students, Boyle and Barranti (1999) found that not much has been written about education for cross-cultural purposes as part of experiential learning options. Rather, several assumptions about the value of cross-cultural engagement are made, including improved understanding of cultural difference and reduced ethnocentrism. In her work on the ways in which mutual empowerment may be fostered through international service learning, Crabtree (1998) found that studies on intercultural learning focus primarily on Northern participants and their individual personal growth. The benefits of intercultural learning are considered in relation to the Northern participants' changing world views and the development of intercultural communication skills (Crabtree, 1988). Based on these findings, Crabtree (1998) claims that mutual empowerment can be achieved by both the "so-called disadvantaged and advantaged participants" (p. 188) when international service learning involves meaningful participation. Communication skills are thus placed at the centre of the practices and outcomes of participatory development, intercultural adjustment, and service learning projects, and the empowerment of all parties involved is foregrounded as the primary objective of each member. To build on this scholarship, I offer findings from my own research as well as insights pertaining to the similarities and differences between these two constituencies in terms of motivations and rationales for improved cultural competence through LVA programmes. Specifically, in this chapter I summarize the narratives from host organization staff and LVA participants from Canada and analyse these experiences collectively.

While there may be a broad consensus on the importance of cross-cultural understanding and the role that volunteer abroad programmes may have for all concerned, it is also important to examine both the motivations and rationales for participation in LVA in relation to cross-cultural understanding from the perspective of the LVA participants who travel to the Global South and the volunteer-receiving staff members who work alongside international volunteers. This chapter explores these perspectives on cross-cultural engagement as a core motivation and also as a rationale for participation in LVA programmes in three parts. In part one the narratives provided by the Canadian youth who participated in this study are explored. In part two narratives pertaining to cross-cultural engagement by the volunteer-receiving organizational staff are explored. Part three provides an analysis of the similarities and differences of cross-cultural motivations and rationales. Specifically, I consider these reflections on cross-cultural engagement in a comparative manner, explaining how references to differences, solidarity, and perspectives on 'culture shock' play out in the reflections on cross-cultural experiences.

The findings from my research with LVA participants (Canadian youth and host organization staff) underscore both positive and negative impacts associated with cross-cultural understanding through LVA programmes. The positive cross-cultural experiences included new appreciations for alternative approaches to development work, host country reflections on the value of alternative perspectives and new ideas and energy, and a general interest in getting to know people and to have rich, intercultural exchanges. There were some challenges and frustrations with the cross-cultural experience noted as well, and these are elaborated below in relation to: the perpetuation of perceived differences rather than similarities across cultures; isolationism or cultural bubbles that international volunteers may form while abroad; and reflections by host country participants in relation to the arrogance and perceived superiority of international volunteers, making the exchange of ideas and shared learning difficult. In research by Reynolds and Gasparini (2015), they noted that community organizational representatives repeatedly highlighted the importance of humility. One of the quotes provided in this context included references to the importance of recognizing the work that is already taking place and the knowledge that exists locally within the host country (p. 44). Nonetheless, these challenges must also be understood in relation to the benefits derived from transnational interactions and encounters, namely the cultural enrichment and exposure afforded through such programmes. These positive outcomes can contribute to improved cross-cultural understanding, solidarity-oriented goals, and global citizenship identities.

The benefits of cross-cultural opportunities afforded through LVA4D may be experienced by both the international volunteers and the host community/host country staff. In their research, Lough et al. (2011) found that intercultural understanding had improved for host country participants as a result of hosting American volunteers because the international volunteers are seen to bring intercultural understanding to the host organization and the communities they serve. Cultural competence of host staff, according to Lough et al.'s study, was enhanced through the presence of volunteers from the Global North. Furthermore, cultural understanding was promoted through practices such as preparing food, sharing music and dancing, and other cultural practices. Lack of knowledge of local language, however, was considered one of the impediments to cultural exchange. The advantages of cross-cultural opportunities provided by international volunteering also contributed to what was perceived as an improved understanding of cultural practices for the participants from the Global North. In addition, cultural exchange provided opportunities for creativity and innovation. Overall, the findings from the study by Lough *et al.* (2011) documented very positive experiences from international volunteer programmes, and the authors reported that none of the staff members from host countries in their study made reference to the significant problems associated with international volunteers from the Global North.

The positive experiences identified by host organization staff in the Lough *et al.* (2011) study are echoed in a study by Graham *et al.* (2011), who documented that: "host organisations felt that international volunteers were able to view situations with new eyes and with different experiences, and were thus able to produce technical and cultural innovation" (p. 16). The example provided in the study by Graham *et al.* (2011) found that the exchange of ideas helps the organization move forward and therefore the benefits of international volunteering and cross-cultural exchange contribute to organizational development. Findings from my research suggest that the cross-cultural exposure in LVA placements also contributed to innovation and new insights, as well as significant emphasis placed on the human connection and the relationships formed as a result of LVA4D. The cross-cultural motivation was articulated in a variety of ways by the more than 300 study participants (Canadian youth and host country participants) and these articulations of cross-cultural exposure highlighted rationales pertaining to individualistic values in relation to some of the global citizenship identities desired. Such analyses offer important insights into the limitations of cross-cultural exposure, but they are insufficient frames of analysis for understanding the rationales of participants that often also include solidarity-oriented goals.

The significance of cross-cultural understanding for study participants

Global North youth are themselves highly motivated to participate in LVA programmes because of the perceived benefits of cross-cultural understanding they expect from these opportunities. In research on LVA carried out between 2007 and 2011, when youth were asked to rank what they saw as their primary motivations for taking part in LVA programmes, the desire for cross-cultural understanding ranked as the 'most important' motivation overall and the highest ranked motivation for women who participated in the interview.

Interestingly, the Canadians who participated in this study consider the cross-cultural experience to also be important to the host organization staff. Thus, there is a perceived value expressed by the volunteers from the Global North that they project onto the host organizations in the Global South. I provide here a quote from one of the Canadian participants – Avery[1] – who noted that in "Ghanaian culture specifically, they [Ghanaians] consider cross-cultural experiences to be particularly valuable as a learning experience solely. I think that they value the relationship in different ways [than the volunteers]." Avery considers the value to be of a different character than her own value associated with these programmes; yet, she does not push any deeper to consider the possibility that her presence in Ghana might be representative of a particular set of interests, just as her counterparts also had a particular perspective on cross-cultural engagement: both are shaped by colonial pasts and continuities and are structured by a range of historical processes. Avery's location of this difference within culture is indicative of the types of concerns raised by Epprecht (2004) and Heron (2007), whereby 'othering' is ascribed or re-affirmed through comparative lenses of the nature of cross-cultural understanding. Zemach-Bersin's (2009) study also found that students were more likely to reflect on separateness rather than similarities across cultures, and the focus on differences (pertaining to class, race, language, and culture) facilitated strong identity formation along nationalist lines rather than notions of mutuality and global solidarity (Zemach-Bersin, 2009).

However, important variations in perspectives on cross-cultural learning were identified. For example, the Canadian youth volunteer participants were asked to consider the potential benefits that they think their host organizations and host communities might see in Canadians coming to volunteer in their country. Specifically, they were asked: What, if any, value do you think your host organization/community sees in this kind of cross-cultural experience for Canadian youth? The responses, ranked in order of most frequently mentioned, include: cultural teaching, relationship formation, professional expertise, and solidarity. Keith argued that the building of relationships is important: "I think that they see the value in building ties across countries." Felicia said her host community "enjoyed our company" but she went on to say that the project is an ongoing one that involves reciprocity and exchange visits between countries, including opportunities for people from the host country to visit Canada each year.

In Lough et al.'s 2009 study, international volunteers were also asked to reflect on potential problems that may have arisen as a result of their presence in host countries. Their findings conclude that some participants thought their presence in the community may have caused some problems or challenges (18 per cent). International volunteers also expressed concerns that they did not share the same goals as local staff (16 per cent). Others mentioned a mismatch in priorities (10 per cent) and a small number expressed concern that the community did not want, nor request, their services (6 per cent). Additional issues observed from this study included perceptions of "cultural imperialism, gender and racial tensions, concerns over local labour replacement, local conflicts, resource consumption, dependence, and challenges resulting from differences in power and privilege between volunteers and host community members" (Lough et al., 2009: 4–5). In spite of these perceived problems, an overwhelming majority of the participants in Lough et al.'s 2009 study (95 per cent) considered international volunteering an important opportunity to expose host communities to different cultures and communities, and "helped them gain a better understanding of the community where they worked, exposed them to new ideas and ways of seeing the world, and challenged their previous beliefs and assumptions about the world" (Lough *et al.*, 2009: 5). The international experience was also correlated with long-term changes in the participants, demonstrating an ongoing interest in cross-cultural understanding, such as increased time spent socializing with individuals from other racial or ethnic groups upon their return from abroad (Lough *et al.*, 2009).

Host country participants in my study also frequently employed references to the value of cross-cultural exchange, as well as some of the limitations of LVA for promoting improved intercultural relations. I turn now to some of the ways that the Canadian youth and host country staff articulated their rationales for participation in LVA in relation to cross-cultural understanding and challenges, examining specifically their reflections on exchange of ideas and friendship formation.

Cross-cultural communication challenges and opportunities

Host organization staff in my study identified several challenges specific to cross-cultural exposure. Two key challenges are examined in this section: (1) cultural adaptation and cross-cultural understanding of volunteers; and (2) arrogance and/or paternalism including problematic attitudes of international volunteers who think they are smarter, more educated, or more powerful than local staff. There were some important opportunities discussed as well, and I turn to those opportunities later in this section. The first cross-cultural challenge observed by the host country participants pointed to general difficulties with adapting to local cultural practices and norms resulting from two key factors: (1) preconceived ideas about what the international volunteers would experience in the host country; and (2) foreigner isolationism and the 'bubble' or 'fish bowl' effect of sticking to other foreigners from the Global North. For the Malawian participants, the importance of coming to Africa to understand 'Africa' better was identified in relation to the perceived desire for cross-cultural understanding within the context of preconceived ideas of Africa and how those preconceptions dictate the extent to which international volunteers can understand another cultural context. As one participant from Malawi noted:

> Yes, I think it's true that white people in Canada, they have all sorts of imagination about Malawi and the developing countries, but when you have Canadians coming to Malawi and other developing countries to work as a volunteer then they are faced with realities, they are able to understand the reality and why it happens, because there are so many things that are shown on the television, so many things that are written in magazines about Africa, about Malawi, without actually explaining why certain things are happening.

The Malawian participant discussed the high rates of HIV and how volunteers from the Global North lack a good understanding of the reasons for the high rates of the disease in the country. The Malawian participant added that the volunteer placement can be a good opportunity for dispelling some myths and said that efforts are made to appreciate the specific challenges that Malawians face on a daily basis. The hope, according to this host country participant, is that the international volunteers will return to their home countries, and that they are able to share what they have learned while abroad with other Canadians in such a way that stereotypes of Africans begin to change over time.

However, not all host country participants were as optimistic about the potential for breaking down stereotypes. Some of the participants in the study argued that the cross-cultural understanding is so complicated that it can be too difficult for an outsider to ever truly understand local practices. One participant noted that a national volunteer would be more helpful to the organization because "she/he would understand the mentality, the reality, how Peruvians think, while a foreigner wouldn't". The Peruvian participant's comments raised questions about the ability for foreigners to be truly helpful in a cultural context about which they know little. A study participant from Guatemala also spoke about the challenges of breaking into the local culture: "Guatemalans are persons with complicated social codes. We are not very open people. Very polite, yes, but not very open and this makes it difficult for volunteers to socialize with them [Guatemalans]."

Another participant spoke about the mentoring required to assist other staff members in the host organization who became frustrated with the local volunteers and their inability to act in culturally appropriate ways. As the Zambian participant noted about interaction styles across cultures, Northerners tend to be "much more straight and frank and it gets to the local staff". The participant from Zambia went on to note that he had to work with his local staff members to remind them that international volunteers had a different approach to communication that is part of their culture. The Zambian participant talks about the cross-cultural experience as "two worlds meeting, two cultures meeting, and different persons also meeting". The Zambian participant demonstrated the great effort and patience required for the cross-cultural encounters with international volunteers.

A participant from Malawi was similarly concerned with the effectiveness of international volunteers in transnational encounters, and said: "Yes we have other foreign volunteers who I think culturally are not friendly, culturally not flexible, they have their own policies, they have their own way of doing things, they don't want to change." It is important to capture these sentiments and to share them in the words provided by the host country staff members themselves. These sentiments show that host country staff members may indeed have some reservations about the potential for cross-cultural engagement when given the opportunity to speak frankly and openly about their own experiences.

Nonetheless, cross-cultural understanding can be improved when Westerners make efforts to spend time with local staff – a challenge articulated by several host country participants. One participant talked about the importance of preventing cliques among foreigners to help them with cross-cultural understanding, and the amount of work that is invested in preventing isolationism of international volunteers. The participant from Jamaica argued:

> They will mix well with local people and I have found that they do. Providing that your, the host country, is careful to … prevent them developing cliques of their own.

The Jamaican host country participants then provided an example of groups of foreign visitors who would skip their placements and congregate instead at a hotel swimming pool. The host staff members were tasked with ending this behaviour in part to ensure that the international visitors were able to adapt to the culture more effectively. He concluded: "Hosting staff has to be vigilant to prevent them developing the cliques of people who either look like them, or [look like other people] from where they come."

Another comment on foreigner isolationism was provided by a participant from India, who remarked that international volunteers tend to associate with other expats. This participant noted that the 'bubble effect' (or expat isolationism) can be detrimental to the host communities by reinforcing 'us' and 'them' divisions. He argued that when foreigners congregate together "then their influence of what Indians are or what Indian-ness is all about comes from there [foreigner perceptions], rather than actual experience". This comment is very important as it highlights the challenges of knowing another culture through conversations and interactions with other outsiders. This way of 'knowing' can reinforce paternalism, 'othering', neo-colonial attitudes, and even racism if not addressed. The comments from host staff about volunteer preferences for associating with other expats was in contrast to many of the Canadian participants' expressed desires. Several Canadian participants left their international volunteer placements disillusioned by the expat lifestyle and made explicit efforts to develop meaningful relationships with people from the host country. At times, these connections proved challenging if the volunteers were not invited to local community events and activities. For many of the Canadian youth who disliked what they perceived to be an elitist expat culture, they indicated an interest in working in Canada to avoid having to be part of expat circles.

An additional – and related – challenge of cross-cultural understanding observed in this study is the perception of volunteers from the Global North having problematic attitudes and superiority complexes. As one participant from Guatemala argued:

> some people [co-workers] get upset because of the wages and special conditions volunteers come with to do the same work they do. Sometimes, they consider they are too quiet or that they treat people in a paternalistic way. Sometimes, people will complain about volunteers wanting to impose rules and attitudes that are valid in their own countries.

This comment reinforces the challenges of working in cross-cultural contexts, particularly when a particular set of values developed in a particular cultural context are foisted onto local staff.

A participant from South Africa reflected on the issues arising from perceptions of who has skills that matter and how the value attached to the 'skills that matter' are culturally relevant:

> From the staff's point of view, it is tricky. On one hand, staff can appreciate the help of volunteers; on the other hand, they might get irritated. Sometimes it entrenches certain perceptions about who has the skills. That might create tension in the workplace.

Perceptions of knowledge and skills vary depending on the individuals. As one Peruvian participant said:

> I have received few complaints, but one complaint I have heard is, for example: the partner organization or its personnel have too ambivalent attitudes about the co-operant [volunteer]. Sometimes they expect them to have information about everything, expert [information] – they have to know, they were educated in Canada and so they have to know. They say 'the expert' when it's convenient and when it's not, then: 'you don't know, you are a foreigner'. This is disqualifying the other because they are a foreigner, it's a cultural thing. Now, I should tell you, this doesn't always happen. They use the two assessments. So this is a problem of negating the qualifications of the other, which is something that they should also know exists. I am not saying that everyone will do it (and does it) all the time, but it happens.

Thus, the critique of cross-cultural understanding and expectations about cross-cultural behaviour also applies to host country staff, according to some of the host country participants in this study.

As the comment above from the Peruvian participant makes clear, interactions with arrogant international volunteers is not the only experience they've encountered. Many positive cross-cultural experiences were also reported. Thus, hosting international volunteers within the organization also presents some important opportunities for cross-cultural understanding as identified by the host country participants. The participants in this study spoke of enrichment and alternative perspectives resulting from cross-cultural exposure.

The participant from Peru remarked: "The eyes of a stranger see things that we don't see." Building on the desire and appreciation for alternative perspectives, the participant from Jamaica said:

> Again too it's not just about finance, it's about the cultural exchange, which is so important for our people. Indeed, in bringing a different perspective too, it really expands the vision of staff, of women participants, of the volunteers

too. … Again we always maintain it's a mutual benefit to be gleaned from these exchanges.

The general interest in getting to know the international volunteers plays out in a number of ways, including generous invitations for volunteers to visit host staff members in their homes. Overall, host country participants noted the high importance attached to getting to know people and learning about their cultures and ideas as a key motivation for participation in LVA4D.

In summary, the findings point to a combination of opportunities and challenges associated with the cross-cultural exposure presented through the encounter between volunteers from the Global North and the host organization staff and overview informants in the seven countries of the Global South participating in this study. The positive experiences reflect on the nature of cross-cultural sharing that takes place and the enrichment that is experienced through this exposure to other cultures, practices, and approaches. The positive experiences must also be understood in the context of challenges experienced and identified by the participants from the Global South. The issues that were identified in the findings include the challenges of dealing with preconceived notions of what life in developing countries is like and stereotypes that develop and are possibly entrenched through LVA experiences. Other challenges include isolationism of foreign volunteers and the formation of cliques and enclave communities that hamper cross-cultural opportunities. Even more problematic, cross-cultural challenges may include arrogance or superiority complexes on the part of foreign volunteers, which can create tensions and prevent a rich cross-cultural experience. Addressing these challenges is essential for improved cross-cultural understanding and exchange.

These findings provide some insights into the perceived value and challenges of LVA programmes in the Global South from the perspectives of international volunteers and host organization staff. The findings also raise some important questions about how we understand culture more generally and how our perceptions of cultural understanding can serve to cloak inequality (Simpson, 2004). For example, poverty and material conditions can be explained away with reference to culture. The cultural understanding that may emerge from these experiences is that people in the Global South are "poor but happy", which can translate into an understanding that "people 'do not mind' being poor, or that happiness is a greater wealth than material conditions" (Simpson, 2004: 159). Through this process, poverty becomes rationalized and obscures the bigger issues of inequality, exploitation and oppression (Simpson, 2004).

An emphasis on difference arises in many of the findings from the international volunteer and host organization research. As Simpson points out in her study on gap year programmes in the United Kingdom, international volunteering is often

infused with a language of cultural difference. However, they risk teaching that all difference is explained through 'culture'. For, without critical engagement, without the search for commonality as well as difference and with an apolitical language, a discourse based on cultural 'explanations' becomes dominant. Within such a discourse, culture becomes the only possible explanation, and one in which questions of material inequality can be ignored under the panacea-justifying cloak of 'culture'.

(Simpson, 2004: 689)

Opportunities for building relationships and forming friendships

One measure of cross-cultural exchange is the extent to which friendships are formed between the volunteers and the host organization staff. In this section I examine the reflections on friendship formation on the part of the Canadian LVA participants.

One way to examine the extent of cross-cultural exchange is to learn about the nature and extent of relationships formed between the international volunteers and host organization and community members. In this study, I asked questions about the nature of relationships formed and with whom the volunteers became friends. Many, but not all, of the youth participants commented on friendships they formed with other Canadians or other foreigners who were volunteering or working abroad. The Canadian youth spend holidays travelling with other foreigners and enjoyed weekend activities primarily with other Canadians, or foreigners from the USA or Europe. There was a distinct preference for associating with other volunteers rather than wealthy expats with whom many Canadian volunteers felt they had little in common. Yet, friendships with the local colleagues they worked with during their placements also featured quite prominently in their discussions of who they considered their friends during the LVA placement. In research conducted by Unstead-Joss, she found that volunteers "did not expect to become good friends with local people" (2008: 16) which "might indicate a volunteer's sense of detachment from the host community before they arrive" (Unstead-Joss, 2008: 16).

Interviews with Canadian youth revealed a mixed response to friendship formation while abroad. Some of the youth participants felt they were able to establish meaningful and enduring friendships with colleagues in their host organization and in their host communities. Other youth talked about difficulties in making friends with locally based colleagues. Several Canadians talked about the busy lives of their colleagues and extensive differences in interests between the volunteer and the host staff. As a result, many Canadian youth sought friendship formation with other foreigners. Nonetheless, some examples of cross-cultural friendship from my study stand out. Adam, for example, reflected on the depth of friendship he experienced with one friend from Guatemala who saved up money to travel to Canada to visit him for a month after the volunteer (Adam) returned home. Adam remarked on the positive experience he had hosting his colleague from Guatemala in this reciprocal fashion. Francois noted that his closest friend during his placement abroad was his boss at the host organization. He said: "We spent a fair bit of time together, and gradually became closer and closer friends. [We] started talking about pretty much everything... . She was the person I went to with all my problems." Francois also noted that he dated a Ghanaian for a while and said: "We were pretty close, but apparently we misunderstood each other's intentions. I thought it was just a short-term thing and she was pretty upset when it all ended. That was probably, yeah, one of the closest relationships I formed as well." At least two of the Canadian participants in my study ended up marrying people from their host country and had moved permanently to live abroad with their new spouses.

Clara, like other volunteers, noted that she made friends with both local part-ners and with other foreigners. She became friends with her officemate, who she described as "a lovely lady with very cute kids". She also said she made friends with the executive director because "we helped each other get to the top of Kili-manjaro". Clara commented on how difficult it was for her to leave behind these new friends, noting "there was some crying on both parts" when the placement was over. Clara said she also developed a close relationship with another foreigner, a guy, a relationship she said made sense "because you're going through everything together, you know we're in the same spot and you have the same frame of refer-ence". For Shelley, her friendships consisted of Filipinos who shared similar interests as her, including a group of rock climbers and Frisbee players; she has stayed in touch with several of these friends since returning home to Canada.

Maci, however, said that "obviously" she made friends with other volunteers who were from Western countries because together they were able to reflect on their experiences abroad. Lindsay, too, said that she made friends with

> mostly expats. A couple of Americans, and [a] few South Africans, Dutch, German, not a lot of local people, which wasn't intentional, but the places where we would go at night happened to be favourites of other volunteers or foreign workers or whatever so you just sort of make friends and get used to that group sort of thing.

Kennedy also noted that she spent most of her time with another Canadian. While Kennedy travelled abroad with the intention of challenging herself and get-ting to know people other than the Canadian she was travelling with, she found it "beneficial" to have another Canadian with her: someone to eat dinner with, work out with, and to travel together. Kennedy noted that the positive experience she had can be attributed to the friendship she made with another Canadian while abroad: "I think my experience would have been much different and probably not as good without her." Philippe said that his friends were "mostly other expats. Almost, almost, well Germans and Canadians I guess, but mostly Canadians which is kind of sad." Margaret also said she made friends with other foreigners – a fact that she regretted towards the end of her placement, she noted. Camilla reflected on what she perceived to be the difficulty of developing relationships with local people, noting that local people "are so different from you in terms of the way you think and what you like to do". For Camilla, the differences were considered insur-mountable rather than an opportunity for pushing her beyond her comfort level.

The reflections on friendship formation noted above offer insights into what the Canadian youth considered important qualities for making new friends. The emphasis on shared interests is significant in these comments. The Canadians talked about the people they could easily befriend as a result of the Canadians' interests in particular activities such as sports, sightseeing, or going out to clubs. The emphasis is on ease of friendship formation, with little attention to stepping beyond what Canadians might consider socially valuable activities. In effect, there was little effort made to embrace a cross-cultural experience in the host country for many of the participants as the expectation of friendship formation was limited to finding friends who were 'like them' and who did things they would do back in Canada. As such, the 'bubble effect' is clearly demonstrated in these expressions of how friendships were formed during the LVA4D placements. In Ogden's (2008) analysis of "today's colonial student", he highlights the physical space of the "verandah" as a metaphor for the colonial approaches and limited intercultural engagement that can take place during student mobility programmes. He concludes with the following statement: "If education abroad is about helping students to learn new ways of thinking and to become more complex, inter-culturally competent individuals, it is not desirable for students to remain comfortably situated on the verandah" (p. 50). Rather, students need to make 'meaningful contact' with the host culture "to learn with and from them, to explore new values, assumptions and beliefs" (p. 50). Volunteers are likely to share accommodations with other foreigners and are unlikely to leave the comfort of what they perceive as safe spaces – physically and culturally. As a result, the volunteers begin to make sense of other cultures and people, observing from afar and through a lens shared with other volunteers.

The 'bubble effect' did not apply to all of the experiences of the study participants, however. Stacey, for example, said that most of her friendships were with local people. Most of these friends, however, were men because friendship formation with women was difficult due to perception of the foreigner's status as more closely aligned to men's status in the local society. Stacey spent some time trying to understand why she had so few women friends, and reflected on the English-speaking skills of the women she met from the host country while she was abroad. She went on to reflect on how the men she became friends with were hotel or restaurant owners and their access to (relative) wealth gave them status that made it possible to be friends with them. Overall, however, the majority of the youth participants noted that it was easier to develop friendships with other expats or foreigners, indicating that they had more in common with other foreigners, and had each other to travel with or to spend time with during holidays while co-workers were busy with their families. Nonetheless, the friendships formed with local staff, while less intense for many of the youth participants, were very important and no less significant. Many of the youth talked about staying in touch with their former co-workers via Skype, email, or phone conversations.

Host country participants also felt that friendships they forged with the international volunteers were important and significant. Several of the host country participants talked about the lifelong friendships made with international volunteers and even noted that some of the interns became involved in intimate relationships with local community members. As Martine from Jamaica noted: "we have had two families who have had children who are married to two of the volunteers who came. As a matter of fact it is two chaps who married to two girls." Another Jamaican participant (Frank) said that the friendships were often genuine and even "led to a volunteer inviting a Jamaican friend to spend time with her in Canada".

Two of the Zambian participants (Kandyata and Wilbur) mentioned that the friendships built between the volunteers and the host communities extended to the villages where the volunteers were placed. Over time, trust and friendship developed such that the village gave the volunteers local names and the volunteers became very attached to the community (Kandyata). Reflecting on the transitions taking place over time, Wilbur found that the volunteers begin to fit in and even spend their weekends interacting with people from the community: "They really change their attitude towards these people when they are in the country after a certain period." One of the Guatemalan participants, Nelson, confessed that he fell in love with a woman volunteer when he was 23 years old. He reflected on the challenges they faced since she was still a student and the relationship lasted for a period of time while they were apart. He went on to note that he developed friendships with many of the international volunteers. "I have been to the homes of many volunteers and I have had the possibility to do some things through this network of friends."

In summary, the interviews with the Canadian youth and international host staff reinforced the argument that both groups considered friendship formation with each other as meaningful and, at times, lasting. However, the Canadian youth frequently spent weekends and holidays with other foreigners, thus limiting the extent to which cultural immersion took place. And while some of the youth noted that they stayed in touch with their colleagues in the host country after returning to Canada, many of these friendships were not sustained over the long term, according to the longitudinal study.

Ogden's analysis of foreigner isolationism (the verandah metaphor) is further reinforced by several of the comments provided by host organization staff. Some of the host organization staff went to great lengths to reduce the 'bubble effect' that arises when foreigners only spend time with other foreigners. The isolationism inherent in many international volunteer placements demonstrates how foreigners "carry the home-grown 'bubble' of their lifestyle around with them" (Ogden, 2008: 38). A related challenge is the extent to which international volunteers invest in cultural immersion and friendship formation in their host communities. Internet access, blogging, email, and other information communication technology that international volunteers have (and many even insist on) raise questions about whether international volunteers ever really leave 'home' in a way that facilitates a rich and deep cross-cultural immersion. The effect of this cultural isolationism and lack of cultural immersion, Ogden argues, creates the "colonial student" similar to earlier colonialists in the Global South (Ogden, 2008). A 'colonial student' risks reinforcing stereotypes of the 'other' – by virtue of understanding local people through the eyes and observations of other foreigners – rather than breaking these stereotypes down by educating themselves through deep understanding with and from local community members.

Yet, despite all the challenges noted in this chapter, intercultural learning remains widely understood as an automatic and likely result of volunteering abroad for many who promote these transnational encounters. The findings presented above do not always resonate with the findings for the literature reviewed in this chapter. Even though important challenges were identified, many opportunities and prospects for deep cross-cultural interactions remain. Nonetheless, several factors must be considered in order to ensure a fuller and richer cross-cultural experience. Lough *et al.* (2011) highlight duration, immersion, guided reflection, and contact reciprocity as key factors required for reflection on better cross-cultural understanding. Others factors to consider include individual characteristics and capabilities, attitudes and predispositions, expectations, and previous experience. All of these factors are key elements necessary to maximize the cross-cultural experience. The findings presented in this chapter also reinforce the need for explicit efforts to 'make meaningful contact' with host communities; to break free from the 'verandah' or the comfortable activities popular among the foreigners; and to establish connections with local community members that demonstrate an appreciation for – or interest in – the activities that are enjoyed locally. For some volunteers, that meant attending church with colleagues on Sunday morning or taking a trip to a rural community to visit someone's extended family for a wedding or funeral. Such gestures of interest in the day-to-day life of host communities are highly valued and contribute immensely to the depth of the cross-cultural experience for both hosts and international volunteers.

The Canadian youth who participated in the LVA study demonstrated some knowledge about the challenges of cross-cultural understanding through LVA programmes. However, the Canadian youth did not identify several key issues that were discussed by the participants from host countries in the Global South. In particular, the challenge of isolationism or creating a 'bubble' around themselves by interacting socially with mostly other foreigners who they may see as more similar to themselves is one major hurdle that could be addressed in pre-departure orientations and programme facilitation. Interviews with staff members from countries in the Global South therefore brought a more complete picture of the challenges of cross-cultural communication than might otherwise be available from the accounts of the international volunteers or the volunteer-sending organizations.

The findings from this research reinforce many of the concerns raised in the critical literature pertaining to neo-colonialism (Cook, 2007; Heron, 2007; Ogden, 2008), exacerbating differences rather than seeking solidarity (Simpson, 2004; Zemach-Bersin, 2009) and also highlight that cross-cultural communication needs to be understood as an important goal of LVA programmes and not an automatic result of such initiatives (Raymond and Hall, 2008). In other words, cross-cultural understanding is indeed a possible outcome of LVA4D. However, it requires management and facilitation to ensure that host staff and international volunteers find spaces and places to engage in deep cross-cultural interactions. Workplaces are not necessarily sufficient spaces for deep cross-cultural learning as offices often take on cultural norms similar to Global North office spaces, and when they don't reflect familiar Global North office cultures, international volunteers often lose patience with their colleagues for culturally relevant practices such as 'being on time'.

Moving from a language of 'culture shock' to cultural understanding

Cross-cultural experience can be one of the greatest challenges in the volunteer abroad experience (Epprecht, 2004). Furthermore, it is generally assumed that these encounters with 'difference' will be overcome in a way that leads to greater engagement with the host community or activist-oriented work in the future (Epprecht, 2004) – assumptions requiring further unpacking (Epprecht 2004; Simpson, 2004).

Scholars such as Crabtree (2008) argue that "international immersion experiences involve intense psycho-emotional, ideological and physiological disruptions" (p. 21). Crabtree provides an extensive overview of a variety of models designed to explain the process of cross-cultural adjustment: "These models include stages or phases of psychological disruption, gradual adjustment and adaptation over time, questioning oneself and one's own culture, and resultant attitude and behavior changes" (p. 21). In the study of LVA participants, several Canadians recounted experiences with reflection on stages of learning largely through the 'culture shock' framework. 'Culture shock' is widely employed to refer to a form of psychological disruption. Challenges identified in these disruptive phases include inability to understand and/or frustration with their day-to-day encounters. To cope in these circumstances, some of the Canadian participants talked about shutting themselves off from the world – and from the local cultural practices – around them. Paulette and Shelley, for example, said they distanced themselves emotionally, employing the terms 'emotional shut down' and 'depression' to denote the physical isolation they sought from colleagues and local community members. One participant, in particular, spoke about shutting himself in his room to escape the psychological challenges of cultural immersion; another, Shelley, said she withdrew from activities she usually enjoys because her experience in a new cultural context made her feel depressed.

Other LVA participants from Canada talked about their frustrations with their inability to understand why things work the way they do in the host country compared to how things work in Canada. What is interesting about these discussions is that none of the participants mentioned having any systematic or structured strategy for dealing with what they perceived to be 'culture shock'. In one case, Paulette said she was advised to retreat from the situation (take a holiday) and seek out peers with whom she could relate based on shared experiences and, thus, further isolate herself from the cultural context by creating or extending her 'bubble'. Taken to another level, one participant talked about 'culture rage' and how she needed to learn how to deal with this rage in order to 'get through [her] day'. This rage was discussed in relation to intense negative attitudes towards the day-to-day cultural practices of her co-workers. Her inability to embrace cultural differences and her failure to consider that her own perspectives on how things should be done are not the only possible way to bring about immense frustration that required facilitation and deeper reflection. Evan also referred to 'adjusting' to cultural differences that he never came to completely understand. Sonia noted that she had a challenging relationship with her host mother because she could not speak back to her in the same manner that she could speak back to her mother in Canada. As a result, she felt powerless and came to terms with her situation by having to 'rough it out'. These examples point to strategies of avoidance and tolerance rather than structured and/ or concerted efforts to understand why cultural practices exist and how acceptance and adaptation may be reasonable responses to difficult situations. Furthermore, these examples speak to the expectations of the volunteers – expectations that circumstances *should* be similar to what they are familiar with in their home countries. In this sense, Epprecht (2004) and Crabtree (2008) express a similar concern regarding the need to better understand how cross-cultural adjustment takes place in the context of volunteer abroad programmes so that learning that comes from this adjustment process is better facilitated by staff. Just 'getting through' or 'learning to deal with' these challenges is not reflective of the type of learning and ultimate engagement that is presumed to come simply based on the experience of cultural immersion.

Heron (2007) equates the notion that the other's culture will be shocking with the implication of a "carnivalesque world that does not make sense and is not quite real", calling into play "previously known spatial tropes that are productive of Othering" (p. 59).

Epprecht (2004) describes the underlying pedagogical theory of work-study abroad programmes in the developing world as being founded on an assumed relationship between cultural immersion and learning:

> Perhaps most importantly, however, the shock of immersion in a foreign culture disorients the student's faith in her/his own embedded assumptions about right and wrong. Such culture shock ideally forces her/him to reconstruct a truly global perspective. Whether that is ultimately harnessed to make the person a socially responsible international banker or an anti-globalization activist largely depends on the other courses offered in the program that shape its vision of good global citizenship.
>
> *(p. 714)*

Furthermore, the language of 'culture shock' and its employment as a means to explain the kind of experience international volunteers have when they encounter the cultural practices of host community staff was considered highly offensive to some of the host staff participants. There are some practices that come as a shock to all people (whether random violence or disregard for human life). However, the day-to-day cultural practices and ways of living should not be, according to the host staff, encompassed in the language of 'culture shock'. Volunteer participants should also be reminded that specific practices, modes of dress, habits, and activities that volunteers display can be perceived as 'shocking' or offensive to host communities as well. Furthermore, the employment of this lens of shock sets the international volunteers up for a particular kind of experience that may not resonate with the participants. The host organizations suggested a shift in language from 'culture shock' to 'challenges of integration' or 'cross-cultural challenges'. The change in language opens up space for reflection on the dynamics of cross-cultural interactions and opportunities to work through these challenges (fluid and reflective) rather than characterizing another society's culture as separate and shocking (fixed and judgemental).

In her work on the gap year phenomenon, Simpson (2005: 461) states that: "[t]he value of the gap year is premised, to a large degree, on the presumed relationship between encountering difference and knowing difference" and that "The notion of 'broad horizons', encapsulates the idea that learning automatically occurs through travel." Simpson is critical of the 'contact hypothesis', a theory based on the assumption that "experience alone (in the form of contact) would be enough to cause a change in values" (2005: 462). Thus, 'understanding' through cross-cultural encounters cannot be taken as a natural outcome of volunteer abroad programmes. Cross-cultural understanding is enhanced through explicit efforts to immerse oneself in the local culture, in taking time to interact with people in the host community and to do so in ways that involve a variety of interactions, including work relationships, cultural events, and personal connections. Host family placements in which international volunteers live with host families, share meals with these families, and take part in the day-to-day life of a host family can be a rich and rewarding way to immerse oneself in the local culture. Many LVA programmes include homestays as part – or all – of the programme abroad. Canadians who have returned from international placements involving home stays often include reflections on what it was like to have a deep relationship with a home stay mother and to feel like a sister or family member in someone's home. Even though such opportunities for meaningful cross-cultural engagement may be made for the international volunteers, several practices may limit the potential for deep cross-cultural experiences. One way that international volunteers may fail to connect with host communities is through the constant communication with friends and family 'back home', through blogging or Facebook posts, etc. All of these practices can be a way of journaling one's experience, but also have the potential negative effect of engaging in cross-cultural experiences for the purposes of shaping a particular image of oneself in relation to the 'other' – a performance performed for the purpose of audiences back home rather than a meaningful interaction and change opportunity while abroad. A second institutional challenge that requires careful examination is the pre-departure preparation received and the way that terms such as 'culture shock' may inadvertently shape the perspective of the international volunteer and his or her ability to connect with people in a new cultural context.

As participants in LVA prepare for their placements, they are often, during pre-departure training, told to prepare for 'culture shock'. The idea of 'cultural shock' is taken as a given for those who travel abroad. Volunteer abroad participants may also be told to prepare for 'reverse culture shock' upon their return to Canada. 'Culture shock' is described as the experience of being confronted with a new cultural environment, or the effect of going from one culture into another. By the time you begin orienting yourself, you could be experiencing the first signs of culture shock. There are four stages of culture shock generally described in pre-departure orientation materials. These stages are highlighted in Figure 3.1 on the culture shock U-curve. The projected experiences of culture shock are mapped out on this inverse curve. Youth who take part in pre-departure orientations may be warned of these stages, beginning with euphoria (or what is often referred to as the honeymoon stage of being abroad, when everything is exciting and new). This stage is followed by anxiety when LVA participants may begin to have concerns about their contributions, or develop issues with their peers, colleagues, etc. The third stage of rejection is deemed the lowest point of the culture shock curve. It is during this stage of rejection that youth are told they may experience some elements of depression characterized by a perspective that the youth do not fit in, are not accepted, or feel different from the 'others' they encounter. The youth participants are told they may feel rejected and/or may feel they are rejecting the culture of the community and organization that is hosting them. The final stage is characterized as the adjustment stage: a time at which the youth participants begin to come to peace with their contributions and place in the LVA programme. Cultural practices are expected to no longer 'shock' the youth participants.

Some of the symptoms of 'culture shock' include feelings of anger, discomfort, confusion, frustration, or irritability and loss of a sense of humour; withdrawal, spending excessive amounts of time alone, spending time only with Canadians or other foreigners and avoiding contact with locals; negative feelings about the people and culture of the host country; compulsive eating and drinking or a need for excessive amounts of sleep; and boredom, fatigue, and an inability to concentrate or work effectively (Government of Canada, 2014). Those who provide pre-departure orientations will likely comment on the variation in experiences and a series of ups and

Culture Shock U-Curve

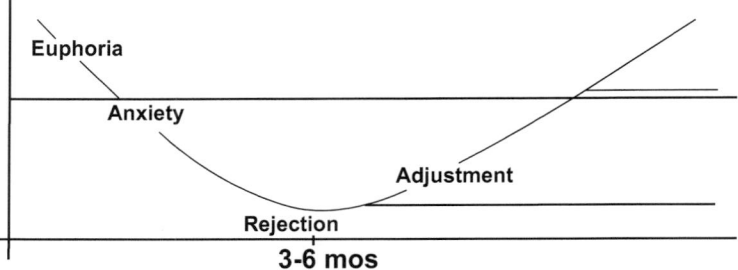

FIGURE 3.1   Culture shock U-curve.

Source: Safety Abroad website, University of Toronto.

downs that youth might encounter while abroad. Some participants are told that they may not experience the lowest lows that their peers may experience, but in any case, before going abroad, Canadians learn the language of 'culture shock' and expect 'culture shock' as a normal part of their time abroad. In effect, volunteer abroad participants learn that it is normal and natural to feel shocked by other cultures.

When doing interviews with host country participants in the Global South, we inquired whether the staff working in the host country organizations also observed the characteristics of 'culture shock' among the Canadian participants and/or whether the culture shock curve resonated with their experiences of hosting international volunteers. To begin, it is important to note that many of the host country participants were offended by the use of the term 'culture shock', wondering aloud why we would consider their culture or any culture shocking. Ronaldo said: "I don't see it as a shock, but a difficult period of adaptation." Raj noted: "I don't know whether it's a cultural shock … maybe cultural difference that they have faced, which might have created some discomfort for some of them." And Madeleine said: "It's natural, part of adaptation, but it doesn't come to this, because the graph shows a deep depression that does not really exist."

Jose Miguel said that language constitutes part of the culture shock he observes in the international volunteers. In addition, he refers to other shocking experiences including food and weather. Julia attributes the experience of culture shock experienced by the international volunteers to the exposure to levels of poverty that foreigners are not used to. While reflecting on the pre-departure terminology of culture shock, some of the interview participants from the host countries highlighted how their exposure to youth from the Global North was equally 'shocking'. Kandyata reflects on things that are shocking about the international volunteers, providing an example of an international volunteer chain-smoking and even smoking inside the offices, despite smoking not being allowed inside the building. The staff members of this organization were shocked by this behaviour and found themselves often going outside to get away from the smoking volunteer inside the building. Rather than adhering to rules (or learning what local rules regarding smoking entail), the host country staff had to deal with different work situations and adapt their work activities and routines. Another host country participant reflected on the culture shock that the communities faced when they were introduced to the international volunteers from the Global North. Examples of things they consider shocking from the international volunteers included the way volunteers dressed or behaved in public spaces. In some cases, host country participants talked about the need for de-briefing sessions for the staff and community members of the host country. The host staff, at times, offered de-briefing sessions for community members who had hosted international volunteers. These community members needed an opportunity to reflect on what they had observed during the volunteer's stay and discuss the 'culture shock' in an effort to mitigate some of the negative effects of hosting them. Other host country participants said they are no longer 'shocked' by the international visitors because over the years they have become accustomed to the culture of Western volunteers.

Manuel explains his own experience working with international volunteers on 3–6-month placements. He summarizes the experience as: accompanying the volunteer, being responsible for the volunteering and for the security of that individual, which can be "a huge shock" for the host country partners. The shock that Manuel is referring to is the nature of the expectations of the international volunteers and the kind of work that is (or is not) performed while in the host country. Manuel's comments highlight the surprise and frustration that comes with the support and meeting the needs of the international volunteers who come for short periods of time, combined with the limited pay-off associated with supporting these three-month placements.

Another host country participant, Sameer, argues that the depth of culture shock is experienced early on in the placement, in the first stage.

> This is more work-related, work culture shock. They realize that I've been here for so many days and realize nothing works in this organization. Every day there's a new thing happening, there's a new agenda. They don't take me seriously. They get a shock of the way the whole organization works, how organic the structure is. If there's a resource crunch, if somebody's teaching painting to children, every day, he or she has to go ask for art material and they are sorry there's no art material, come back tomorrow … they get frustrated how the organization works sometimes.

For many of the host organization staff, there was considerable effort put into orienting the international volunteers to alleviate any culture shock, but more work could be done to better prepare international volunteers for greater adaptability and reduced expectations of what can be accomplished, given the structural constraints and limitations of working in contexts where access to resources is unreliable.

Other staff members noted that culture shock was either not an issue in their experience, or that it had been effectively mitigated through pre-departure or on-site orientations. In one case, the host country participant noted that a great deal of time was invested in providing orientation to the international participants:

> because in the orientation we take them to the bus stop, we really do not just (give) a lecture kind of orientation, we physically take them to different places so that they can understand and see … how they sit in the plaza and see how people relate. We do a language session with them, that kind of thing. So culture shock hasn't really been a real issue.

Other host organization staff also commented on the orientation sessions the volunteers receive before travelling abroad so "when they come to us they are already oriented" (Grace). Generally, the host organization staff members were less comfortable with the term 'culture shock', opting to use terms like 'familiarity with cultural differences' or 'adaptation' to describe the range of experiences the youth participants might have while abroad.

The comments provided by the host organization staff raise questions about the use of the culture shock U-curve as a pre-departure orientation tool and the use of the language of culture as potentially shocking. In any case, the experience of immersing oneself in another culture provides a rich opportunity for personal growth and developing adaptation skills. Both the Canadian youth and the host country staff members highlighted the importance of adaptation while abroad as central to the personal growth experience for both the hosts and the volunteers.

Cross-cultural immersion as personal growth

Personal growth is mentioned by the Canadian participants as an important motivation for going abroad. On its own, the notion of personal growth is difficult to define and is highly linked to other motivations such as cross-cultural understanding or skills development. Some of the challenges attributed to the motivation of personal growth include the emphasis placed on individualistic changes, the focus on the international volunteer's personal growth, and the ambiguity of the term itself.

The Canadian youth who participated in the interviews offered a number of examples of how they thought they had grown as a result of their LVA4D experience. Examples of personal growth included greater understanding of different ways of doing things, greater adaptability and resourcefulness, and more maturity resulting from greater independence and expectations of performance from host staff.

When host organization staff members were asked if they saw evidence of growth of character with the volunteers they hosted, many of the host participants said they had. The Canadian youth also had a clear sense of the value that personal growth had for them individually. There was little critique, however, about the one-directional nature of this personal growth experienced by the Canadian youth. The personal growth that young Canadians were able to achieve through LVA experiences was thus used as a rationale for taking part in these programmes and also articulated as one of the most significant motivations for choosing to go abroad. The benefits of personal growth are discussed in this chapter; however, these reflections on personal growth and shifts in identity provided by Canadian youth shed little light on the broader implications of justifying egoistic motivations for going abroad.

Cross-cultural understanding for global competency and global citizenship

LVA4D programmes offer much potential for the promotion of cross-cultural understanding, and this improved exchange of ideas can foster global competency (ability to act ethically, effectively, and conscientiously in global contexts) and foster a sense of global citizenship and international solidarity. Participation in international service learning is believed to foster more engaged citizens. In an analogy offered by Bringle and Hatcher (2011), the authors consider the pedagogical approach of international service learning (ISL) as central to global citizenship. They note that "ISL holds the potential and may be a pedagogy that is best suited to prepare college graduates to be active global citizens in the 21st century" (Bringle and Hatcher, 2011: 3). Since the early 1990s, the language of global citizenship has increasingly been adopted to reflect the desire to learn about the world and to travel to far-off places. The concept of global citizenship – and its implications for social change versus egoistic benefits – is examined in greater detail in Chapter 7. As has been highlighted throughout this chapter, there are limitations in cross-cultural understanding when experiences abroad are constituted as culturally shocking, or when isolation or avoidance of cultural immersion takes place. Addressing some of the challenges highlighted in this chapter will be an important first step in improving LVA programmes to ensure that cross-cultural engagement is more effective in future initiatives.

Summary: rationalizing cross-cultural engagement

This chapter has highlighted many of the challenges and opportunities of cross-cultural communication for LVA4D. The Canadian and host country participants offer important reflections on both the motivations for cross-cultural engagement as part of the reasons for participation in LVA4D as well as pointing to the broader rationales for intercultural competence as part of development solutions. Motivations for cross-cultural engagement can be egoistic in nature in terms of specific skills development for the participants in this study. For Canadian participants, the skills acquired through cross-cultural engagement on LVA4D may be central to other aspirations, such as personal goals and/or finding a job in international development and community development contexts at home or abroad – a subject for the next chapter. Host country participants may also be motivated to engage in cross-cultural communication for the purpose of improved job performance working in international contexts, as well as for personal goals of shared understanding across cultures.

The value of cross-cultural engagement is rationalized by diverse actors and in a range of discursive contexts from volunteer-sending organization advertising campaigns to international development scholarship. Cross-cultural understanding can be rationalized as a means to entrench systems of inequality by focusing on personal relationships at the expense of changing structural inequalities. It can also be rationalized in the context of contributing important learning and reflexivity-oriented approaches to global change. Of all the motivations expressed as very important to the Canadian participants in this study, cross-cultural communication stood out as the most common motivation. Host organization staff members also referred to cross-cultural exchange and learning from international volunteers as a valuable aspect of volunteer abroad programmes, with numerous references by host country staff to the value of learning new ideas and alternative ways of doing things from the international volunteers.

While there are important challenges and limitations to the cross-cultural dynamics that occur during LVA4D, there is also much promise for improved cross-cultural understanding, global competence, and solidarity through LVA4D. Out of all the motivations examined in this book, and in relation to the important rationales for participation discussed throughout the chapters in this collection, cross-cultural communication stands out as one of the most promising elements of LVA4D because it has the most potential to contribute to enhanced learning and shared understanding required for mutuality and social change.

Addressing several core challenges remains significant in the way forward, including improved understanding of how cultural practices are steeped in historical relations within and between countries. Searching for – and finding – similarities between volunteers and host partners is also important for reducing the 'othering' that can happen when volunteers focus exclusively or extensively on the differences they observe when comparing the culture they feel they know from their own life experiences and the culture they have recently encountered.

Most importantly, a solid cross-cultural experience prioritizes the learning component of LVA over the 'helping' or volunteering aspect (I turn to helping in greater detail in Chapter 6). Volunteers returning from medium-term (3–6-month) placements abroad will not return as experts on the cultural practices of the host country. Nor will those volunteers who have spent two or more years abroad. Many long-term volunteers, in fact, may say that the longer they spent immersed in the culture of the host community, the less they felt they understood. Here, the iceberg analogy is a useful model to consider as there remains so much under the surface that is difficult to see and comprehend. Nonetheless, medium-term LVA4D offers potential for improving cross-cultural understanding and is rationalized by the volunteers and hosts alike in both individualistic and solidaristic terms.

Note

1 Pseudonyms were used for all study participants.

4

SKILLS DEVELOPMENT AND TESTING A CAREER CHOICE

Capital accumulation and perceived benefits

Introduction

Participants in learning/volunteering abroad for development (LVA4D) expressed a broad range of overlapping motivations pertaining to competencies that are acquired through participation in these programmes. Among these competencies are cross-cultural communication skills (discussed in greater depth in the preceding chapter), practical skills development that enable the Canadian participants to find employment or test an academic background or career choice, and personal growth attributes. There are also important learning and skills-building opportunities for host community and organizational staff, including new perspectives on approaches to development work, learning new skills or technical abilities through information sharing with volunteers as well as competencies acquired in the process of learning to negotiate and communicate with people from diverse cultural backgrounds.

In Chapter 3, I highlight the significance of skills development and testing an academic background or career choices as one of the most important motivations highlighted by the participants in my research. For young Canadian men who participated in these interviews, testing a career choice ranked as *the* most important motivation for participating in learning/volunteering abroad (LVA) and ranked as the second most important motivation overall for women and men combined. In this chapter I provide a deeper analysis of the significance of a motivation of career advancement and related motivations such as 'skills development' from the perspectives of the Canadian participants in LVA programmes and host country staff. These motivations are important to consider in the context of other rationales in the context of international development more broadly and in relation to the host country perspectives of skills learned more specifically, which are examined in this chapter. This chapter begins with a discussion of building skills as part of the LVA4D programme, as this was one of the most frequently noted benefits identified by host country staff and volunteers alike.

Factors that contribute to career advancement

Interview respondents from Canada and the host countries agreed that participation in LVA programmes facilitated skills development for both the international volunteers and the host community staff. For the Canadian participants, the skills developed or honed while abroad were generally considered valuable skills for entering the job force and pursuing a career. The youth participants noted that participating in LVA programmes enhanced skills and also affected their career goals and plans. For some Canadian volunteer participants, the experience abroad deepened their resolve to continue working in a career that involves international development work; others decided that working internationally was not for them, opting to find work in Canada (Tiessen, 2014).

Some of the participants mentioned the relationship between their experiences abroad, their career goals, and their academic focus. A total of 20 participants (17 women and 3 men), or 19 per cent of the Canadian participants, noted that their experience abroad affected their academic focus. In total, 23 participants expressed an interest in graduate studies or furthering their education as a result of their experience abroad.

Some of the participants learned that before they can begin a career, additional education is required. Some participants thus indicated an interest in graduate work in international development while others expressed an interest in learning more skills-oriented material through an MBA or nursing degree. Erika, for example, said:

> Definitely, I'm going to be doing my masters. I don't think I would have done my masters in international social work without [the experience abroad]. I think it has made me passionate about international social work. I feel like, especially in developing countries, community work is interesting.

Katrina originally thought the completion of an undergraduate degree and a CIDA internship would be sufficient to get a job in international development, but realized after her internship that she needed more education. Most of the participants who said they would return to school said they were planning to pursue a Master's degree. Others decided that additional graduate research (pursuing a PhD) would be postponed or abandoned. Tracey, for example, said she didn't want to pursue a PhD after living abroad. Based on her experience observing students conducting fieldwork in the country where she was placed, she noted that:

> academic research can be extremely intrusive and often when we apply it to our theories and when we write it up it really loses all of its meaning and value for the people that we research and so it kind of put a bad taste in my mouth.

Some who decided not to continue with postgraduate education favoured a role that involved a more helping orientation upon realization of the intrusiveness of graduate research in the developing countries.

Many of the participants talked about the desire to build skills and a career path in tandem with the motivation of helping others. Volunteering abroad, particularly among youth, is therefore widely considered to be a way to "help others" as well as to "explore career options and to increase the likelihood that they might be able to pursue the career they want" (Stukas *et al.*, 1999: 11). I return to the significance of helping desires in Chapter 6, but it is valuable to point out the interrelationship between motivations as highlighted in Chapter 2, and the challenges of singling out specific motivations or ranking them without consideration of the deeper rationales that underpin motivations.

Testing a career choice

One of the core findings from this research is the motivation expressed by many of the participants, and especially the male respondents, to use the international experiential learning programme as a way to test their academic background or career choice. Throughout the interviews, participants referred to testing a career choice or academic background in several interview responses. Ingrid said:

> I first went over essentially testing whether I wanted an international career. That was one of the reasons I guess for going and after my experience there I decided that it wasn't appropriate at my level of expertise really to be working overseas yet, in a development capacity. So my aim is to work in development in Canada for the next ten years and then re-evaluate whether I have the interest and the capacity to work overseas again and so now I've come home and I'm working for the closest thing to a microfinance organization in Calgary.

Ingrid's reflections on her experience abroad in relation to her career offered some positive insights into the importance of LVA4D as an educational opportunity for young Canadians who may feel qualified to do international development work but are able to learn, based on their medium-term exposure abroad, that their contributions are minimal, and possibly even counterproductive.

Isabelle said her experience abroad taught her that she didn't have the right personality to do the work she had dreamed of doing throughout her undergrad. She said: "I used to think I wanted to do very grassroots work with people in developing countries but I realized I'm not as charismatic – or outgoing enough – to do that. Which is fine." In this way, 'testing the waters' through meaningful medium-term volunteer abroad options allowed the participants to consider their own abilities early on in their careers.

Other participants noted that they had a negative professional experience while on LVA4D programmes. Some said they were no longer interested in non-governmental organization (NGO) work and decided to pursue something either completely different or somewhat related (e.g. policy research). Some participants turned to – or returned to – a domestic focus because of personal values, treatment by hosts (good or bad), a revelation of the complexities of international development, and personal capacity (homesickness, challenges with adapting, lack of capacity for cross-cultural understanding), among other reasons. Ernesto said:

> I'm probably more reluctant after working in Zambia to … pursue a career in NGO work. Certainly in local level NGO work, I don't think that's my calling. I think that's something, I'm not precluding anything but it reaffirmed my interest in pursuing kind of other angles … so it was quite valuable from a career standpoint.

Other participants noted that they felt they could have a bigger impact working in Canada than internationally. Stephan noted:

> Before I wanted to work strictly in international development. When I came back to Canada I was working with youth that were new to the country. One of the challenges on the volunteer trip was that I was not very culturally relevant. I did not leave a lasting impression. Had someone locally been given the same opportunities by the Argentina government rather than the Canadian government, they might be better off. So I learned I was much more culturally relevant in the community where I grew up, which is why I'm working in Toronto now.

The findings also reflect that international experiences have become an important benchmark of achievement. The experience is important for many in terms of looking good on a resumé, getting into grad school, or finding employment. As Wendy argued, her international experience was the "perfect" opportunity to get experience in one country (South Africa) that she could then apply to her work in another country (Chile). Most important, Wendy noted, is that the work experience abroad builds her career portfolio which will lead to better jobs. While Wendy noted quite specifically that this is a highly "selfish" motivation for working abroad, she sees it as a necessary stepping stone for building a career either internationally or in Canada. As such, the building of a portfolio and development of a CV are central elements of capital accumulation. "Her CV is now differentiated from others in the pile when a prospective employer seeks a new hire with that most fashionable of qualifications, a social conscience" (McGloin and Georgeou, 2015:12).

McGloin and Georgeou (2015) examine expressions of "looks good on your CV" in relation to neoliberal rhetoric in voluntourism or short-term volunteer/tourism programmes, noting that "neoliberalism privileges individual autonomy and responsibility over that of the collective" (p. 6). As such, the volunteer abroad experience is understood in terms of 'corporate' citizenship whereby individuals are the consumers of a particular product (career advancement) rather than political actors (McGloin and Georgeou, 2015: 6). The experiences abroad in LVA4D build social capital that can be translated into economic capital through better pay and better jobs. Building on the argument of capital accumulated through voluntourism, these authors consider the "flow-on effect" defined by a change of values among the voluntourists that also and subsequently translates into changes in lifestyle for them (p. 10). Similar criticisms emerge in the analysis of the LVA4D or medium-term participants who articulate their experiences abroad in relation to the capital (social or economic) accumulated. Several of the male participants expressed a motivation for participation in LVA4D because they were able to earn money and make a financial profit from their experience abroad by saving their per diem allowances. Beyond the life-changing experience abroad for the voluntourism participants is an assumption that the lives of the people in the host country have also been changed. As McGloin and Georgeou (2015) note, this is not always the case as hosting international volunteers, particularly voluntourists, can do more harm than good as in the example of orphan voluntourism in Cambodia.

The comments provided by the Canadian youth shed light on two very practical career-related motivations for going abroad: (1) going abroad is important for building CVs and will help them get the jobs they want; and (2) going abroad helped the youth make sense of whether working in international development (at least in the Global South) was their true goal. Host country partners also recognized these practical motivations and the capital that international volunteers were able to accumulate through LVA4D programmes. Several references to LVA4D programmes as opportunities for career advancement for the international volunteers were made. Often, these remarks were accompanied by disillusionment due to the structural inequalities that prevent the host country partners from enjoying such benefits as well.

Is going abroad on LVA4D essential for the skills learned?

The Canadian youth participants were asked to reflect on whether the skills learned in their international experiences were skills they think they could have learned while in Canada. A minority of the participants said the skills they learned were distinct from skills they would have learned by volunteering or working in Canada. As Amy noted, the importance of being in a cross-cultural context and out of your "comfort zone" means that everything abroad is an adventure and different, including a trip to the bathroom. Acquiring language skills was an important difference in the responses. Those individuals who considered language skills to be among their key skills learned felt strongly that the international experience was essential. As Felicia noted:

> No, for me language skills definitely … advanced a lot quicker when I'm surrounded by people and am forced to speak the language … it's completely different when you go to a foreign context and apply those skills. We have lots of multiculturalism in Canada and obviously we interact with many different cultures everyday but to be in a completely different cultural context and reconcile your values and ways of communicating is a different experience.

Many of these skills could be learned, however, in a local – or Canadian – context. The degree of learning or speed was considered more significant in an international placement. Language stood out as an important skill developed while abroad due to the perceived need for immersion. Nonetheless, many of the youth participants recognized that a lot of the other skills could be learned in Canada.

The Canadian participants also considered the skills learned abroad to be highly transferable to work they might do back in Canada. The transferability of skills, however, requires careful examination. In a study by Thomas (2001), the author found that volunteers from the UK who participated in gap year programmes abroad may find it difficult to transfer skills they learn during their volunteer abroad programmes to their work experiences back home (Thomas, 2001). Thomas attributes the lack of skills transfer in international volunteering to the employers' reluctance to acknowledge the international volunteering experience as a form of career development or as a legitimate form of transferable skills development. The time spent away in another country is seen as time not spent learning skills in the UK to be applied to current work experience. However, for employers interested in hiring individuals who claim to have developed skills in adaptability, open-mindedness, and intercultural teamwork, volunteer abroad programmes may indeed give a boost to those starting a career.

Some of the participants in the LVA4D study presented in this book did consider the skills learned while abroad as distinct from the skills they could have learned by volunteering or working in the Canadian context. For those participants who responded that the skills are distinct from skills that could be learned in a volunteer or internship opportunity in Canada, many reflected on the importance of cross-cultural immersion to gain a new perspective, looking at the world differently, gaining cultural skills, critical thinking ability, and problem-solving skills, among other ways the volunteer abroad programme challenged them. On a professional level, some participants said they developed a special skill-set, practical language experience, field work experience, and gained more responsibility. Dalia, for example, said she is "very critical of people who work in development who have never been in a developing country" so she concludes that going abroad is essential for skills development but doesn't elaborate on why or how. Katrina argued that she could not have learned the same skills if she had worked in Canada, instead noting that it is much more competitive in Canada and much harder to get access to the jobs that will give her the skills she was able to learn in her host country. Thus, LVA can be seen, based on Katrina's observations, as a way to jump-start a career in international development by gaining experience quickly. Joan also remarked on the ability to get work experience abroad that she does not experience in Canada. Joan noted: "If somebody gave me the chance [to work in Canada], yeah." Joan's point emphasizes the privilege and opportunity that going abroad presents. Many youth may be pursuing international experience so they can learn skills since they can't get positions in Canada that teach them these skills. It presents some ethical issues though, because Canadian youth are often put in positions while abroad that may otherwise be reserved for nationals with more experience.

Several participants reflected on comparative skills-development training in Canada. Alice, for example, reflected on the potential to learn no matter where you are. She went on to suggest that working in Nunavut (a Territory in Northern Canada) was a similar cross-cultural experience to that of volunteering abroad. Nunavut, she argued, is "a whole new world" for her. Alice gave examples of other ways that individuals can experience a 'culture shock' similar to that experienced by going abroad, pointing to the possibility of urban people living in rural parts of Canada. For Shane, the skills he learned were not specific to living in another country. He said: "I don't think it matters too much where you click a mouse." Shane commented specifically on skills in the workplace and does not privilege the other skills one might learn by living abroad and being immersed in another culture. April noted cultural diversity in Canada as a way to immerse oneself in other cultures and to gain a similar experience as that of going abroad. She said: "I think so. We're so culturally diverse, especially … in Vancouver [and] there's so many opportunities to chat with people from anywhere." April continued with some reflections on the large number of opportunities for cross-cultural exposure within Canada. Nonetheless, April's time in Malawi confirmed for her that living abroad offered a *more* challenging cross-cultural exposure. She employed the language of 'culture shock' to expand on her experience of cultural immersion in another country and the exposure afforded when she observed the way people live on a daily basis in that country. Other Canadian participants highlighted the potential for cross-cultural exposure by meeting people within Canada who have recently moved to the country. Irene, for example, shared that working with immigrants in Canada is one possibility for cross-cultural skills development. Like April's comments, Irene agreed that Canadians have to be highly motivated to seek out opportunities to develop cross-cultural skills within Canada.

Clearly there are many benefits to putting oneself in a different cultural context, learning to adapt to different circumstances, and gaining independence and maturity through these experiences. However, as the findings above suggest, going abroad for volunteering is not always necessary for learning the kinds of skills that the youth learned while abroad. Yet, in terms of skills development and their application, there is a perceived benefit to going abroad as it relates to gaining employment. Many of the references to skills development, in fact, were directly related to employability. As such, skills development for the Canadian participants were articulated in relation to the capital accumulated: social capital that can be translated into economic capital resulting from paid employment.

Host community perspectives on volunteer skills contributions, skills development, and career advancement

There are indeed a range of experiences with LVA participants and the nature of skills these volunteers bring with them, according to the host country participants. Several host country participants made explicit reference to the positive attributes of international volunteers particularly in terms of critical thinking skills, new or fresh ideas, and new energy. In reviewing interview transcript data from the host country participants with reference to the benefits of hosting international volunteers, the term 'skills' was flagged 95 times. References were made by host staff members about the importance of international volunteer skills in relation to complementing the team. Others talked about specific skills such as computer or information technology (the most frequent reference to a specific skill-set), and writing or documentation skills. Host country participants noted that there are such skilled individuals within the country but that the organization may lack the resources to fund skilled employees, thus explaining their reliance on international volunteers to fill those positions.

In discussing the value of skills-sharing, one participant from Jamaica highlighted the need for international volunteers to also recognize the skills that the Southern organizations provide to the volunteers from the North, and the importance of being respectful of those skills. In fact, many of the references to skills were followed by the word 'sharing', suggesting that the two-way exchange of skills was considered very important to the host country staff members. Others made reference to skills transfer, highlighting the importance of transmission of skills to the host organization staff to ensure the sustainability of the organizational staff and their capacity to continue to perform specific tasks. In other words, the host organization staff considered the skills shared with local staff to be important and not just the exposure to individuals who temporarily brought such skills to the organization.

Other host country participants offered a more critical assessment of skills on offer with a clear sense of inequality of opportunity afforded to international volunteers who offer little and gain so much in terms of career advancement. Participants from the host countries were thus well aware of the skills-oriented and career-related opportunities that volunteer abroad programmes offered those who were pursuing jobs in international development and/or community service. For some of the host country participants, the advantages earned through LVA bordered on exploitation of host communities for personal gain. One such example was noted succinctly by a participant from Peru, named Madeleine: "They come with very little work experience. They forge their future here." This participant's comments, while brief, encapsulate quite well the structural challenges observed by several of the host organization staff who worked with international volunteers. These structural challenges relate to the global inequality of opportunity: volunteers from the Global North are able to advance their careers, develop skills, and gain capital as a result, while Global South partners experience few, if any, capital gains (social or economic). As the host partners elaborated, the Western youth who participate in LVA programmes are seen as generally having few tangible skills when they arrive in the host country but they learn important skills while abroad and use this experience to gain good jobs (capital) back at home. A participant from Malawi, Joseph, expanded on this point: "Another challenge is that these volunteers come here not for volunteering but only to look for greener pastures." By greener pastures, the participant is referring to the ability of the youth volunteers to return to the Global North and use their experiences to start or advance their careers.

Not all volunteers from the Global North used the LVA experience as a career-advancing initiative. However, it is clear from both the participants and the broader discourse surrounding LVA, that the experiences in the Global South, regardless of length of time abroad, are perceived (by the volunteers and the hosts alike) to improve their CVs and to give them a "leg up" when applying for jobs, and that systemic (perhaps neo-colonial) challenges prevent the host country participants from some of these same rewards. Some of the youth participants from Canada also noted that international internships were pivotal to career advancement or getting into a profession. And while there is a general and growing *perception* that LVA is crucial to finding a job, it is less clear whether these experiences abroad actually result in finding meaningful careers. Previous research by Lough *et al.* (2009), nonetheless, documents a correlation between international volunteering experience and the defining of educational and career objectives. LVA programmes, according to Pires (2000), are an important aspect to launching academic, career, and volunteer commitments. Other evidence of the correlation between skills development, LVA programmes, and career goals can be found in the study conducted by the Institute for the International Education of Students. The authors of this study demonstrated the long-term impact of study abroad in relation to additional academic pursuits, career choices, language skills and personal development, noting a direct correlation between career trajectories and study abroad opportunities (Norris and Gillespie, 2009). Most of the Canadian youth interviewed for my study considered LVA opportunities as fundamental to finding a meaningful career and that participation in LVA generally looks good on a resumé (Tiessen, 2014). However, there is need for additional research in the Canadian context to document the correlation between volunteer abroad opportunities and employment or career advancement.

Throughout the interviews with Canadians and host country staff, there was significant emphasis on learning 'cultural' or 'personal' skills rather than 'technical' skills. These 'soft' skills were generally very valuable to the Canadians and host partners alike, and speak to an agency-oriented analysis of some of the benefits of LVA4D. Several positive experiences are highlighted in the research findings and the significance of cultural enrichment and the alternative perspectives cannot go unrecognized. In fact, the positive cross-cultural experiences are to be celebrated, encouraged, and further developed. However, we cannot be we cannot get caught up in the promise of cross-cultural enrichment and ignore the important structural challenges that must be identified and addressed.

Skills identified by Canadian youth

The kinds of skills learned by many recent graduates of International Development Studies programmes or related fields may not be momentously linked to poverty alleviation in immediate or large-scale terms. However, there is indeed potential for the skills learned in a social science degree to foster improved international development work. Practical tools learned in educational programmes, including the day-to-day skills of researching and communication of ideas, are essential for international development work. Practical skills learned through more technical educational opportunities may give participants in LVA programmes an advanced vocabulary and experience with specific techniques, such as results-based management or log-frames, or participatory rural appraisal (PRA) toolkits.

Personal growth as linked to skills development by both Canadians and host partners

References to the benefits of participation in LVA in terms of personal growth abound and apply to a range of motivations from cross-cultural exchange to travel and adventure. The term 'personal growth' is used frequently to refer to the amount of self-understanding and self-reflection that will arise from volunteering abroad experiences. Thus, volunteer abroad programmes often employ the language of 'an experience of a lifetime' to both promote their programmes and signal to the consumers that this experience of personal growth – this journey of the self – is a once-in-a-lifetime experience that can fundamentally transform people. Upon returning from abroad, many volunteers note that they feel their placements abroad were life-changing for them individually and that they had grown as a result. There is no clear articulation of what aspect of them has grown. It could be spiritual awareness, overall maturity, a new-found cynicism for development, or some combination of these and other aspects of personal change. While the maturity of understanding that can come about as a result of living in a new cultural context is a highly valuable skill, much of the focus on personal growth is individualistic and egoistic, rationalizing the fact that the sojourners will benefit much more than they will contribute. Furthermore, this focus on personal growth overshadows the importance of achieving development outcomes and ending poverty and inequality, and requires some careful attention in terms of whether personal growth of volunteers is also experienced by host country staff and therefore may contribute indirectly to some development outcomes of empowerment, for example.

Research on personal development and exposure to a new culture by Weinmann (1983) and Carlson (1991) expressed personal growth in terms of identity change in relation to tolerance of other cultures, greater compassion and understanding of other people, and an enhanced global perspective contributing to new insights, beliefs, and behaviours. Anderson (1994) refers to the experience abroad as a rebirth whereby those who travel abroad can be 'reborn' by the experience (Anderson, 1994). Personal growth is also examined in relation to the development of a different person whose perspective and world view changes profoundly and transcends his or her indigenous culture. Various authors, therefore, attempt to define personal growth through LVA as the qualities of someone whose horizons extend significantly beyond his or her own culture. An 'internationalist', for example, has been defined as a person who trusts other nations, is willing to cooperate with other countries, perceives international agencies as potential deterrents to war, and who considers international tensions reducible by mediation (Lutzker 1960). Others have studied the international orientation of groups by measuring their attitudes towards international issues – e.g. the role of the UN, economic versus military aid, international alliances, etc. (Campbell *et al.*, 1954). And at least several attempts have been made to measure the world-mindedness of individuals by exploring the degree to which persons have a broader international frame of reference rather than specific knowledge or interest in some narrower aspect of global affairs (Sampson and Smith 1957; Garrison 1961).

Personal growth and the skills that are associated with it are frequently used to describe a person who is inclusive of different life practices and welcoming of diverse ways of doing things. Adler (2002) refers to such an inclusive person as a multicultural individual who is not defined by the languages he or she speaks or the number of countries visited. Rather, the multicultural individual is characterized by his or her outlooks and world view on the value of global interconnectedness in thought and action (Adler, 2002). Individuals who combine their personal development with benefiting others through the sacrifice of time and resources are more likely to see a shift in their self and personal identity throughout their lives. The nature of living in a different cultural context, at times in a different language, far from home and facing new challenges, can all contribute to "a transformative experience in the lives of volunteers" (Sherraden *et al.*, 2008: 15; Grusky, 2000) and thus can transform personal values and shape the intellectual and emotional growth of the participants. Such a shift in personal identity may translate into changed behaviour that promotes and ensures solidarity-oriented actions, or it may contribute to highly egoistic values and rationales.

In her study of returned Voluntary Service Overseas (VSO) volunteers, Unstead-Joss (2008) found that a main motivator for pursuing overseas volunteer work in the developing world centred on the desire for personal growth. The returned volunteers (RVs) in this study associated personal growth with overcoming a 'challenge' and/or an 'adventure' which would be more readily found in a developing country than it would in another developed country:

> People's wish for personal growth underpinned their decision on where they went overseas. By going to a developing country, as opposed to another developed country, RVs explained that this would satisfy their wish for a 'challenge' and/or an 'adventure'.
>
> *(Unstead-Joss 2008: 11)*

This study once again illustrates the ways in which volunteer abroad participants satisfy a desire for travel, adventure, and challenge through their experiences of being culturally immersed in a host community and host organization in the developing world.

The personal growth and challenge that one does experience overseas, however, may be perceived as equally intense or even more intense in a developed country, as in Shannon's case. Shannon compared her experience in Guyana to that of a previous experience in Germany. For Shannon, the language barrier was more significant in Germany than Guyana and she also places a lot of emphasis on the open and friendly nature of Guyanese people, implying that this was not her experience in Germany. This is an important observation because it helps breaks down some of the assumptions related to all forms of travel and volunteer work in the developing world and the presumption that physical, cultural, and emotional challenges will automatically be present and therefore necessitate a period of cultural adjustment that will then lead to a deeper understanding of the host community/country/culture and somehow inspire the participant to become more engaged in the experience and the future of the host community/country. The quest for a challenge was a common theme for many of the participants – such as Andrew, who said his participation in the volunteer abroad programme was partly motivated by his desire for an adventure but also to "get out and do something ... challenging".

While some of the youth participants talked about what constitutes their personal growth, others talked about their personal growth in more introspective terms. Vanessa, for example, said that the personal growth aspect was the most important part of her experience abroad, adding:

> the things that you find out about yourself and what it reveals ... your strengths and your weaknesses and who you are when you're in those kinds of situations when you are on your own and you're basically learning and struggling through and you know you're making your way and it becomes a lot clearer to ... get to know yourself a lot more.

Sonia reflected on her personal growth in terms of becoming more patient and relaxed, bringing a lifestyle she had while abroad back to Canada. Sonia ended her reflections on personal growth to note that she "really got a lot more out of it than I thought I could have ever gotten". In reflecting on her personal growth, Felicia noted:

> I had adventures, I travelled, there was time off to travel and explore the country as a whole as opposed to just the city that we worked in and I met my mother's family. I made new friends. I have really closely bonded relationships now ... in India and I feel like I have a new home to return to in the future. So all of those things definitely contributed to my own personal growth.

However, if personal growth is articulated in the context of having an experience of a lifetime or for opportunities for adventure and travel, then the focus is much more squarely on individualistic or egoistic rationales for participation in LVA4D; this is a topic to which I turn in Chapter 5.

These findings on skills development (concrete skills and personal growth) and career advancement resonate, in part, with Epprecht's (2004) argument that the profits (benefits in terms of personal growth, job skills acquisition, etc.) rest primarily with the Northern volunteers. While we can understand the benefits of personal growth and skills development for Canadian youth, we need to also understand those benefits in relation to the impacts in developing countries. Building on the idea of individual, one-directional flow of benefits to the Northern volunteers, Nadine argued:

> you want to make a difference but once you're there you realize that you can't do that much. It really is just for yourself that you're going. So, I probably would have had more selfless goals when I went there but then looking at what I can do ... I realized that it's pretty much ... me wanting to go on an adventure and be out there and understand a different culture and my own personal growth.

Belinda reflected on the importance of personal growth as a first step in doing "development work properly ... the need to reflect on yourself before you can help others". These are just a few examples of the many comments provided by the youth participants on the value they placed on personal growth and how it was articulated in egoistic or individualistic ways.

There is, however, a self-realization and self-critique attached to this personal growth motivation whereby the participants recognized egoistic justifications and the, sometimes, selfish nature of personal growth. Yet, LVA programmes were still rationalized by the youth participants because of a believed importance of personal growth for cross-cultural understanding and as a first step to have an impact and positive contribution to development. Personal growth of the Canadian youth can also be a rationale for LVA programmes that are known to be development failures – or failures in meeting the objectives of the host communities – and enable volunteer senders and the volunteers themselves to cloak themselves in the feel-good rhetoric of personal growth. Heron argues that the personal growth defined in relation to cross-cultural skills may actually entrench stereotypes rather than create open-mindedness (Heron, 2007) – an argument that makes justifying LVA programmes much more difficult. In any event, the focus on personal growth reinforces the one-directional nature of LVA programmes. The one-way direction of benefits of these programmes is a point noted by many of the host country participants who participated in interviews for this study. However, a range of responses pertaining to the challenges and opportunities of personal growth rationales were identified in the interviews with host country participants as well, and I turn to these comments in the following section.

Host country participant reflections on personal growth

When considering the benefits of hosting international volunteers, only one host country staff member referred to the value of personal growth for his own benefit, noting that hosting international volunteers

> gives me the experience of how to treat people, how to resolve ... perhaps not huge conflicts but ... small problems, and personally it helps me because I can see that each person is different in their own ways.

Mixed in with these personal dimensions of growth are also references to concrete skills for conflict resolution and problem-solving, as well as interpersonal/intercultural relations. Most of the references made to personal growth provided by the host country participants were observed with the volunteers they hosted, saying they noticed growth and a maturity among the participants over time. The host country participants were not asked explicitly about personal growth among the volunteers, but were asked if they saw any changes in the volunteers over the course of their stay in the host country.

A participant from India, Sameer, reflected on how foreign volunteers become more street-smart and less naïve over time. A Jamaican participant, Nicholas, also noted that over time the volunteers become less naïve and grow accustomed to culture and day-to-day life. Another participant from Jamaica, Shanice, commented on the improvement in coping skills of volunteers he has witnessed over their stay. A participant from Zambia remarked that in his experience, many of the youth volunteers lack maturity for the nature of the work and placement abroad. "They are fresh from school, they are full of enthusiasm … [but] the maturity levels are quite low." Another Zambian participant named Bernard noted that the volunteers' attitudes change over time and they show greater maturity when they "come to realize that people [in the host country] are more advanced, people are developed, people are educated and people are civilized, so they change their attitude towards people".

This participant from Zambia went on to reflect on the attitude changes experienced by the youth volunteers, who begin to realize

> there are actually people who are out there and doing better than them and maybe those are the people they have actually come to help, so their attitude changes and now they start thinking 'why am I here to help them when they can do this on their own?'.

Not all of the participants from the countries in the Global South would come to the same positive conclusions as the Canadian participants about personal growth for foreign volunteers. Furthermore, there was a clear understanding among the host country participants that the idea of personal growth was the purview of the foreign volunteers: an individual gain that was meant for the volunteers exclusively. Some of the participants in the recipient countries expressed concern for this one-directional flow of benefits and personal growth. Others argued that personal growth of the Northern volunteers is not a justification for LVA programmes in developing countries, where poverty rates are high and the needs for basic goods are so great. Thus, there were some critical comments raised but these speak to a broad set of structural issues beyond the volunteers themselves, such as the asymmetry in opportunity for hosts and volunteers. Many of the host participants, however, felt that there was substantial personal growth among the volunteers they observed and they maintained hope that the personal growth – and cross-cultural skills and understanding that comes from it – will make for more sympathetic citizens who are more willing to give development aid, and/or advocate for greater development commitments in the future – a solidarity-oriented perspective. In essence, the underlying assumption is that youth abroad programmes will make the volunteers better citizens, possibly even better global citizens, and lead to some form of structural or social equity changes. In the section that follows I examine what the youth consider to be their identity changes.

Making sense of diverse skills from practical competencies to personal growth

Given the responses from the Canadian youth, there are data to reflect the individualistic and egoistic rationales for participation in LVA4D in relation to skills development, particularly as those competencies translate into capital for the Canadian youth (in terms of personal growth, skills development, employment outcomes, or career advancement). While the value of personal growth, maturity, and improved understanding of international development contexts and issues is clear to the international volunteers on LVA4D, it may be less clear for the hosts of these programmes who may see the value of international volunteering in relation to development outcomes, poverty alleviation, and social justice. Heron (2007) interprets one of her participants' desire for a "real challenge" as an explanation of her pursuit of international development work as evidence of her consumption of the world in her "quest for herself, trying to find out 'what kind of person' she would be amid Others, somewhere else" (p. 50). Heron further develops our understanding of the relationship between place and the concept of authenticity when she notes:

> This quest for self is, of course, equally an actualization of class privilege. Implicit is our desire for the racial Other, which has as much to do with our constructions of self as with exoticized attraction to difference. Both are legacies of bourgeois subject formation from the era of empire, although the latter has been constructed in somewhat changed terms by the discourse of multiculturalism and the marketing of foreign travel destinations. Our yearning for 'authentic' (read exoticized, racialized) difference is very much productive of our desire for development and bound up in our enthusiastic reactions to the commonplaceness of the opportunity to do development work. Longing for relationship with the Other and experiences of Otherness are implicit in participants' acknowledgement of wanting adventure, the experience of living in another culture, of 'something different.' However, the encounter with the Other that is sought – that seems to count – can only be obtained by going to the spaces of the Other.
>
> *(p. 51)*

In her analysis, Heron (2007) highlighted the significance of travel and interaction with "Others" in authentic spaces (in the host countries) as key motivations. In the next chapter I return to some of these critiques and their implications for motivations pertaining to travel and adventure.

Summary

Experiences of personal growth, skills development and career testing hold a lot of value for those who feel transformed, matured, and better skilled as a result of the volunteer abroad experience. However, these motivations can be highly egoistic and one-sided in nature and, thus, do not reflect the structural challenges inherent in volunteer abroad models that give opportunities for those with relative privilege to consume such opportunities. However, the interviews with Canadian youth and host partners also pointed to a perceived value in 'skill sharing', mutual understanding, and increased maturity, even if the benefits were largely realized by the international volunteers rather than the hosts. Host country staff and community members reflected on the gains experienced by the international volunteers in larger, systemic possibilities: that the exposure to life in another country could build long-term commitments to partnerships and the potential for future opportunities for all.

Taken together, the findings from the host country participants and the Canadian volunteers pointed to a more nuanced analysis of the role that skills development plays in the context of international development. The Canadian youth may present their motivations of personal growth and skills development in highly individualistic terms; however, host organization staff, overall, expressed great interest in the skills-oriented rationales for participation in these programmes. As such, skills development and its relationship to career advancement and personal growth (for the Canadian volunteers and host partners alike) must be understood as potentially valuable and a component of agency-oriented reflections on mutual gains through volunteer abroad programmes. The bigger picture of structural constraints and inequality of opportunity (such as career advancement opportunities for the international volunteers but not for the host organization staff), however, are ongoing international injustices that do not get fully addressed through reflections on skills-sharing opportunities in LVA4D.

Scholars interested in the broader range of volunteer abroad programmes have cautioned that programmes like voluntourism (short-term or 1–2-week volunteer/adventure abroad programmes) are at their core still embedded in neoliberal approaches to development. As such, inequality is a prerequisite for market-based growth (Jones, 2011). LVA4D can also be examined in this critical assessment. Those who participate in LVA4D must be equally mindful of the neoliberal logic and justifications for participation. The range and diversity of perspectives on the value of hosting international volunteers in the context of skills development, however, offers glimpses into a potentially deeper political and solidarity-oriented set of rationales for mutual benefit, with some benefits being more immediate and others perceived as long-term (at least in terms of deeply held hopes for the future of international development). The next chapter explores what, if any, benefits can be derived for the host country partners in relation to the motivation of travel and adventure as articulated by the Canadian youth who ranked this as the next most important motivation for participation in LVA4D (after cross-cultural communication, testing a career choice, career advancement, and personal growth)?

5

IT'S ALL ABOUT THE TIMING

A 'place' for adventure and travel

Volunteers who travel abroad need to be adventurous in spirit. They require a particular openness to learning new ways of doing things; a desire to experience different foods, customs, and practices; and a commitment to making the most out of situations they may find difficult or unfamiliar. Travel and adventure are therefore natural motivations for going abroad. When choosing a location for a learning/volunteer abroad (LVA) placement, the volunteers may be thinking about the nature of adventures they might have while abroad, and for some, the country they choose to visit will be based, in part, on the opportunities for adventure. Advertisements for volunteer abroad options may also highlight tourist attractions in their promotional material, thus potentially contributing to a particular set of motivations or desires, as well as the rationales that underscore decisions to go abroad. Therefore, the notion of 'finding a place for adventure' can be important to some volunteers choosing their overseas destination. Host organization staff also understand volunteers' motivations in relation to adventure and travel, and noted the value of exploring the wonders and beauty that the country has to offer, and encouraged volunteers to find time for travel and exploration. However, the host organization staff also stressed the importance of the *timing* of travel and adventure or its *place* relative to other motivations and commitments such as project or work-related requirements.

Careful consideration of the needs and priorities of the organization and/or project when choosing when to travel and have adventures is therefore crucial to volunteer success. In this chapter, I unpack the narratives provided by host organization staff and Canadian volunteers on LVA programmes around the themes of motivations for travel and adventure and the reactions of host community staff to this particular motivation. I begin, however, with some reflection on the broader context (the imagery and discourse that promotes volunteer abroad options) in which volunteers are making decisions about going abroad, and often the choices about where they may wish to go. The larger marketing context and advertisements of volunteer abroad programmes provides an entry point for considering how the rationales for participation in LVA4D programmes are developed and play a role in shaping what volunteers might expect to get out of their volunteer abroad placements in addition to other benefits and contributions.

The broader context of rationalizing LVA4D in relation to adventure and travel

An important starting point for an analysis of travel and adventure begins with consideration of the broader context in which participants are making choices about going abroad. Volunteer abroad programmes' advertising strategies employ a range of visuals as part of their competitive approach in a rapidly growing sector. Thus, images depicting volunteer abroad programmes may often include visuals of wildlife, beaches, and mountain tops. Using a Google image search, the frequency of adventure-oriented images becomes apparent, with examples of young adults climbing to the tops of mountains or interacting with wild animals.

Specifically, a Google image search was conducted each year over three years to learn about the most common (first 100) images that correspond to the keyword search 'volunteer abroad'. The language of advertisements for volunteer abroad programmes also employs the language of adventure and travel. One volunteer-sending organization in the UK, for example, advertises their programmes in relation to conservation, education, and exploration. Under the theme of adventure travel, the website promises opportunities to "Explore Central America or Southeast Asia on an exotic adventure trail or see the sights of amazing Mozambique on a horseback safari" (www.frontier.ac.uk). One of the largest volunteer-sending organizations, Cross-cultural Solutions, promotes its programmes as "Volunteer abroad trips … that allow you to travel, see the world, and do good, all while having the time of your life" (www.crossculturalsolutions.org).

There are numerous images, brochures, and programme pamphlets encouraging us to have an adventure abroad, whether in Europe, Asia, Latin America, Africa, or elsewhere. Internet sources are easily accessible for opportunities to take part in international volunteering abroad programmes and "glossy posters depicting faraway locations urge students to spend a spring break, summer, semester, or year encountering new people, places, and languages in a destination of their choice" (Zemach-Bersin, 2009: 303). In her research on volunteer abroad options, Zemach-Bersin (2009) noted that, in the United States, American undergraduates have unconsciously and consciously absorbed thousands of images and advertisements before they finally decide on their destination of choice. The messages that are relayed to the prospective participants in LVA programmes may, however, differ from the aspirations of global educators and the desires of recipient organizations, thus undermining some of the goals of learning/volunteering abroad for development (LVA4D). The advertisements both shape our understanding of the world and reflect common, and often false, understandings of the world. The images in advertising brochures and websites provide an interesting starting point for analysing how and why youth are motivated by a desire for travel and adventure in LVA programmes.

An internet search of LVA programmes will uncover thousands of opportunities for diverse experiences and build-your-own adventures. Many LVA organizations present their programmes as adventure-oriented, with images of backpackers hiking through deserts or rainforests, young people working with endangered or dangerous animals, or youth paddling boats down a stream or climbing a mountain. One image retrieved through a Google image search led to an article from *Verge Magazine* and from the organization Travellers Worldwide. The caption for Travellers Worldwide read: "Volunteer Abroad – Your Adventure Starts Here." Accompanying this advertisement is a picture of a young person wearing a baseball cap and lying on a wooden pier with three young lions. One of the lions is lying beside him and looks to be about to lick his hand (or possibly eat it). The young person in the photo is smiling and the background depicts a beautiful, natural setting. Travellers Worldwide is based out of the UK and advertises that "no qualifications or previous experience is necessary, just a good dose of enthusiasm". There is no caption for this picture so it is unclear if it is from actual work done with the Travellers Worldwide programme or what that work entails. Volunteering with wildlife organizations can be an important contribution to nature conservation. However, the picture depicts the young white person in the photo as the only person working on this project. In analysing this photo, we are left wondering: Who runs the programme? How does this programme contribute to environmental or economic opportunities in the host country? What are the safety measures in place? What is the purpose of this programme beyond giving Northerners an up-close interaction with dangerous wild animals? The summary of the programme explains that this project is in Zimbabwe:

> You'll work on the world's leading programme for the release of lions back into the wild. You'll walk alongside lions as part of the pride and enjoy the exhilaration of being part of a hunt as the young cubs learn to stalk their prey. And more, you'll experience the African bush in a very special way. You will be actively involved in a number of conservation activities.

Thus, a great deal of important information is left off the page. There is no reference to the local experts who run these programmes and who facilitate the volunteer's work. There is also no discussion of the broader challenges farmers face in relation to wildlife preservation strategies. The emphasis is exclusively on the experience and adventure that the participants will have, devoid of any interaction with local experts or community development strategies.

Many of the images of volunteering abroad include working in wildlife centres, or use pictures of wildlife to promote their programmes, even if conservation programmes are completely unrelated to the volunteer abroad programme. The image of the sea turtle, for example, is used on a number of international experiential learning programme websites. The CADIP (Canadian Alliance for Development Initiatives and Projects) Volunteering Worldwide programme (www.cadip.org)

offers a range of options, including working with volunteers and environmental conservation. When you click on the turtle icon, however, the project that comes up is one for "volunteers for equality and social justice" in Mexico, working with "local youngsters in different activities oriented towards community support, promoting equality and social justice" (www.cadip.org/volunteer-in-mexico.htm). In this case, the sea turtle has little to do with the actual programme description but is used (perhaps rather effectively) as a way to entice potential participants to volunteer for their programmes.

Images of young white people sitting on top of mountains overlooking the farms and fields below are also common. The image evokes the potential for conquering other lands. In a photo from the website for The Travel Cuts Gap Year Abroad programme, the options are promoted as more than backpacking; they are, rather, "seeing the world with purpose". However, the purpose of the volunteer abroad programme is never articulated in this instance but rather left to the consumers' desires (www.gapyearabroad.ca/04-%20Volunteer/Volunteer%20Abroad.asp).

Many of these critiques are explored in the scholarly literature on volunteer abroad marketing strategies and visual representations. In Zemach-Bersin's (2009) analysis of advertising material, she reasoned that the Western, white youth is seen generally as a paternalistic figure positioned at the centre of an image. In many cases, the white subject is located at a higher elevation, such as on a mountain top or in a victorious position with arms stretched out wide or raised in victory. What is emphasized in these images, and therefore the core message that is being relayed, is that the white, Western sojourner is the most important part of the image, always in the foreground, and "positioned as even larger and more profound" than the expansive landscape, mountains, or nations visited. African countries are frequently depicted first as 'Africa', devoid of different national boundaries, and second as vast landscape largely devoid of humans (particularly adults) and covered in safari parks. Other symbolic representations of specific regions exist. Nepal is frequently represented with an image of mountains (again devoid of people) and small island countries are represented with vast – but empty – beaches and sunsets. There are seldom any images of cities or development infrastructure presented in these pristine images, thus reinforcing stereotypes of the Global South as uncharted, untouched territories waiting to be 'discovered' by sojourners from the Global North.

Images that include volunteers working with people in the host countries frequently employ images of white Westerners playing with black children. Zemach-Bersin (2009) calls this imagery ubiquitous, with a common image of a white student

> with blond hair in a clean, collared shirt surrounded by smiling African children who appear to be eager to be photographed or the White female student ... standing in the centre of the image surrounded by out of focus, blurry black bodies. The viewers' attention is drawn in both cases to the White American students, as if to suggest that non-white locals are background props or passive scenery to be enjoyed by their guests. Local hosts are

depicted as an undifferentiated group, apparently nameless and often unworthy of being shown in focus.

(Zemach-Bersin, 2009: 308)

She continues her line of argument, noting that the Westerner is always the centre of attention, and presented as the superior and powerful figure in the image. Clost (2014) extends a similar analysis to images of Canadian-based volunteer abroad programmes. Clost employs the framework of the "visual economy of volunteering abroad" to examine how marketing strategies entice Canadian participants. This visual economy is structured around 'binary oppositions' positioning young, often white volunteers as 'helpers' while local, non-white communities in the Global South are depicted as 'weak' or in need of this help (Clost, 2014: 250). The adventure of 'helping' or having an authentic experience (by way of working with children who may have a different skin colour than the volunteer) in 'exotic places' is therefore central to the imagery generally employed and may influence the motivations for participation in volunteer abroad programmes.

Other messages relayed in the advertisements for LVA programmes include the desire for personal achievement and success of the Western participant and an opportunity for adventure and to experience the exotic (Goudge, 2003). Ellyn Clost (2014) refers to these marketing strategies as part of the "visual economy" that reinforces and then sells stereotypes of "development" for Northern consumption. In the chapter that follows (Chapter 6) I return to the imagery employed to promote helping opportunities and return to Clost's analysis, which builds on the critique of colonial continuities or the neo-colonial project of volunteering abroad (see Heron, 2007; Cook, 2007). Through the consumption of these images, volunteers may then reinforce these same stereotypical images by the photos they take while in the host country – photos that are then shared with and consumed by friends and family upon their return (Roddick, 2014). It is important to point out that different volunteer-sending organizations will employ a range of images and not all volunteer-sending organizations use problematic imagery to the same extent as others. However, there are very important lessons to take away from reflecting on the kinds of images employed to depict the volunteer abroad experience. Images and discourses used in volunteer abroad advertisements reify the importance of travel and adventure and minimize the significance of cross-cultural understanding and solidarity. The scholarly literature offers important cautionary considerations of the structural inequalities and neo-colonial practices that can be perpetuated through the practice of volunteer abroad programmes, starting with the marketing of these programmes by the volunteer-sending organizations to the practice of volunteering abroad as well as the telling of the experience upon return to Canada.

A critical analysis of the 'visual economy' was also provided by host country staff in the Global South who participated in my study. Host country participants frequently made reference to volunteers' desires to obtain a specific set of photos before returning to their home countries. In order to ensure the volunteers had the 'right' or 'perfect' photos, host staff often had to create opportunities for – or allow time for – the volunteer's adventure and travel as part of their experience. Examples provided included visiting rural communities to capture images of 'authentic development' (which I turn to later in this chapter), or going on safaris or excursions.

When host country staff members were asked to reflect on what is perceived as one of the primary motivations for youth volunteers travelling to the Global South, a participant from Zambia, Godfrey, said that acquiring specific images by taking photos is a primary motivation. In Godfrey's highly critical assessment of international volunteering he argued that volunteers come under false pretences, saying they wish to volunteer but being more interested in gaining information about – and confirming stereotypes of – the host country.

> Then they will take advantage of that time to get pictures and things like that. So usually they don't understand that issues in HIV need a lot of confidentiality and we respect the person whether they are infected or not and sometimes they just get the photos and they take them wherever they are taking them.

In this context, volunteering abroad can be understood as a consumer-oriented activity whereby the extraction of information and the documentation of a particular set of images are performed for the purpose of gaining cultural capital for the volunteer when he or she returns home and can share his or her evidence of international volunteering.

Social media sites such as Facebook provide spaces for people to highlight all the countries they have visited on a world map and to reveal the accumulation of places as part of their cultural capital. In the satirical newspaper *The Onion*, a writer poked fun at the narcissism and egoist rationales for participation in voluntourism programmes with a joke news headline: "6-Day Visit to Rural African Village Completely Changes Woman's Facebook Profile Picture" (*The Onion*, 2014). The article highlighted the problematic imagery noted above with the smiling white woman surrounded by black children. The messages conveyed in similar but real blog posts reinforce the way that experiences of adventure and 'helping' in less developed countries contribute to the sojourner's status (social status as well as Facebook status) and cultural capital. While similar critiques were provided by host country staff, there were a broad range of perspectives on the value and limitations of travel and adventure (with or without the photos taken). Throughout this chapter, critical insights and constructive analyses of the motivation of travel and adventure are articulated by the Canadian youth who volunteered abroad and the partner staff who hosted volunteers. The findings point to several important structural and neocolonial considerations, as well as important agency-oriented reflections on the value of exploration and discovery in the host country.

Youth perspectives on the quest for travel and adventure

It came as little surprise that young Canadians who go abroad for learning/volunteering opportunities have a desire to travel. A critical analysis of the Canadian participants who expressed an interest in travel and adventure included reflection on how the Canadians justified their yearnings for going abroad as a desire to fulfil a "little girl's dream" or to live out a "lifelong dream". Some of the Canadian participants said they had always wanted to travel to a particular country or continent such as a desire to "experience Africa". Others noted that they had studied a particular country or region and wanted to learn more by also travelling there, again in terms of lifelong dreams to travel to Africa. Specific countries that were priority destinations and long-term dreams of volunteers were talked about, in some cases, as if they were trophies to be acquired. Volunteers may be assigned to one particular country but may use that opportunity to travel extensively in the region (at times including travel and adventure during work days as noted by some host country participants and discussed in more detail below). The number of countries visited says little about the content of one's experience, the depth of exchange, or extent of knowledge-sharing. The desire to visit many countries, "to do" Tanzania or Rwanda, to check off a list of major wild animals seen (the Big Five, for example), etc., can be analysed as a reflection on the question for cultural caché and acquiring a kind of cultural capital among friends rather than about having a meaningful, cross-cultural LVA opportunity. However, in reflecting on these comments, it is important to note that the references to desires for travel and adventure were discussed as one motivation in addition to other motivations. Overall, the desire for travel and adventure ranked sixth out of the eight most commonly cited, and the most important motivations for deciding to take part in LVA programmes, and it must also be understood in that context as one of the least motivating factors for this sample group in their decision to take part in LVA. However, the reflections on the value of travel and adventure offer important insights into why travel and adventure are motivations at all.

Africa calling

Based on the findings of my study, Africa holds a certain kind of mystique for those wishing to volunteer abroad. While the participants in this study took part in a range of programmes in Latin America, Asia, and Africa, many of the participants noted a long-standing desire to travel to – or "to do" – Africa. More Canadian participants from the sample of 138 Canadians travelled to the African region than any other region in the Global South. For many, travelling to Africa was a lifelong dream, no doubt shaped by exposure early in life to images of Africa as well as news of the extent of poverty and insecurity covered in media sources. One participant, Alison, summarized this expression of interest in travelling to Africa quite well in her absence of reasoning for wanting to travel to an African country. She noted: "mainly because I'm interested in travel and I … honestly I just wanted to go to Africa". Other youth participants knew they wanted to have a long-term career working in Africa, in particular, but still felt the need to 'test the waters' through a short experience on an LVA programme. As Jane said:

> I decided to go to Ghana just because I had this idea in my mind that I wanted to work in Africa one day but I thought I should probably go there first and

see if I didn't like it, and I just found that it's probably the most rewarding thing I've ever done.

Even for those who did not express an explicit interest in travel to Africa, the idea of travel itself was important, as Cheryl reflected:

I guess I've always been interested in people and travel. It's always been an interest of mine ever since I was a little girl and I always wanted to see everything and I'm quite an adventurous kind of person.

Thus travel was an important motivation, but most of the participants expressed their desire to travel in relation to other motivations such as the combination of wanting to travel but also to "work with kids", to "make a difference", or to "test an academic background". Therefore, in many cases, the motivation of travel and adventure must be considered in relation to other motivations identified.

For others, volunteering abroad was equated with travel opportunities combined with paid work (many LVAs and international volunteers receive a stipend for their internship work) and this was an important motivation for some participants in LVA, particularly for male respondents in the Canadian study.

Adventure abroad as the antidote to boredom at home

Another justification for travel abroad, as explained by the Canadian participants, included wanting to get out of a "bubble", or leave a small community; some referred to having "itchy feet". In one comment, the participant noted: "I was feeling that I was probably in the same place for too long and I wanted to go to a completely different place that was very far away from where I was." Interest in travel was also linked to boredom with life in Canada: "I was kind of tired of being in school for a long time"; here, travel and volunteer abroad became key motivations in pursuit of something different. Other references to travel highlighted how travel itself can be an addiction: "The more you travel the more you find you feel the need to travel." These sentiments reinforce a particular privilege accorded to those who have the luxury of boredom, too much education or the resources to travel. Zemach-Bersin's research participants also noted a desire for 'escape', noting a "desire to take a break from school" or "I was ready for change" (2009: 310). As a break from academic responsibilities, the youth take part in a privileged act of leisure accorded to very few people in the world. The structural inequality between the Global North and Global South stand out in these privilege-oriented comments. In summary, boredom with life in Canada therefore served as a significant motivation for many youth participants wanting to go abroad. This suggests that there is an expectation that life will be more interesting – or adventurous – in another country. As such, the students may create a conscious or unconscious demand for excitement and thrills by going abroad.

Time and lack of responsibilities as key facets of privilege

In Chapter 1 of this book, the significance of diverse forms of privilege is summarized. The range of privileges identified corresponds to sex and racial identity as highlighted by McIntosh (1989), as well as privileges corresponding to time, mobility, affluence, and position. For some of the Canadian participants, the privilege of time, mobility, and affluence were presented as reasons for going abroad. Several of the Canadian participants referred to their privilege of having few responsibilities or obligations keeping them in Canada. Lisa, for example, noted:

> I don't have any personal obligations [or] commitments that I can't just put away for three months. I basically don't pay mortgage yet, I don't have kids, I don't have anything that … would be a really tough thing to put on hold.

Or as Fran said: "Well, I guess because at this time I am young, and … have no obligations to anybody else." These responses need to be considered in relation to the amount of time abroad. Long-term programmes abroad of 1–2 years generally require a sacrifice of time and significant planning, while medium-term programmes of 3–6 months are seen as more convenient; even shorter-term programmes of 1–2 weeks provide few, if any, significant interruptions for the volunteers. Therefore, the nonchalance expressed by participants around their lack of obligations at home reflected important global inequalities of opportunity. The luxury of time is not shared universally, and understanding the nature of this privilege and why it is accorded to some and not others in the world is an important point for reflection for the Canadian youth. Such reflection could be at the heart of both pre-departure and ongoing facilitated learning throughout and following the placement abroad.

'Authentic' adventures and real experiences

Another common reflection in discussions of travel and adventure in volunteering abroad was the quest for 'authentic' experiences. The kind of travel that one expects to get from a volunteer abroad programme is considered by the youth to be different from other forms of tourism or travel. Many going abroad on LVA programmes were excited that this experience would enable them to have an 'authentic' experience and to travel to places that the average tourist or traveller is unable to see. One participant noted that she had a desire "to see different parts of the world maybe that we wouldn't go normally as a tourist". Chaim Noy's (2004) study of short-term, travel-abroad narratives among Israeli backpackers revealed stories of personal change around a similarly constructed notion of authenticity. The study involves interviews with Israeli youth backpackers searching for an 'authentic' experience separate from tourism, who in fact promote a neo-colonialist and consumerist discourse. This leads Noy to argue that "backpackers should be viewed as a variety within, rather than outside, modern mass tourism" (p. 79) and raises similar questions about the short-term volunteer. However, even the authentic tourist, the tourist who wants contact with what is 'real' in other cultures and environments, perhaps degrades and even destroys the authentic with their presence (Kelly and Freysinger, 2000; Kelly and Godbey, 1992).

An authentic experience may often, from the perspective of young people, encompass a particular set of risks and dangers. The stories that volunteers told about their 'authentic experiences' while abroad included very difficult personal moments such as illness, facing death, experiencing theft, and other observations of disorientation and cross-cultural misunderstandings – all of which contributed to the perception of the authenticity of the experience. The subtext of these reflections is the importance of the uniqueness of the experience and for volunteers to encounter the 'real' experiences and/or communities in the Global South. Volunteers set themselves apart from tourists in this example as becoming ill while abroad is often seen by volunteers as a rite of passage, compared to tourists who may claim no 'benefits' from being sick. The stories told by the Canadian volunteers can then be used to separate their experiences from the stories of tourists who they perceive to have not had a 'real experience'. Simpson (2005) discusses the paradoxical nature of the element of risk associated with travel in the developing world, emphasizing that youth actively seek out danger in travelling because it is a 'marketable commodity' that is actively sought out by volunteer abroad participants as a story or series of tales to share with other foreigners or once they return home. Furthermore, as Simpson elaborates, the industry of volunteering abroad relies on stereotypes of a dangerous Global South to rationalize the role of volunteer-sending organizations and can thereby 'sell safety' to prospective participants and their parents (Simpson, 2005: 458).

In addition to being motivated by a desire for adventure, travel, and even experiences of 'culture shock' and/or danger, the stories that are told about these encounters became highly valuable cultural capital that are traded with other foreigners on weekend retreats or over drinks, often at fancy hotels. Such tales of survival may also be used as part of the re-telling of their experiences when they return, facilitating social capital for the volunteers who can take pride in their new-found heroic status.

Tales of survival

A major theme in tales of adventure for volunteers begin with survival stories, whether surviving unbearable heat for one hot season or surviving experiences in communities with high crime rates. When Felicia, one of the Canadian volunteers, arrived in India, she was overcome with the heat she witnessed and the traffic, which she found shocking. She believed: "I would die every time I would step out onto the road and the heat was unbearable to me. It was about forty to fifty degrees every day and we didn't have electricity." She elaborated that when the electricity was on she would freeze water bottles and put them against her body to stay cool. She then talked about surviving food poising. For another Canadian volunteer, the experiences with crime were notable, which she considered her biggest concern while abroad. She relayed two experiences in which she was not hurt but was scared by her encounters with people she did not trust. The experiences of Lana and Felicia are examples of the kinds of stories that participants were able to share with friends and family members either in blog posts while abroad or upon their return. The stories reinforce the significance of adventure during volunteer abroad programmes. However, in all the youth's experiences with challenges, there was a failure to explicitly acknowledge that these experiences were temporary for the international volunteers but are part of daily life for local people of the host country (not all of whom survive experiences of crime, food poisoning, or excessive heat). The Canadian participants talk about a relief to return to their normal life back at home without, in most cases, explicitly recognizing the privilege that is attached to the ability to escape the sometimes difficult aspects of adventures during international travel.

Sørensen's (2003) observations of backpackers resonate with the experiences of the youth volunteers who are "(future) pillars of society, on temporary leave from affluence, but with clear and unwavering intentions to return to 'normal life'" with nearly all of the volunteer abroad placements having a "fixed return date, typically defined by their flight ticket" (2003: 852). The temporariness of medium-term, 3–6-month placements provides Canadian youth, such as Lana, with a means of coping with negative or challenge experiences while abroad. The predefined length of time of volunteer abroad programmes is often at the forefront of the volunteer's mind – and used as a means to get through the difficult moments.

Furthermore, tales of adventure, when considered the key moments or pivotal experiences, can overshadow other important experiences and learning opportunities while abroad. Shelley refers to her experience of being mugged as a "breaking point". It was during this breaking point that she began to isolate herself and noted that she "got frustrated with all my Filipino friends and then I just starting planning a bunch of trips". The depression lasted, in her estimation, for a significant portion of her time abroad (four months). She was able to escape some of her 'misery' and frustration with people in the country by travelling and sight-seeing (advice she had received from the volunteer-sending organization supervisor). While adventure and tourism provided Shelley with an escape from her frustrations with day-to-day life with people in the Philippines, she did not reflect on the privilege that was accorded to her in this instance – a privilege not shared by her Philippine counterparts. She did note that she felt guilty because she was taking holidays and using resources that were ear-marked for her volunteer placement-related work. The focus on the negative experience as the pivotal one or a 'breaking point' elevates the Canadian youth's experience to the fore of international volunteering and reinforces egoistic or individualistic rationales for participation. Furthermore, the stories that volunteers tell upon their return or through blog posts shape the rhetoric of LVA programmes in terms of survival, adventure, challenges to overcome – all in the context of the sojourner's experience, with little attention to the inequality of opportunity that these experience represent, nor to the nature of the stereotypes that may be reinforced through the selection of stories shared upon return.

For many of the Canadian participants, the idea of adventure may also include the seeking out of danger while simultaneously having to articulate how that danger can be overcome with the appropriate precautions and planning. This challenge–victory dichotomy is discussed in the work of Hudson and Inkson (2006). The adventure/ challenge must exist, but only to an extent that it can be overcome – as this overcoming of the challenge is how a successful experience is defined by the volunteer; if there was no chance of successfully overcoming the challenge, the experience would be much less appealing. Simpson (2005: 459) states that a

> sense of danger is an integral part of a gap year experience for many partici-
> pants. The ability to survive the experience and successfully negotiate risks
> and fears are all part of establishing one's credibility, and acquiring the life
> skills supposedly learnt. When discussing with participants in Peru and Ecua-
> dor why they chose particular destinations, issues of risk, difficulty and danger
> were often expressed.

However, risk and security are prominent features of volunteer-sending organization materials (websites, brochures, etc.). Heron (2005a) is critical of the ways in which non-governmental organizations (NGOs) emphasize security and risk and management in their pre-departure orientation programmes for volunteer and study abroad programmes. Heron (2005a: 790) claims that:

> preparing students for these realities by talking frankly about risk can inad-
> vertently centre their own apprehensions rather than equip them to com-
> prehend the underlying reasons for the complexities they may encounter
> in their placements. While immediately at stake from volunteer participants'
> point of view is their interest in taking up international practicums in Africa,
> focusing on students' possible encounters with development hazards can also
> serve to eclipse their sense of injustice at the vulnerability of people they are
> going to be learning from and for whose benefit they will be working. In
> this process a kind of othering may occur, since the predominant concern
> is how Canadian students can be safeguarded against the conditions appar-
> ent in another country. At the same time, the notion of risk to Canadian
> students implicitly references old colonial tropes such as 'darkest Africa' or
> the fear of contagion. Inherent in such concepts is a sense of timelessness, of
> a place where nothing ever changes, which stands in direct contrast to the
> lived experiences of local people for whom change has primarily been, and
> continues to be, calamitous, rapid and transformative.

This focus on the student/volunteer's experience is evident in some of the Canadian youth's comments regarding their preoccupation with their own safety both before arriving and during their volunteer experience. While concern for the participants' personal safety should factor into the preparation and planning of the volunteer abroad programme, Heron's concern is that if the challenges related to staying safe are perceived – as indicated by the Hudson and Inkson (2006) study – as challenges to be overcome by the Western volunteer (ultimately leading to a sense of accomplishment at the end), then a greater appreciation for social justice and the daily conditions under which the residents of the host community/country live are diminished. For Shelley, as documented above, the experience with danger or perceived risk is about her ability to cope by telling herself that she is only there 'temporarily' – these comments further emphasize Heron's concern that students/volunteers participating in these types of programmes fail to appreciate that members of the host communities live in these conditions every day and do not have the luxury of leaving when they are ready, when their contract expires, or when they have had enough of coping. Shelley does not mention how this violence or danger might affect her co-workers or host family on a regular basis, reinforcing some of the critical analyses provided by Heron (2005a), Simpson (2005), and Epprecht (2004), who have documented how cultural immersion does not necessarily move a volunteer/student to a place of empathy or understanding that might result in their desire to become more actively engaged in social justice issues. Similarly, Judy is focused on the difficulty of treating her illness when she is living in the countryside, yet does not reflect on what this might mean in the context of daily life for members of her community. Other stories of 'survival' include Felicia's reflection on her experience with unbearable heat and how she had to use frozen packets to stay cool. Her analysis does not include a reflection on her access to a freezer in her home nor the sparse electricity in the country during these heat waves – electricity that she had the privilege to enjoy, on occasion, in order to freeze water in her water bottles which she could then use to keep herself cool. The broader context reveals that these are conditions that kill people on a regular basis, conditions that are inescapable for the majority of people in the Global South, and without the luxuries of frozen water as a means to cool down.

The motivation of adventure and travel therefore overlaps in many ways with other motivations such as cross-cultural exposure. Some of the Canadian participants examined their interest in cross-cultural experience in relation to consumption discourses. The desire to 'consume' culture was no more apparent than in the quote from Janelle, who employs the language of "indulging" or "gorging on culture" as though her short period of time in a cross-cultural context is an adventure involving taking in as many cultural experiences as possible. The use of specific words such as *indulge* and *gorge* in reference to experiencing culture signal an excessiveness of consumption or an unrestrained gratification. Other study participants expressed similar interests in cultural consumption but with reference to their desire to consume that which they deemed 'authentic' or 'real' in nature. In particular, the participants were seeking something separate and distinct from the kind of experience a 'tourist' might have.

Other participants highlighted their motivations for participation in volunteer abroad programmes as ways to set themselves apart from other sojourners from the Global North such as tourists, backpackers, or voluntourists, putting the emphasis of authenticity onto the volunteers themselves, as more 'real' than others, reinforcing Chaim Noy's (2004) analysis of authenticity noted above.

Articulations of authenticity

The quest to explore the 'authentic' or 'pure' life in less developed countries reinforces simplistic understandings of places as rural and remote. Thus an 'authentic' volunteer placement is frequently seen as a rural experience. Even when volunteers spend most of their time in large, modern urban communities, the pictures they bring home are more likely to reflect rural villages and extreme poverty. The quest to experience 'the real Africa', for example, symbolizes the desire to explore and possibly reinforce deeply held, constructed notions of Africa as rural, dirty, hopeless, and comprised almost exclusively of women and children. Images of skyscrapers, well-dressed Africans in business attire, modern conveniences, and fast-food chains do not suit the stereotype of Africa that many people choose to recreate in the images and stories they bring home.

The notion of experiencing the 'authentic' is therefore about reinforcing deeply entrenched stereotypes of what the 'real' Africa looks like – the Africa they are likely to see on posters and website photos. Accessing their own version of those images gives people the opportunity to obtain social capital and perceived credibility in the development community of having completed a 'genuine' development experience or work placement.

References to heroism, sacrifice, being at one with the poor, and 'roughing it' in rural communities in the developing world are perceived by some participants as ways to separate those who do 'desk work' from those who are 'in the trenches' of development assistance. The division between urban desk work and rural 'get your hands dirty' work is a gendered one in which the perceived 'hard' work of rural living reinforces notions of masculinity. Furthermore, masculine tropes of the 'authentic' experience play out when Canadian youth expose themselves to dangerous situations, health problems, and other challenging contexts: challenges they are able, for the most part, to conquer. There are elements of nurturing or stereotypical feminine characteristics depicted in imagery and expectations of international volunteers as well, particularly in those images or expectations of being surrounded by happy and comforted black children – for example, the 'Madonna complex', or what Clost summarizes as "the role of white women as rescuers or caregivers" (Clost, 2014: 243). Heron's assessment of these feminized representations is articulated as white women's convictions of helping and thereby "performing appropriate bourgeois femininity" (Heron, 2007:154). Clost argues that volunteers may emulate the figure of the Madonna (a figure representing virginity and protection in Christian thought); thereby recycling powerful colonial images of the missionary values and Christian saviour complex.

Translating adventures into cultural capital

The consumption of adventures combined with a collection of places travelled can translate into cultural capital for the traveller, as I highlighted earlier in this chapter. "The main way travelers convert 'collecting places' into cultural capital is through a narrative of personal development and authoritative knowledge about the world" (Desforges, 1998: 189). "Collecting places" refers to "framing the 'Third World' as a place where individual knowledge and personal experience can be gained through travel" (Desforges, 1998: 183). Cultural capital means collecting knowledge and experience that can be converted into economic capital, namely employment and social class, for example in the form of social solidarity with other interns and travellers (Desforges, 1998). The term was first introduced by sociologist Pierre Bourdieu in reference to a socially valuable set of beliefs and practices that function like economic capital (Li and Bolaria, 1993). The danger of cultural capital and collecting places is the potential to see the world as a series of differences from home, which can create more division and misunderstanding, as opposed to seeing similarities and being in solidarity with communities in countries visited (Desforges, 1998). The differences from home are essential, however, to 'Othering' and thus reinforce, rather than break down, stereotypes of the poor, helpless, and often rural communities the volunteers seek out as part of their 'authentic' experience. One of the Canadian volunteers, Susan, expressed a desire to "see how other people live" and this reinforces other participants' expressions of interest in understanding the 'Other' through binary divisions of 'us' and 'them'. More specifically, "it is a question of 'them' being known by 'us' and being assessed by and understood through our 'standards'" (Heron, 2007: 34).

Feminist critiques also challenge the notion of consumerism inherent in the quest for experiences abroad. Adventure travel is a form of high-priced consumerism desired by people regardless of location but accessible only by a few (Beezer, 1995). Thus adventure travel or travelling abroad for the purpose of short-term volunteering is a luxury that is affordable to Westerners but not most people, and is tied to Western values of personal growth and worldliness.

In the process of consuming culture, the Western participants in volunteer abroad programmes also engage in a process of othering. The ability to be adventurous and to explore other cultures must also be read in relation to how the world is depicted as a series of places waiting to be explored, consumed, discovered, and/or conquered. Those living in the countries to which adventurous youth plan to travel are depicted as

> oblivious, sleeping or passively waiting for American students.... Such rhetoric inadvertently evokes the sexual and gendered language of colonialism, in which foreign lands are characterized as passive, needy, undeveloped, and submissive as a justification for exploitation and domination.... American students are not just more important, but far more active, real, and powerful than the world beyond the borders of the US.
>
> *(Zemach-Bersin, 2009:306–307)*

In so doing, the 'others' who are visited and observed in the less developed countries visited by Westerners become objects of development assistance and/or globalization rather than global subjects (Tiessen, 2011). Lewin (2009) summarizes study abroad in a largely cynical way, noting: "study abroad is nothing more than commercial travel masquerading as academic experience ... a kind of poverty tourism that reinforces stereotypes of themselves and others" (Lewin, 2009: xv).

Some of the comments raised by youth further reflect the consumption, othering, and problematic aspects of international experiential learning when it is pitched as an alternative form of tourism and an act of adventure. However, as documented in the previous chapter, international experiential learning programme opportunities are increasing in number while the demand for such opportunities also grows. The issues raised in this chapter point to important ethical implications of volunteering abroad when the participants are motivated by travel and adventure. The desire for travel and adventure further reflect an egoistic and self-oriented experience.

Scholars such as Zemach-Bersin have posed the question: Is this a glorified vacation under the guise of volunteering abroad? In their review of the sociological work on tourism, Lyons and Wearing (2008: 5) note that

> while the examination of the self continued in the cognate area of leisure studies, in the tourist literature, these arguments became diverted into a debate about the authenticity or otherwise of this experience (cf. MacCannell, 1976; Cohen, 1988), serving to focus attention on the attractions of the tourist destination. Such a shift objectified the destination as place – a specific geographical site was presented to the tourists for their gaze (Urry, 1990).

The authors claim that this shift to a focus on place and its authenticity became the means by which mass tourism became classified in the 1990s and "ensuing debates about tourism have critically linked the debates about authenticity to broader macro-social issues associated with the globalization of mass tourism" (Lyons and Wearing, 2008: 5). These debates have led to a critique of global tourism that emphasizes the consumptive nature of tourism, especially with respect to tourism in areas where the recipients have "little or no ability to influence its construction" (Lyons and Wearing, 2008: 5). Lyons and Wearing (2008) claim that these critiques have led to the emergence of "alternative conceptualizations of tourism" (p. 5), whereby the tourist destination is reconfigured "as an interactive space where tourists become creative actors who engage in behaviours that are mutually beneficial to host communities, and to the cultural and social environment of those communities" (p. 5).

This analysis of the shift towards alternative forms of tourism highlights the similarities between alternative tourisms such as volunteer tourism and the more development-oriented medium-term volunteer abroad trips. Although we do not tend to classify volunteer abroad participants as tourists, we can see that, by Lyons and Wearing's definition of alternative tourism, the LVA participants experience place and space in a very similar manner to the alternative tourist to which Lyons and Wearing refer.

Sørenson's (2003) ethnographic study of backpackers also helps us draw many similarities between the backpacker quest for adventures and the volunteer abroad participants' desire to experience the challenges and adventures provided by a short-term volunteer placement in the developing world. Sørenson (2003: 853) noted that

> many backpacker journeys can be described as self-imposed transitional periods, and for many, self-imposed rites of passage. Such an understanding of backpacker tourism is well in line with contemporary scholarly views on situations and rites of passage in modern societies.

However, Sørenson noted that these theories do not fully account for why an individual would choose a backpacking trip as a rite of passage and recommends further inquiry. As there is a clear link between backpacker mentality and the desire to volunteer abroad, my research on the motivations of those who volunteer abroad helps to deepen our understanding of why youth choose to study and volunteer abroad in the developing world.

In summary, the critical reflections on authenticity, privilege, and inequality provided in this chapter offer a glimpse into some of the negative attributes of volunteer abroad programmes. The motivations of adventure and travel may translate, for the volunteers, into desires for taking risks or encountering dangerous moments. The stories that the volunteers compile become important forms of social capital as these stories are relayed as challenges to overcome. It is important to point out that not all of the returned volunteers reflected on their challenging experiences in positive ways. Some individuals were highly traumatized by break-ins they had experienced. Others expressed deep concern for the well-being of the friends and community members they had come to know.

An important general analysis of the Canadian youth commentaries, however, reinforces the need for return de-briefing sessions with volunteer abroad participants to give them the opportunity to reflect on privilege and inequality of opportunity and to find ways to strive for deeper and more fundamental systemic changes so that routine crime, illness, and oppressive conditions are reduced for those in the host country and that these 'stories of survival' become less common among the international volunteers.

Host country partners who work with international volunteers from the Global North also reflect on the opportunities and risks of travel and adventure during volunteer abroad placements and those reflections are summarized below.

Host country interpretations of the value of travel and adventure

Positive reflections on adventure and travel

The desire for adventure and travel among Northern sojourners is well understood by the host organizations and host communities in the volunteer-receiving countries. Several of the participants in the Global South talked about a sense of adventure in a very positive way. A participant from India claimed that his experience with volunteers has been quite positive, noting that the volunteers

> are very open and they have a liking to travel to different places in India. They have very strong willingness to learn also. They are fascinated to go to rural places. One volunteer even was lost in Orissa during his work. I liked all these qualities among the foreign volunteers.

Others marvelled at the sense of adventure of foreign volunteers, noting that they found Western volunteers much more open to travel and adventure than they could imagine for themselves.

As long as the sense of adventure was matched with an equally strong commitment to completing the work for the organization, most of the participants did not seem to mind that travel and tourism were rationales for participation on the part of the volunteers, noting that they appreciated the volunteers' interest in the natural beauty and historic sites in their home country because, as one host partner said, "it is nice to see the eagerness and the interest in wanting to learn about new culture". A respondent from Peru, Ricardo, for example, highlighted the way that volunteers worked hard and played hard:

> Youth tend to combine work with taking the maximum advantage of their weekends, to go on the Inca Trails. They always come back on Mondays saying, 'I've been in such and such place.' There's constantly a sense of adventure, etc. That's something we notice, but they have a high respect for work. Additionally, they come with clear rules, with responsibilities.

The respect for foreign volunteers' sense of adventure was thus frequently followed by a qualification that adventure was respected when matched with a commitment to the development work required.

Host country concerns

There were, however, several concerns noted by the participants in the countries comprising the Global South for this study. These concerns are important to highlight because they challenge us to re-think the way we offer and/or take part in international volunteering programmes. One of the challenges identified by a Guatemalan participant is the set of expectations of travel and adventure that volunteers bring with them. Manuel noted:

> For example, some of them come already with their calendar of activities and everybody else has to adapt himself to this calendar and they wonder why there is nobody to accompany them to Tikal, for example. These things are sometimes difficult for us.

Some of the participants even mentioned that they were not terribly motivated to have international volunteers, noting that the volunteers are a burden for the organization when their demands for travel and adventure are so important. One Guatemalan participant said:

> it does take an extra effort [facilitating the volunteer's travel demands] and this normally isn't taken into account or planned, nor by the volunteer or the organization who backs him up. This is a reason why the organizations or NGOs are not motivated to have volunteers and also because volunteers normally come here to learn, to visit, and it is normally hard for them to commit for one specific task.... Most of them come here and they want to learn and travel all over the country, and some say, for example, 'these are free holidays' and sometimes it is difficult to identify the real interest of the organization to have a volunteer.

Of great importance to several of the participants in this study was that volunteers could be inconsiderate with the timing of their holidays or their inability to stay in touch with the office while they were away. As one Guatemalan participant, Adolfo, reflected: "What mostly affects me is when they say 'I'm taking vacations' or 'I'm leaving the country' and they go just like that, and they take their time without thinking in what stage of the work we are in." A similar concern was raised by one of the Jamaican participants, Roger, who argued:

> We tend to have volunteers [for whom] this is a vacation.... They come for the nice, big sunshine city, sometimes, and they just live it up. And sometimes that can cause a dip [poor performance in work] because you are saying that this person is not serious. It is a strain on you because the organization gives you a project to do and at the same time we have to be doing the project or providing too much supervision and that can create a problem.

Many of the host country participants noted that there were distinctions to be made between various groups of volunteers (students versus interns, young versus mature, or short-term versus long-term). One host country participant from Peru noted that youth who participate as short- to medium-term (less than six months) volunteers often treat their time in Peru as a "long vacation". Another participant from Peru added that, for the students, "their main motivation is tourism. As in any situation, there are some who do things well and others who have different motivations." This participant from Peru went on to provide an example of a volunteer who came primarily for the vacation and who would not "respond to schedules and to his responsibilities". In addition to accommodating the schedules and travel plans of the volunteers, some of the host country participants also noted the challenges of family members and friends visiting the volunteers and the impact this had on their work time. Madeleine argued:

> Yes, one of the things we always talk about is that these young men and women not only come to work, they also have to make a schedule for

tourism. Their families take advantage that they are here in order to come and so, during certain seasons, there are a number of leaves: one week to be with my dad, another week for my sister, another week to be with X. In a way, this creates stress among the others, who don't have the exception volunteers enjoy because they have to fulfil a schedule.

This telling example speaks to some of the frustrations experienced by host organization staff as they fully recognize the distinct advantage – or as the hosts called it, the "exceptions" – volunteers have because of their privileged position.

Participants from Southern Africa also remarked on the issues or concerns they had with the travel schedules of volunteers using important work time for tourism-related activities and also the challenges of reaching participants when they leave on extended holidays. As a Zambian participant, Mercy, noted: "When they [the volunteers] are on leave, they are on leave and it is rare that they will really want to come in or answer to your request."

A South African participant, Ibrahim, said:

> you find others who come here who want to get a week off to do a tour of Cape Town. I don't mind that. While they're here they must see the country. But if they do that at an inopportune moment when we are busy, they create a bit of a problem. Because they are volunteers and we don't pay them, it puts me in a hard place as well.

In another interview with a South African, the participant provides a more frustrated response: "They [the volunteers] must realize that 15 years into democracy South Africa is not all peaches and cream. South Africa has big problems and not some big safari", remarked Nhahlala. The issues with work–holiday balance are echoed in the comments provided by a participant from Zambia, Bernard, who commented: "I have got nothing against holiday but it is like you will see it even as they are doing their work."

Some of the host country participants even questioned the primary motivation of the participants. As the participant from Peru, Ramon, noted, he had an experience working with a student who said she chose this internship so she could "visit Machu Picchu, and meanwhile I will do my work". The Peruvian participant goes on to say she doubts that the volunteer can do a good job in these cases. There is a tendency among some of the volunteers to make decisions for volunteering abroad based on what is in it for them in terms of what exciting adventures they can have or what visits to world landmarks they can scratch off their 'bucket lists'. The Jamaican participant, Jeremiah, noted that volunteers find all sorts of excuses to travel around the country:

> they also want to explore Jamaica more, so you find that they use every excuse, you hear they are going to go to Negril when they should be here; going to Montego Bay when they should be here, and then they come and they say they are sick; but in truth and in fact they went all over the place. You

find that sometimes they want to get the ganja [marijuana], because I have had that situation. Sometimes they even ask the guys to take them into the inner city communities to see what it is like and I am afraid sometimes when they do that, because I don't know what can happen.

These latter examples of desired travel include high-risk adventures. These same adventures can have unintended or disastrous outcomes, including imprisonment, deportation, or personal harm. When there are no negative outcomes from these 'wild adventures', the youth participants return home armed with exciting tales of their exploits, as well as a subtext of heroism and survival.

Not everyone can pick up their knapsacks and go where they want

Another Jamaican participant, Dominic, marvelled at the adventurous spirit of the Northerners she has met, but also the inequitable set of options available to those from the Global North and the Global South:

> I find people from abroad are far more adventurous than us. They will come from any part of the world and go everywhere else – [but] we are not moving. We are not going to take our knapsack and just go overseas, jump on a plane and go to a place where we don't know a soul and expect that we are going to be taken in and treated well. We have issues with that. Maybe they are far more trusting than we are.

This comment reinforces the concerns held by host organization staff surrounding the lack of reciprocity and the inequality of opportunities for volunteer abroad programmes. In addition to the lack of opportunities afforded to the host partner staff, there are also sentiments of a perceived lack of privilege that would benefit them if given opportunities to travel abroad. For example, the latter comment about expectations of being helped by local communities applies only to the Western youth and is perceived to be an unlikely privilege accorded to a Jamaican even if he or she decided to go abroad, thus highlighting concerns of mistreatment due to racial inequality. Partners from the Global South reflected on perceptions of mistrust of visitors to Western countries from the Global South. Many host partners commented on the lack of a level playing field for travel, and the privilege accorded to those who are from countries in the Global North that do not extend to those from the Global South, in large part because of a belief in race-related discrimination.

Other participants from the Global South talked about the need to meet the expectations of the volunteers in terms of their quest for an 'authentic' experience or the chance to see the 'real Africa' (a motivation noted above). A Zambian participant, Roger, said:

> If you take them on a trip, you will see this person really happy and appreciative of what they are seeing because that is what they perceived. When you

are going to Africa, what was in mind was the animals, the grass thatched house and so on.

Roger's comments highlight the significance of preconceived ideas of what the volunteers' experiences in Africa would be like. The real adventure begins, for the volunteers, when they begin to observe something that is extremely different from what they are used to at home and also what the images of Africa told them their experiences abroad would entail.

The theme of age and maturity surfaced over and over in the interviews with participants in the Global South. All of the countries in this study made reference to the distinctions to be made between the younger volunteers and the more mature ones. As the participant from Guatemala, Carlos, argues:

> The older ones are more centred. They do not come to pass their vacation and are more serious. After 30 years old, they have better knowledge and have master's degrees for example or doctorates and more maturity and capacities.

A participant from Malawi, Sigele, also distinguished between the challenges of the younger volunteers and the significant contributions of the older ones:

> yes the older volunteers are good because those older volunteers have got vast experience in terms of work and even education. They have a lot of experience unlike the younger volunteers [who are] sometimes … childish [and] they like fun unlike the older volunteers.

Therefore, the desire for adventure was perceived by host organization staff to be more important for the younger volunteers.

In reflecting on the volunteers who are the most or least serious workers, a participant from Jamaica, Cassell, argued: "I think probably the least serious are the university ones because nothing is tied to it." One of the Zambian participants, Kenneth, noted that the young volunteers can be very adaptable and adventurous. However, the adventurous spirit is often limited to certain experiences and their ability to adapt does not always apply to their contributions in the organization. She added that the

> younger ones, as young as 18, 17, who have been left out alone with the families in the communities, have adapted very well particularly for those that come to stay for longer periods of time. And also younger ones tend to see it as adventure away from their norm, their usual, so to come to Africa and integrate in that community becomes more adventurous for them … [for the] younger ones, it is more of adventure first. So you wouldn't really say they are fitting in well because they are a bit adventurous.

According to a participant from India, Arun, the older volunteers may have already had a great deal of travel exposure and may be more aware of conditions before coming. For the younger volunteers coming to India for the first time, they are more tempted by travel and sight-seeing. India "is full of temples and beautiful sceneries and all that and beaches. So if someone has come with that perspective as well … it depends on the maturity."

Two different participants from Zambia (Reuben and Bernard), when reflecting on age and maturity, noted that having young volunteers was a particular challenge for the organization because of their need for 'social entertainment' to the extent that "the younger ones, they go into it so much forgetting even their work to that extent. While the older ones are more dedicated even if they have a desire to take vacations, they are able to mix holiday and work", noted Bernard. The Malawian participant, Anzanani, also talked about the demands of younger volunteers who require a lot of 'socialization'. She said that the younger ones: "they will demand things which will suit for them but the older ones they understand the situation. The younger sometimes they don't understand the situation." A participant from India, Sameer, reflected on his experience with volunteers who were in their eighties when they came to India for a volunteer experience. The volunteers in their eighties came for two weeks. They were "well-to-do people who could afford to travel and were in decent health conditions to travel to a developing country". This group of volunteers came for the

> touristy part and then during the day do some constructive work. So there was very little, sort of, value added by such volunteers. I was more scared about them [worrying about their safety], of course they're very adventurous to come in their eighties.

He goes on to note that "A lot of younger volunteers who come, they could be backpackers, they could be very vague with what they could contribute with. They are like student volunteers."

A Guatemalan participant, Eva, had a different perspective on the student volunteers and she distinguished between those she thinks are coming for solidarity reasons and those coming for tourism reasons. She noted:

> it depends according if they are short-term or long-term volunteers because some of them come for charity, while others that are in College come here because of solidarity with our country. It depends a lot on the person because some volunteers come only for tourism and others want to know the country and study it deeply.

The host country participants overall made a distinction between the age of the volunteers as well as the length of the placement as factors in relation to whether they perceived volunteers to be helpful or more interested in travel and adventure. For a participant from South Africa, Sikelela, the short-term volunteers were more like tourists. For them, she continued, "it's more like being on a holiday".

The host country participants, however, did not provide a definition of 'younger volunteers' or 'older volunteers'. Based on the interview transcripts and overall comments throughout the interviews, 'younger' came to be defined as anywhere from 18 to 30, and 'older' as anything over 30. Since all of the Canadian participants in my study were in the 18–30 age bracket, the comments about younger volunteers can generally be applied to the sample here. It is important to note, also, that host country staff members facilitate volunteer placements often for a large and diverse group of individuals. It was difficult for the host staff to distinguish between different 'kinds' of volunteers, indicating that they had not been making such distinctions in their analysis prior to the interviews. Short-term for the host country participants was generally defined as anything less than six months; long-term was seen as usually more than one year. Again, within those categories there is a great deal of variation.

In order to cater to an increasing interest in spending more time doing tourist activities (in part because of the shorter period of time that volunteers are spending abroad), the host organizations are doing more to find activities in their work schedule that expose the volunteers to cultural activities and field trips:

> What we have done is to give them more information, to put them to do cultural activities and less office work, so they can be in touch with the people and the reality. For example, we bring them to Mayan ceremonies where they can be in direct contact with the culture, the communities and persons.

This example is a good reflection of the extent to which host country participants were actively finding ways to 'entertain' the volunteers from abroad and ensure activities that meet the demands and preconceived notions expressed by the volunteers they have observed over time. This comment is somewhat problematic, though, as it reinforces a client–service provider relationship that frames the volunteers as the clients (capable of purchasing an experience and dictating the informal rules of what is expected) in contrast to the service providers (those who must sell their services and must adjust to the demands of the consumer). This theme comes up again in Chapter 6, where the idea of 'helping' is deconstructed in greater detail.

Summary

The responses provided by the participants from the seven countries in the Global South who participated in this study provide a range of responses and diverse experiences. There are some positive reflections provided, including an admiration for the adventurous spirit of the volunteers they have encountered. However, there were many concerns raised by the participants in relation to the priority attached to travel and adventure for certain volunteers and the way that adventure-related activities can come at the expense of the work that needs to be done. These concerns need to be taken very seriously. Participants from all of the countries in this study expressed concerns they had with the work–travel balance of the volunteers and the challenges of catering to the travel plans of many of the volunteers from the Global North. The major lesson to take away from this is the need for Northern volunteers to carefully evaluate their motivations for travel and adventure in volunteer abroad programmes in relation to the needs and priorities of the host country partners. There are other ways for youth to travel and gain an adventure through regular tourism and backpacking. However, there is growing evidence to suggest that the combination of desires for volunteer opportunities and adventure/travel is an important (though not among the most important) motivation for participation in LVA and volunteer abroad programmes more generally.

The desire to combine travel and adventure with a volunteering opportunity can be linked to the individual wishes and desires of the participants themselves, in part resulting from their adventurous spirits but also from the perpetuation of a particular kind of experience widely promoted in advertisements used by volunteer-sending companies and organizations. Taken together, the findings from interviews with Canadian youth who have been abroad and interviews with host organization staff in seven countries of the Global South highlight some of the structural inequalities on a global scale that play out in relation to inequality of opportunity, privilege, and colonial continuities that facilitate perceptions and stereotypes of dangerous places from which survival stories will emerge. However, the host country responses also signal the need for a more nuanced analysis of the agency and complexity of adventure-oriented experience that can be understood as valuable opportunities for the volunteers to learn to appreciate the host country in important ways.

Host country participants, however, saw the value of adventure and travel when it pertained to volunteers exploring their beautiful countries and sharing their experiences and excitement with staff members upon their return, so long as this personal motivation did not interfere with the important work of the organization or the needs of the communities. There is a place for adventure as part of the volunteer abroad experience, as noted by the host country participants, but there is also a time for adventure. Some level of frustration and disappointment can be discerned from the host country participant responses. In particular, the desires of volunteers to be able to collect certain kinds of photos, to visit certain places in order to meet expectations of an 'authentic experience', or missed work to accommodate family/friend visits and travel around the country or region. The reflection on the comments provided by the Canadian youth must be understood as part of the broader critical analysis now widely employed in much of the scholarly literature. The motivations for participation encompass a wide range of reasons from boredom to desires for adventure and cross-cultural understanding.

The critical literature offers some valuable insights into the potentially negative consequences of such motivations when they are largely egoistic in nature, lending support to the cultural capital of the volunteers themselves, helping with the advancement of only the volunteers and not the communities they are expected to assist, and potentially reinforcing stereotypes of an imagined space where adventure will take place, whether in the 'dark Africa' that Heron deconstructs or the 'real Africa' imagined in the dreams of a young girl. Such a critical analysis serves an important purpose in providing opportunities for critical reflection and self-awareness of the volunteers as they begin to sort through ethical implications and privileged positioning in an inequitable world. Such a deconstructive theoretical exercise has great value for reflecting on the broader structural and systemic processes that perpetuate inequalities. However, these critical analyses do not speak to the agency-related comments provided by the host community members who see some value in cross-cultural exposure in hosting international volunteers; who admire the sense of adventure and the desires of the volunteers to learn about the diverse cultures and landscapes; and who have a healthy critique of the challenges of adventure-oriented desires for international volunteers as well. Overall, the host country staff tend to express their desires for having more volunteers because of the benefits of hosting international volunteers in relation to capability-oriented approaches to development outcomes. As such, the freedoms to assess the advantages of the volunteers' contributions to the organization and/or programmes and also host staff members' ability to assess their own desires to engage with international volunteers must be constructed around notions of their freedom to do so, their freedom of choice in making the decision to host international volunteers. Critical scholarship, on the other hand, can be dismissive of these actor-oriented desires and paternalistic in the evaluation of volunteer abroad programmes if careful attention to agency, freedom of choice, and human capabilities are not also considered. A similar analysis applies to 'helping' narratives, as examined in the next chapter.

The arguments highlighted in this chapter point to important ethical issues and a sound critical analysis of the motivation for travel and adventure when it is at the expense of meaningful contributions and/or combined with neo-colonial and/or egoistic experiences for volunteers in the Global South. The allure of adventure is thus both natural and misplaced in this analysis. Those considering or taking part in LVA programmes are encouraged to reflect more critically on their own desire for travel and adventure and how it fits into the volunteer experience in a way that is acceptable to the recipient countries and host organizations.

There are other important factors to consider, including the increasing desire for a particular kind of 'experience' abroad, discussed in Chapter 4 as an 'experience of a lifetime'. Travel and adventure may be considered secondary motivations for many volunteer abroad participants – or perks, really. At the heart of these desires for participation in volunteer abroad programmes is a broader range of motivations and rationales. In preceding chapters (Chapters 3 and 4) and in the present chapter the findings from my research have explored the diverse – and overlapping – rationales of solidarity and individual gains. There have been important critiques emerging from the scholarly literature and the interview responses alike. Many of these critiques have highlighted structural inequality, privileges accorded to some and not others, as well as systemic challenges that perpetuate inequality through the re-telling of particular narratives. There are also, however, important reflections pointing to windows of opportunity that can bring about improved global relations and communication across cultures, as well as respect for diverse approaches to development and change. Next, I turn to helping motivations. The motivation to 'help' ranked, overall, fairly low as one of the 'most important motivations' expressed by the Canadian volunteers (more details are provided on the ranking of motivations in Chapter 2). The motivation to help did, however, come up often in the interviews with both the Canadian youth and the host partners referring to helping narratives in a broad set of ways that I will turn to next, in Chapter 6.

6

HAVING AN 'IMPACT' AND OTHER HELPING NARRATIVES

Introduction

Volunteer abroad programmes are often structured around strategies for 'making a difference' or 'having an impact', and employ 'helping' narratives to describe their programmes. Learning/volunteer abroad for development (LVA4D) programmes may also facilitate helping discourses and practices, though perhaps more likely in the context of development strategies and outcomes. Thus, the impulse to help or make a difference is a common motivation and a likely rationale for participation in learning/volunteer abroad (LVA) and other volunteer abroad programmes.

How the idea of 'helping' gets constituted in practice and how it is perceived or received by host communities are important considerations that are addressed in this chapter. A simplistic, but useful, framework for analysing 'helping' rationales in volunteer abroad work begins with the charity versus development dichotomy. I will return to this framework later in this chapter in an analysis of the research findings. A second important lens through which to make sense of the helping impulse is the way that poverty and inequality in the Global South may be explained as 'problems' requiring 'solutions' from well-meaning individuals in the Global North. The employment of South–North and problem–solution dichotomies in volunteering abroad can perpetuate colonial continuities that marginalize people in the Global South from the resolutions to their own development challenges. Merely constructing the Global South as the site of development problems perpetuates a singular vision of inequality that fails to acknowledge the socioeconomic and political relations that facilitate that inequality through unfair trade arrangements, resource extraction that benefits few at the expense of many, and other imperialist and/or neo-colonial practices facilitated by elites, corporations, and Northern governments alike.

In this chapter I summarize some of these critiques and reflect on their relationship – or significance – to the research findings with Canadian youth and host

organization staff. I also examine the helping initiative in relation to national identities surrounding perceptions of how and why Canadians should or could 'help'.
The national identity is an important extension of what we imagine to be our best
selves. In their employment of the helping identity, volunteer-sending organizations, in their marketing strategies, are able to tap into these individual and national
identities, in part by constructing an image of the volunteers who go abroad as
giving, nurturing, and generous.

A third useful analysis pertaining to the helping imperative derives from the
perspectives of the host country participants and their reflections on what, in fact, is
considered helpful and how this assistance may or may not promote solidarity. This
final analysis builds on the critique provided at the end of Chapter 5, where I reflect
on the limitations of critical theory, post-colonialism, and neo-imperial critiques in
relaying the sentiments expressed by many of the host participants as they pertain
to helping discourses and practices. Building on a normative framework of human
capabilities and empowerment discourse, this analysis reflects on the value of the
deconstruction of systemic challenges while also calling for more agency-oriented
analyses that enable the participants in volunteer abroad programmes to express
themselves outside the confines of critical theory. I begin my analyses by reflecting
on the broader context in which motivations to 'help' are created and perpetuated
through the images and marketing texts used by volunteer abroad programmes.

Selling the helping imperative

The motivation to help must be understood in the broader context of the messages
received and interpreted by those who take part in volunteer abroad programmes.
Advertisements for volunteer abroad opportunities employ the language of 'helping' and 'making a difference' to promote their programmes as much as, if not more
than, the rhetoric of adventure and travel (discussed in Chapter 5) or personal
growth and having an 'experience of a lifetime' (examined in Chapter 4). A review
of Google images for 'volunteer abroad' searches reveals that in addition to volunteer abroad website images of wildlife, safaris, mountain climbing, and other adventurous activities (as highlighted in Chapter 5), an even more popular image used
by volunteer-sending organizations is that of young white people providing 'help'
to black children. These images correspond with adventure-oriented identities of
'authentic experiences' as well as helping narratives. For example, Crosscultural
Solutions captures the helping imperative in the language of: "doing meaningful
work that addresses a specific need" (Crosscultural Solutions, 2014). The Global
Volunteer Network (2014) advertises its programmes with the phrase: "Make a
Real difference in the lives of others." A third example is "Impact your world", the
catch phrase for one advert for International Student Volunteers (2014).

Usually, the helping takes the form (in the images used by a wide array of
volunteer-sending organizations) of a young white woman holding, greeting, or
carrying small black children. The desire to help in the Global South is very intimately linked to a sense of helping or assistance, and a specific kind of experience

abroad that is imagined in volunteering abroad programmes. The imagery depicting volunteer abroad programmes forms an important part of the context that, in part, explains and shapes the volunteer abroad experience. Based on the imagery, one might expect that a 'helping imperative' (Heron, 2007) serves as a crucial motivation for taking part in volunteer abroad programmes.

The images of helping that are perpetuated in photographs, as well as the corresponding language used to describe volunteer experiences abroad, have come under intense scrutiny in scholarly literature (for example, see Clost, 2014; Heron, 2007). Barbara Heron, in her book *Desire for Development*, employs critical race theory, postcolonial studies and feminism to analyse primarily white middle-class women concerned with inequality in the world and a desire to make a difference and promote change. Heron argues that the colonial project of othering remains intact in volunteering abroad programmes whereby white women are able to assert their own value by virtue of helping the oppressed 'other'. Such narratives of helping are often constituted in rationales of altruistic values. Heron's work raises the question: What is altruism? She says: "Our altruism is also contingent on positioning the Southern Other as available to be changed, saved, improved, and so on, by us, thereby ensuring our entitlement to do so" (Heron, 2007: 44). These analyses grow out of a broader body of literature and a longer historical critique of missionary work and notions of charitable giving (helping) that have been criticized as poor development strategies in international development studies literature. Yet, the rhetoric of having an impact in the world, making a difference, doing meaningful work, etc., can also be criticized in the same way when it is used to mask helping narratives.

Critical newspaper articles and scholarly literature on volunteer abroad and voluntourism have picked up on this critique, noting the relationship between voluntourism and 'geographies of care' (Mostafanezhad, 2013: 487) – a relationship which is fostered as a result of celebrity endorsements and the celebritization of humanitarian work. Mary Mostafanezhad (2013), for example, documented the 'Angelina effect' (based on Angelina Jolie's humanitarian and personal activities) in her research with volunteers in Thailand. In her analysis, Mostafanezhad explains the growing interest in humanitarian and development work. Thus, on the one hand, there is a wealth of imagery depicting a particular 'helping imperative' that is popularized, and to some extent actualized, through a range of volunteer abroad opportunities. The imagery promotes a simplistic, and paternalistic, set of expectations of what the volunteers will observe and do in the Global South.

Ellyn Clost (2014) argues that there are three significant issues worthy of analysis in the images of LVA marketing for which we must better understand the ethical and sociocultural implications: the photographer as 'owner'; the location and significance of white and non-white bodies in photographic space; and the specialized role of female Canadian volunteers as child caregivers. She describes and analyses these three key issues in the context of the "visual economy of volunteering abroad". Her findings reinforce some of the critical scholarly debates from a postcolonial lens: white women are frequently positioned at the centre of the page – the subject of focus and often surrounded by black children. These white women are often depicted as caregivers, perhaps holding a baby, carrying a child on her back, administering medicine, food or, school supplies, etc. The photos of white women caring for black children are then consumed and internalized by other white women as normal and natural feminine contributions to development outcomes.

Marketing strategies that depict volunteering abroad in the manner noted above celebrate the volunteer and put him or her at the centre of the solution to development problems. Employing imagery of children (and seldom of adults in the Global South) further reinforces paternalism and enables the focus on those from the Global North (often white, young, privileged individuals) as the bearers of development solutions. Whether or not volunteers aspire to a celebrity status through their volunteer abroad work, they become 'popular' figures, often lacking anonymity and having high visibility in the community, and this kind of attention can perpetuate a celebrity-like status of participants in Western volunteer abroad programmes.

In addition, the 'fame' of volunteers abroad must be understood in the context of – and a motivation inspired by – celebrity humanitarianism performed by musicians and movie stars engaging in charitable work and often promoting volunteer abroad programmes. In *Celebrity Humanitarianism: The Ideology of Global Charity*, Ilan Kapoor (2013) argues that celebrities currently play a significant, though highly problematic, role in shaping the debates in humanitarianism, an argument that can be extended to development work more broadly. Kapoor argues that celebrity humanitarianism legitimates and promotes global inequality by depoliticizing it. In this vein, development challenges are constructed as problems requiring straightforward and simple solutions that can be easily measured (such as more health clinics, provision of micronutrients, improved proficiency with computer technology, etc.) rather than political issues that require deeper commitments to social justice.

While a highly valid critique worthy of further exploration, the visibility of celebrities such as Angelina Jolie provides an important media context to help make sense of the growing interest in volunteering abroad among young, primarily white, women from the Global North. Within this larger context of critiques of the helping impulse of young, white women is a series of articles in newspapers and magazines documenting the negative impacts of Northern volunteers working with children in orphanages. The *Independent* ran an article on January 12, 2013 titled: "Brangelinas need not apply: A Cambodian orphanage is leading the march against 'voluntourism'", following a series of articles examining the negative impacts of the voluntourism – and 'orphan tourism' (tourism and volunteering linked to caring for orphans) – industries arising in the Global South to meet the demands of Western white women to help and hold babies. *Al Jazeera* reported in June 2012 the findings of two reporters (Juliana Ruhfus and Mat Hanna) who travelled to Phnom Penh to investigate the 'orphan business' that has sprung up in Cambodia – a business that is fuelled by the rapid growth of voluntourism.

Other negative news stories about the 'problem' of voluntourism have surfaced in the popular media, usually focusing on one anecdote of a volunteer abroad experience that went poorly, or one person's opinion based on a negative experience of volunteering abroad that is used to explain the broad range of diverse volunteer

spoke with confidence about the significant contributions they made to their host organizations. Felicia, for example, said:

> Yeah, definitely … yeah because my projects were useful to them … definitely had in mind what the organization needed over there as well as the development of new projects and … so to the extent that they were completed and they were completed well, I think that was definitely helpful to the organization.

Arrrggghhh!

Helping in indirect ways: friendship formation and role-modelling

The second most common beneficial impact articulated as a form of assistance or helping noted was relationship formation. Many participants saw the benefits in terms of day-to-day activities, cross-cultural exchange, and the relationships formed, especially in the case of home stays (living with host families). Aisha said she was able to have a positive impact: "because I just came there with a loving attitude and I contributed what I could and I … fit in their flow".

Canadian participants also noted the importance of having exposure to Westerners and Western ways of thinking as forms of helping in order for the Global South to be able to develop. To elaborate on this point, one of the participants noted that "cross-cultural understanding on their [the host organization's] part" was important because "they [host organization staff] got a good dose of … what it's like working with a foreigner and all the baggage of that". Interviews with host country staff members also highlighted relationship formation and cross-cultural exchange as valuable components of their learning process. Jean-Paul reflected on a number of ways he felt he was able to help:

> Helping them kind of look at things in different ways hopefully helps them build their organizational capacity and their professional capacities.… I stayed in the village … and did overnights there to try and not only to help understand what it's like living in the village but also to have an intercultural exchange with people who might not normally get that with a Westerner and help try to … deconstruct some of those stereotypes and misperceptions.

This is interesting because Jean-Paul talks of a two-way transfer of knowledge and cultural exchange, but never really identifies what it is he gained from the host community, but instead focuses on what he was able to contribute to the organization and how he 'helped' the host country staff have a different perspective on Westerners.

The third most common perceived positive impact noted by the Canadian youth – related to the point about exposure to Westerners noted above – was teaching an outside perspective. The youth participants saw the LVA programmes as an opportunity for people from the community or organization to learn a new and/or different way of doing things. This came up quite often whereby volunteers were teaching organizations new skills or improved methods in a specialized field or a better way of doing things that they had just learned from university. Initially, these responses by the youth may come across as arrogant, so it was interesting to see that the host communities also considered LVA programmes to be a great opportunity to be exposed to new ideas. Ronaldo from Guatemala said that international volunteer placements are good for Guatemala because it fosters international relationships, "and it has helped us with international lobbying because it generates networks and those kinds of things", as well as bringing financial help to the organization, said Eliza from Guatemala.

Chusilo, from Malawi, also noted how volunteers have helped the organization acquire funding from donors by assisting with successful funding proposals. Ompie, from Zambia, recalls the assistance of a Voluntary Service Overseas (VSO) volunteer who helped set up an accounting system that resulted in increased funds from donors.

Some of the Canadian participants saw their stay as beneficial in terms of the money and material they brought with them from Canada, either to the host organization or to the host community in the form of gifts or the funding that came with their internship. A Canadian participant, Brad, said his only beneficial contribution was

> the amount of money that I spent in the community. I mean I hate to be cynical about this, but the organization, I mean even if I did do some work at the organization, even the organizations where I helped other VSO volunteers, you know I didn't put in place any sustainable solution ... it's very difficult to get people interested in learning the technologies that I was dealing with.

Brad went on to explain the problems he encountered, problems he said were experienced by previous interns who had worked in this organization and not by/ with him. In the end, he said his experience wasn't all bad because "I was there [and] I was spending money in the community which is helpful, I mean it's a very, very poor area right?" Isabelle echoed these remarks in her reflection on the financial contribution she felt she made to the orphanage where she stayed:

> this is practical, they got money. I know not a lot of volunteers think that but for what I paid, what I paid per day was my stay doubled. So instead of $6/day they got $12. That is a source of income that allows the orphanage to keep doing things they wouldn't otherwise be able to do.

Clarice also discussed the financial help she offered the host community by paying rent while living abroad. She thought the host family made a profit off the volunteers so they could redo their kitchen.

Western enlightenment: the perceived value of exposure to volunteers from the Global North

Cross-cultural understanding was also construed as a way of helping on the part of the Canadian volunteers. Some volunteers considered their time abroad an educational opportunity for the host communities and a chance to 'enlighten' host community members about life in North America because, as Clarice noted, host community members "have a very twisted view on it" because they think North America is an ideal world. While she claims to have dispelled the myth of the American dream to her host family, she is also reinforcing it by her presence by virtue of the fact that she has a disposable income, privilege, resources, and freedom of movement that enable her to get on a plane and leave her home – a luxury that most people in the Global South cannot afford.

Small contributions

Another small contribution that Canadian volunteers considered valuable included the little things that the volunteers brought from home as charitable gifts for host communities and host country staff. Stacey gave the example of medication for children that she brought along or her efforts to bring children to the hospital on occasion as efforts to make a difference. She commented, however, that the larger challenges within the communities were beyond her ability to assist. Another – and related – way of contributing identified by the Canadian youth was providing much-needed extra personnel or "free labour" for the organization. Jade expresses this in her analysis of helping, noting that:

> A lot of people were working many hours and that was based on funding, how much funding they had for people they could hire and so having a volunteer there, someone they didn't have to pay was really helpful for this organization but at the end too you're leaving them in a bit of a quandary because they have to find ways now to continue on with several of the duties that you were [doing] and they didn't have another volunteer coming this year, so from that perspective it was pretty useful for them, just extra hands.

Several other Canadian participants talked about small gestures of helping, including references to helping kids to learn to speak English, or unskilled labour such as washing dishes in the orphanage kitchen. The multiple references to the free labour they brought to the host country are devoid of any reflection on the implications and ethical dimensions to consider in the act of providing free labour, how that is perceived as privilege and connected to bourgeoisie identities. Practical issues such as the wealth of free labour within the host countries, and the high unemployment among university- and college-educated people are rarely brought up.

The notion of helping by virtue of serving as a role model came up on many occasions during the interviews, particularly from women who considered themselves important mentors for other young women from the host country. There were specific examples provided during these interviews of Canadian volunteers coaching their female colleagues on how to 'stand-up to their bosses' and assert themselves in the workplace. Another participant thought she was "being a good example" by showing women it is "okay to talk to the boss" openly and candidly. Some of the participants mentioned that serving as a role model enabled them to motivate the people they met in their host countries or host communities "to keep working hard". These mentorship identities were not considered, however, in the context of larger structural forces and societal implications at play that may prevent women and girls from being able to exert the types of freedoms the Canadian volunteers had. There are also implications for encouraging host country women to behave in a particular way while the Canadian volunteer is present – a strategy that may backfire on these women once the volunteer is no longer around. Gender sensitivities require a much broader societal and organization commitment that does not necessarily get addressed when volunteers encourage individual women to change their behaviours in the workplace.

In some cases, a rather problematic language of helping the host organization staff "get outside of the proverbial cave" was used. This participant goes on to say she was able to "help ... co-workers explore new ideas and different ways of doing things ... helping them kind of look at things in different ways". Another participant noted that she was able to bring

> a little bit more consideration, a little bit more humanity to the project because ... others [the local community and local staff] ... are so accustomed to seeing that kind of poverty and are not affected by it anymore so they don't make efforts in certain ways that people who aren't used to seeing that kind of poverty would do.

This statement suggests that the volunteer may not fully understand how local community members process and cope with poverty.

In summary, approximately half of the Canadian youth participants thought their overseas placements had a positive impact and they measured this positive impact in terms of helping in the forms of exposing local communities and local staff to Westerners, cross-cultural exchanges, bringing new ideas or fresh perspectives to the organization, acting as role models, and small contributions here and there in areas that are not adequately filled by local staff.

Host country participant reflections on helping and having an impact

Host community staff members confirmed that there was 'help' provided by the international volunteers. When reviewing data coded for the 'benefits of volunteering' and searching for references to 'help' in the 82 pages of transcribed reflections from host partners, the word 'help' was mentioned 148 times. Specific references were made to "valuable financial help to the organization", as well as assisting with understanding relations between countries or improved international perspective. Specific skills were also identified, such as improved technical capacity.

Most commonly cited in reference to the 'help provided' were the comments about the help in terms of human resources or extra hands in the organization to assist when they are short-staffed and need the volunteer support. Most often, the references to helping were expressed as "helping us". In other words, the organizations talked about helping as something that was received and less as a matter of what was provided to the volunteers. Other similar references such as 'impact' (having an impact) were also noted throughout the interviews. In fact, when referring to the benefits of hosting international volunteers, 'impact' was mentioned 33 times. The references to the impact of hosting international volunteers were made in positive terms in relation to impacts on the host country partners, the organizations, the programmes, and even 'society at large'. References to 'assisting' were less frequent, with only 14 comments pertaining to expressed benefits of hosting international volunteers.

Charles, from Malawi, commented on the expertise that volunteers bring: "They bring the expertise from the developed countries. They also help us to have the checks and balances because we know we are somehow answerable to the organization which has sent them to us." Ceasar, also from Malawi, said the volunteers

give you an opportunity to assess yourself from different perspectives in terms of performance as an organization … working with the volunteer that's the part I like most because it gives you different perspectives because what happens is that it helps you to balance southern nongovernmental organization and northern nongovernmental organizations. It helps to know how other organizations are doing it and your organization can cope up. They help you on how you can put your organization at global level not only seeing it as it is in Malawi only.

Jorge, from Peru, also reflected on the value of an alternative perspective:

To have another perspective that helps you to re-think your own, and also to establish connections. I believe that this idea of globalization – I don't like the term – is a reality. So, to have the possibility of making contact, have a dialogue with another person, e-mail for me is of key importance. It helps a lot in finding contacts, in looking for information, in being sensitive to other realities, because we can no longer ignore them and think that all life is here. I believe that's important.

Participants from Zambia (Reuben) and Jamaica (Shanice) both remarked that the cultural exchange is valuable and provides assistance in terms of improved comprehension of other cultures, work attitudes, and exchange of ideas. Mikul from

India added to this notion, noting that the Western volunteers come to India with an "openness to understand, to learn" and that the "cross-cultural learning that takes places is enriching". The fresh perspectives are considered of particular value, according to Shreya from India. As well, she noted that the volunteers bring "a certain amount of objectivity" in the way that things are examined and understood because "they are able to look at things, you know, from a distance, but at the same time, since they are here, so they are able to sort of explain that ... if anything is different, why is it or what is it." South African host staff (Neill, for example) reflected on the information technology skills and equipment the international volunteers bring with them and the significance of these technologies for connecting the South African organizations to the rest of the world. Guatemalan participant Eliseo said that the youth volunteers from the West add "energy and strength to the organization. For the communities it is also good, because they can start to relate with other cultures and have other types of experiences." Andrea from Guatemala said that the youth volunteers bring cultural capital that they can share through their intercultural exposure. Several of the participants from Peru, South Africa, and Guatemala commented on the importance of the volunteers who bring their solidarity values to the organization. Raisa noted that the solidarity approach helps connect the North and South, allowing for what Itzel from Guatemala calls "a cultural interchange".

Host country responses echoed some of the sentiments of filling in gaps in the organization where there were no staff to do the work, noting that Northern volunteers did indeed bring extra hands or prestige to the organization, which enabled them to get funding. "So donor confidence is also one advantage that comes with some of these volunteers, especially if they are given key roles to play." Kandyata, also from Zambia, remarked on the importance of volunteers for perceived credibility, noting that it "adds on to our reputation out there in the foreign missions. So to us it is about marketing. Also it opens up some opportunities for funding especially if they see that there is something that we can benefit, you find they will share this information with us." Albertina from South Africa said that having volunteers "does help to bolster your capacity so that the other full-time researchers can work on other areas because they're getting assistance". A participant from Jamaica, Amoya, noted that any volunteers are welcome because the organization relies on volunteers to survive. The international volunteers, therefore, are perceived by host country partners as bringing a particular "richness" that is appreciated.

Difficulties with hosting international volunteers

Nonetheless, the experiences of hosting international volunteers were not described exclusively in positive terms. When reflecting on the difficulties of hosting international volunteers, host country partners referred to instances when the volunteers had "their own personal issues and we have had to try and *help that individual dealing with their challenges*". Other participants in host countries mentioned the challenges of 'helping' volunteers to settle in, to find suitable accommodation. Others referred to challenges they observed in relation to the motivations of participation, as one Malawian participant noted: "Foreign volunteers should finish their time when they come, and not leave us on the midway because that does not help us at all. They should also come to volunteer not for other reasons", such as travel, adventure, personal gain, etc.

The host country staff did not always agree that women volunteers acted as good role models. Several of the participants talked about the problematic clothing worn by Northern volunteers in spite of their efforts to educate them on appropriate attire for the office and/or the communities. Khumbo from Malawi argued: "Some volunteers would dress in a way that is not culturally accepted here in Malawi." Rasheeda in India said that the staff at their organization discuss appropriate attire with the volunteers but even those discussions have not proven sufficient, noting that community members were shocked by the attire, as were organization staff. Rasheeda welcomed additional orientation sessions for volunteers by the sending organizations in advance of the placement. A Zambian participant, Gideon, commented that the dress can be too casual in some instances: "A situation where Zambians expect there should be some formality depending on who one is going to meet or the occasion." Other participants from the host countries reflected on what they considered inappropriate behaviour of youth volunteers from abroad who were seen kissing in the street, moving in with their boyfriends, and getting into relationships with community members that they hardly know. These concerns are in direct contrast with some of the reflections from the Canadian youth who consider themselves role models, and who see these role model responsibilities as being helpful.

Several of the host country participants also provided insights into the amount of help that Northern volunteers are able give. A Zambian participant thought: "When it comes to direct contact with the people in the community I think they haven't done much except like maybe in the organization management and stuff." The Zambian participant went on to argue that the Northern volunteers he has encountered are hardworking: "You will see them working all the time and they want to see people working all the time." He, however, provided an important critique of the Northern volunteers as well, noting that some

> volunteers … want to come and boss everyone around, like this person would come because they think they are very educated and because of the colour of skin they think they have been given all the authority and so some of them you find they want to do everything themselves because they feel maybe they can do them better than anybody else but not all of them.

A second Zambian participant, Emmanuel, commented on the 'bossy' aspects of Northern volunteers, noting of the volunteers from the Global North:

> some of them they feel that they are more superior than others. They feel that being from the Western world, they know a lot of things so they think that,

they take it that you as an African or you as a black person you know little, or you know nothing at all. So they will always want to, for instance, oppose the opinion of you.

Another similar critique emerged from the interview with a South African participant, Sizwe, who points to a form of exploitation carried out by some of the participants on LVA programmes. The South African participant said that some communities oppose having researchers coming into their communities

> with a view that international visitors are just coming in to exploit them, collect their data, write up their research and collect their PhD. There is no giving back so there have been communities that have shunned international visitors in their communities.

The host community staff also noted the self-oriented nature of the volunteer experience for those coming from the North. In a critique provided by one of the participants from Peru, the participant argues that some Northern volunteers do not come to help at all, indicating that one experience with a Northern volunteer suggested the volunteer was there for purely personal interests:

> The person seemed to me to have some health problems; it was an effort for her to integrate, her attitude was very much like 'well, I have to do this, I have to do research' but as something that was very much her own individual interest which, well, was very difficult for us.

The critiques that have emerged from both the Canadian youth and the participants in the Global South shed light on the concerns they share and the matters that need further exploration.

Honest reflections on not helping at all

Several Canadian youth participants provided insightful and honest reflections on their failure to 'help'. Louisa, for example, said that she didn't "have the impact that I would've liked because my position there was so much different than what I was told it would be, that I was just really basically, most of the time in an office writing a paper". Louisa's comments speak to the expectations she had of what she thought she might accomplish or what she might be able to do to help. Susan also expressed concerns about an inability to help, arguing that:

> the money that they spent sending me over would've been better served providing it to those girls [that the organization was serving]. They didn't need me there at all…. I went out with the whole mentality of helping others but now I don't know anymore. And that's not to say I wouldn't do it again, because I probably would, for my own selfish reasons.

It is interesting to highlight Susan's latter comments, which suggest that the idea of helping is important but the fact that there is potentially no positive change or difference made through the volunteer placement is inconsequential to the Canadian youth. Evan was also unsure of his ability to provide help:

> I don't know, like I would love to say yes, absolutely, I had a positive impact, I was really great … it's difficult for me to know whether I had an impact at all. Well I probably had an impact, but it's difficult to know if that impact was a positive one.

Finally, Ross' reflections on his ability to make a difference point to a good understanding of the limited impact anyone can make in short-term, three-month placements abroad:

> I feel like maybe I had a negative impact because despite how much positive work I did it wasn't sustainable and it was a waste of their time just to have me come … whereas they could have invested in someone who could have been going abroad for a long time and doing a lot more work. So maybe I was a waste of resources to the community through wasting the organization's resources and networks. I think most of the benefits came back to me, not the community.

Sheila also questioned the allocation of financial resources for short-term volunteering programmes. Sheila, who took part in a four-month placement, wondered if it was the best use of funds. Sheila wonders if the money could be put elsewhere and would have a greater impact.

Francois took his analysis of helping abroad further and expressed some concern for his complicity in development, saying: "Well I worried a lot about reinforcing stereotypes and … patterns of dominance just by my presence…. And I was worried that my very presence there was helping to encourage that system." Francois and other youth comments reflect the concepts that Heron (2007) outlines – essentially that despite the ability of participants to critique the development discourse, they participate anyway and then find ways of rationalizing their involvement by suggesting they went about their placement in some alternative manner. Francois did this by stating that he got his degree is African Studies rather than development, as if he made a moral choice to pursue something other than development, yet doesn't really explain how that translates to his volunteer abroad position as more effective or 'helpful'. Similarly, Natalie justified her experience abroad by saying that at least she's probably doing things in a more ethical manner than someone else who may have been put in her position, suggesting that there are worse alternatives to her and other youth who 'care' about people in the Global South. None of these participants offered true alternatives to the development discourse they critique nor did they consider whether they may have been able to take on a role in a capacity other than as a volunteer.

The critiques emerging from youth who considered their time abroad as helpful (often framed in terms of 'having an impact') and those who were more critical of their ability to 'help' support some of the scholarly critiques in development studies and international volunteering. Development studies literature offers a comprehensive analysis of many of the failures of the development enterprise, including ineffective projects and highly paid Western 'experts' in development who may not have a real, nor a practical, commitment to altering the status quo of global inequality (Heron, 2007). The findings presented here from interviews with Canadian youth reinforce a conclusion that Barbara Heron draws in her own research on Western women working in Zambia. Heron argues: "Interestingly though, regardless of how unexceptional our postings might be, most of us see our work as representing in at least some respects an alternative to what is going on around us" (Heron, 2007: 103). Heron called this the "myth of alternative development" in which volunteers separate themselves from what they claim not to be: the problematic development workers.

Emphasis on devotion, hard work, commitment, and compassion of international volunteers obscures the broader challenges of the growth industry of going abroad. In so doing, volunteers distance themselves from other expatriates. Yet, one of the only real factors that distances the volunteers from other paid development 'experts' is the amount of financial remuneration received for similar work combined with often very different placement periods (with volunteers generally having much shorter placements abroad than development professionals). Similarly, through these differentiations, volunteers distance themselves "from the development enterprise as a whole, so that our critiques of it have the effect of enshrining us in virtue" (Heron, 2007: 103).

Heron's analysis of development volunteers (a category in which she includes herself) suggests that the most insightful contributions to a self-critique involve questioning "whether their work might have meant they were implicated in, rather than an alternative to, their own criticism" (Heron, 2007: 135). Beyond the argument of complicity in the development enterprise, development scholars have also articulated additional challenges that can be brought about through the steady stream of volunteers posted to the Global South, as has been addressed above with references to 'othering' and perceptions of dependence.

From the responses provided, it is clear that the youth have a self-critique and have engaged in some reflection on their imagined impact related to 'helping'. The participants came across as open and conflicted. They were not, on the whole, sure they had made a meaningful impact while volunteering abroad and some realized that they may have had very negative impacts on individuals, even if they felt they were acting to address community-level issues. The negative impacts identified by the Canadian participants cannot be ignored. They require rigorous investigation and thoughtful reflection. The identification of negative impacts serves as a mere starting point for challenging youth volunteers to be more careful when making decisions that can affect the lives of people. In one example, a young Canadian woman volunteer told about her potentially negative impact when she spoke to the school headmaster about two teaching colleagues who were subsequently fired. She realized she had a significant negative impact on the teachers' respective lives but considered her actions justified because of the performance of the teachers she had observed. Such complex ethical issues require opportunities for thoughtful reflection and pre-departure preparation. International volunteers need to be encouraged to seek the advice of local and international experts who may have more knowledge or understanding of the local circumstances in order to avoid causing harm.

Furthermore, the youth cannot see themselves as community-level experts, particularly given their short time in the host country, but they must also be cognizant of the power they may wield by virtue of their privileged position as guests in the host countries as well as representatives (perceived or real) of Northern-based development organizations.

Many of the participants reflected on how the placements had a positive impact or 'helped' the Canadians themselves more than the host countries. Benjamin, for example, said

> I think at the end of the day if I were to ... do the cost/benefit [analysis].
> I would say it's more beneficial than negative. But it's hard to say because it's
> beneficial for us, those who are able to go and travel, in terms of those in the
> partner country. ... I got to learn, I got to go personally, I got to travel, I got
> to build relationships and be moved and see poverty and it shaped my life
> but I guess I don't really know that kind of converse relationship in terms of
> those that I worked with or met or saw.

References to 'not helping at all' were made by the host country participants as well. As a Zambian participant noted: "they don't help ... I don't see any help, maybe at Head Office but at my level when we go in the community, there is nothing they do." Nonetheless, the reflection on 'help', assistance provided, or impact must be understood in the contexts in which international volunteers were considered useful to the host organizations. There were some instances where the challenges or difficulties of hosting international volunteers revealed that there were significantly unhelpful aspects of volunteer abroad programmes. However, in reference to cross-cultural communication and interpersonal relationships, the role of 'helping' played a highly positive role. Host country staff members appreciate the fresh insights or alternative perspectives that the volunteers bring. They enjoyed the additional support provided by volunteers in those cases where volunteers could be helpful. It is to be expected that not all volunteer placements are going to be a perfect match for the needs of the organization, but when the match is made well, the host staff had generally positive things to say about the value-added of international volunteers both personally in the benefits they experienced in the work they do, and more systemically in terms of the perceived benefits of having a Western presence in the organization.

Expectations of the potential longer-term impacts and helping after the volunteers return home

Host country participants throughout the interviews highlighted what they perceived as an important part of supporting the international volunteers in their homes, countries, and/or organizations: the message that these volunteers might bring back to their home communities to forge a lasting relationship and continued communication and support.

For many decades, donor governments have funded international volunteering and internships in the Global South through development assistance programming. In recent years, there are fewer and fewer such 'funded' opportunities for youth, and the volunteer-sending community has found it increasingly difficult to prepare for and deliver programmes in the midst of funding uncertainty. Yet, there is a supposed greater value attached to the LVA programmes: they promote cross-cultural understanding, build lasting relationships, and create a committed Canadian community dedicated to fighting poverty and inequality by virtue of their exposure to these challenges in the Global South. There is no evidence to suggest that there is a direct correlation between volunteering abroad and long-term support for development assistance, although a CUSO study tracking former volunteers did make the link between volunteering abroad experiences and high levels of long-term volunteering commitments in the volunteers' home communities (CUSO, 2007).

Other participants noted that it was beneficial to Canadians more generally since the volunteers were able to bring what they've learned back to Canada. These justifications are significant in part because they reflect the emphasis on the Canadian youth's experience and very little on the impact on the host countries or host communities. As such, the findings raise questions about the implications of programmes that may do little to improve the quality of life of people in developing countries and are justified as important learning or personal growth opportunities for Canadian participants.

Several Canadian participants said they were confident that their ability to help would play out upon their return to Canada, where they could share information and raise awareness based on what they had learned. The concept of being able to share information/knowledge/understanding upon their return home is advocated as a benefit of international volunteering programmes in other countries. International Voluntary Services (IVS), for example, views returned IVS volunteers as important means of improving cross-cultural relations or resolving conflicts. International volunteers have the perceived distinct advantage of global understanding, open minds, and a broader perspective on international development (Fuchs, 1967; Hutchings and Smart, 2007). International volunteers, according to some of the scholarship, are also valued for their ability to shape new perspectives of Westerners, enhance communication across cultures, and to facilitate global action (VSO, 2006; Sherraden et al., 2008).

While the motivation of helping did not rank among the top motivations for going abroad, such as cross-cultural exposure and skills development or testing a career choice, the helping imperative was an integral feature in the reflections of the

Canadian youth and the insights provided by host communities. The language of having an impact was often employed to articulate matters that reinforce helping imperatives. In addition to a desire for helpful contributions in the Global South – or making a difference – youth and host communities alike had a fairly well-developed critique of the challenges of helping and the problems associated with the self-oriented gains for Westerners and the neo-colonial global practices of which LVA programmes are a part. These findings resonate with those of Cook (2007) and Heron (2007), who note that Northern women's desire to do development work has important personal implications but also can be understood as the projection of a larger development construction or enterprise whereby individual identities are also linked to an identity as a global 'good guy' who makes a positive difference in the lives of needy 'others' by implementing Western-derived reform. To build on the conclusions of Zemach-Bersin (2007: 24), the findings from this study demonstrate that development volunteers, like students who study abroad, join the ranks of "missionaries, colonizers, anthropologists, and humanitarian aid workers who have served as 'goodwill ambassadors,' promoting the soft power interests of the metropole". Heron (2007) said that the primary motivation for overseas placements is, at its heart, driven by a desire to actualize "the colonial continuities of entitlement and obligation to intervene globally" (p. 88). Is the desire to help a win–win situation for the volunteers and the host communities? Nancy Cook asked this question in relation to the benefits volunteers ascribe to their personal growth and their contributions 'in the field'. If volunteering to do development work (or LVA4D) is inspired by motives of self-development as well as the helping imperative, then in 'helping others' volunteers can simultaneously help themselves.

Scholarly debates on the impact on 'helping' have ranged from critical analyses of the neo-colonialism of 'helping imperatives' (Heron, 2007) to more positive expectations of volunteer impacts in terms of service delivery and cross-cultural exposure (Lyons and Wearing, 2008), as well as those bodies of scholarship that have reflected on the positive and negative impacts simultaneously (Devereux, 2008; Sherraden *et al.*, 2008). The findings from this study are best situated in this latter body of literature. There are indeed some important challenges and critiques to consider, as examined in this chapter. However, the responses of the host organization staff and also the Canadian volunteers allow for a deeper reflection on the potential for positive impacts. The host organizations continue to choose to participate in these programmes and while there are distinct structural limitations and inequalities of opportunity, the host staff have chosen to continue to participate in these programmes because they provide some opportunities for interpersonal relations, organizational strengthening, engaging globally and forming their own identities of global citizenship (a subject of greater discussion in Chapter 7).

Situating the findings in the theoretical debates

The images that we internalize and replicate are an important reflection of how we see ourselves and how we wish others to see us. Images of helping people in the Global South (or more accurately presuming to be helping while holding a black child in a photo-op) appeal to our sensibilities as kind, generous, and good people. In Barbara Heron's insightful analysis of aid workers, she refers to this perception of self as an expression of innocence and bourgeois identity. Heron's work to date theorized that development work is reflective of white women's desire to claim a bourgeois subjectivity by demonstrating their "superior moral sensitivities" and she suggests that

> development work constitutes a particularly compelling expression of inno-
> cent knowledge because it addresses the issue of how to act in the world, as
> well as how to fulfill the imperative to "help" or "improve" [which she associ-
> ates with a white woman's bourgeois identity]; in other words, participating
> in some aspect of the development enterprise – as a helper – seems to guar-
> antee a place on the moral high ground of white middle-class subjectivity.
> At the same time, bourgeois subjects are assured that when we intervene it
> is an innocent undertaking … [and] our actions bear no connection to the
> perpetration of domination or other immoral processes or relations. Quite
> the contrary, 'helping' in this context is a manifestation of the moral fabric
> of bourgeois subjectivity, as colonialism's civilizing mission was in its day.
> Planetary consciousness and the related sense of entitlement and obligation
> to intervene elsewhere appear to be unproblematically 'good'.
>
> *(Heron, 2007: 126)*

Reflecting on the bourgeois morality of the helping impulse, Nancy Cook noted that:

> This philanthropic pull factor – for privileged Western women to provide for
> the needy – can be understood as a positive aspect of a discourse of bour-
> geois morality and femininity, whether the benefactors are inspired to do the
> devout work of development of Christianity.
>
> *(Cook, 2007: 88)*

Cook argued, however, that despite their desire to 'help' local women, her participants remain relatively uninterested in, and disconnected from, the day-to-day lives
of the women they claim to be helping. In general, Cook found that her participants stressed the factors that 'pushed' them to Gilgit (compelled to help), rather
than the 'pull' factors, some of which are associated with the notion of altruism
mentioned above.

Othering

The helping imperative (however articulated as having an impact or positive
change) implies that the helpers have in mind those people they think are in need
of help as well as the notion that the 'other' is faced with problems requiring the
solutions of foreign volunteers; and thus facilitating simplistic divisions between

'givers' of help and 'receivers' of assistance (Mostafanezhad, 2013). The portrayal of those being helped in discourses and images surrounding LVA are 'othered' because they generally remain nameless and/or are presented as the objects of development assistance. Urry's (1990) notion of the humanitarian gaze is a helpful construct for making sense of power dynamics, binary divisions, and hierarchy that play out in LVA encounters (Mostafanezhad, 2013; Urry, 1990). Yet not all volunteer-sending organizations can be painted with the same brush. Several organizations have made key discursive shifts in an effort to change the balance of power and establish a more level playing field for development assistance. One such example is the impressive work by CUSO to change the language of 'recruits' to 'cooperants' and to employ the language of 'partners' when referring to local field staff. Other organizations, such as the 'Breaking the Silence' initiative by the Tatamagouche Centre, promote an ethic and practice of solidarity – an approach to volunteering abroad that was highlighted and valued by the participants from the host organizations in Guatemala interviewed for this study. Discursive shifts such as the one advocated by the Canadian Council for International Cooperation (CCIC) calls for an approach of "interdependence and connected destinies" (2007). The CCIC claims that the use of international volunteers and the concept of transferring money, technology, or knowledge are all reflective of a benevolent/charity-based model that can have the negative impact of "hammer[ing] home a single message – the endless need of the South" (2007). The CCIC argues this discourse can be changed by a broader framework of global citizenship (discussed in greater detail in Chapter 7).

In a similar vein, Ehrichs noted that:

> Even with such changes in discourse, however, the framing of locals in the South as the Other, the one needing help, remains largely the same. What the Western volunteers have learned, or need to learn, is to improve, or mitigate problems of poverty in their own societies and communities – which is not explicitly addressed in many of the volunteer sending organizations.
>
> *(Ehrichs, 2002: 7)*

In doing so, the problems that require solving become global issues that exist in the Global North and the Global South. Addressing these issues begins by understanding global dynamics that perpetuate poverty and inequality and finding solutions on a global level that involve resolutions both 'at home' and abroad.

In addition, breaking down the notion of the 'other' is essential. Drawing on the work of Escobar and Foucault, Ehrichs made the following statement in regard to how volunteerism can contribute to transformational change: First, volunteer action that transforms rejects the notion of an Other, or the subject/object paradigm, in favour of a subject/subject construction of discourse, and creates what Escobar calls a counter-discourse (1984: 392). The ability to do this depends largely on the critical consciousness of the volunteer. Therefore the second aspect expands on the process of conscientization and perspective transformation (Ehrichs, 2002).

Discerning ways to enhance mutual or shared power and learning is central to this strategy (Ehrichs, 2002). In conclusion, Ehrichs states that:

> volunteer work in development, and the humanism that distinguishes it, has made attempts to change discursive practice and the power and knowledge inherent in it. But this change is as yet superficial. Volunteering began in the modernisation paradigm as all development work, and in the 40-ensuing years has begun to reject the 'othering' of locals but commitment to this counter-discourse must deepen manifold, especially at the level of personal consciousness.
>
> *(Ehrichs, 2002: 11).*

In her study of volunteer motivations and their implications for international development, Unstead-Joss explains the need to recognize relationships of power as inherent in the altruistic desire to help others: "A post-modern critique argues that if volunteering is to contribute to transformational change, then voluntary action must recognise that within general motivations to 'do good' there are issues of power and powerlessness" (p. 4). Building on the work of Illich and Rahnema (1997), specifically that social responsibility is the "soft underbelly of a weird sense of power through which we think ourselves capable of making the world better" (Illich and Rahnema, 1997: 108), Unstead-Joss argues that if volunteers are motivated by rationales of improving and changing the lives of others, the 'others' in this case are perceived by volunteers as powerless to effect change in their own lives and are therefore dependent on the help of outsiders (Unstead-Joss, 2008).

Erikson-Baaz (2005) found that her research participants (Norwegian development workers) position their Tanzanian partners as "spoilt by aid" or "passive aid recipients", which she claims is a more recent version of the colonial stereotype of "the lazy native" (p. 121). While the participant comments in this chapter do not seem to invoke these images of passivity or laziness, there is significant evidence of an assumed aid-dependence as the outcome of their volunteer work. As such, some volunteers may invoke the notion of charity to describe what they do and how they carry out their volunteer work.

Charity versus development: what kind of helping takes place?

The helping imperative expressed by youth is central to the discourse surrounding LVA programmes. While the notion of helping ranked relatively low as a motivation that the youth considered 'very important' to their reasons for going abroad, a discourse of helping surfaced during many points of the interview, with a range of references from explicit mention of helping to other terms such as having an impact or making a difference; thus, shedding light on important desires for development and also on some central critiques of the helping impulse. The host country participants reflected on the ability of youth to help and noted ways of helping that are less widely covered in the volunteer abroad scholarship. In spite of the self-criticisms of helping identified by the youth, the host communities, and articulated in the literature, host communities continue to ask for more volunteers, arguing that the disadvantages do not outweigh the advantages of hosting Northern volunteers. The nuances and complexity of the relationships forged through international volunteering require more careful consideration in light of structural and systemic challenges and agency-oriented realities as articulated in the comments by both the Canadian youth and host country staff. Perhaps the cross-cultural exposure that is experienced through the volunteer placements facilitates a different kind of identity formation for both youth and host communities; this notion of global citizenship identity is examined in the next chapter.

While a more complicated reflection on the diverse helping experiences that the Canadian youth and host country partners encountered is warranted, the broader context of a particular discourse and imagery of 'helping' most definitely plays out in volunteer abroad literature, imagery, discourse, and through celebrity humanitarian propaganda. There is good reason to expect young would-be volunteers to be influenced by this imagery and to enact these tropes in their LVA experiences.

There are distinct marketing strategies employed by volunteer-sending organizations and these techniques vary from one organization to the next. For-profit organizations may have a different approach than not-for-profit volunteer-sending organizations, and the mandates of diverse organizations must also be taken into account. In any case, it is likely that the marketing employed by volunteer-sending organizations plays an important part in the creation of a demand for volunteer abroad experiences, but these same images do not account for, in their entirety, the nature of the experience abroad. A growing number of young Canadians – and youth around the world – are sensitized to the harmful discourse and practices of the 'helping imperative' and seek ways to mitigate their potentially negative or harmful impacts. Furthermore, a range of participants with diverse experiences and backgrounds take part in LVA programmes. The training (whether through academic studies, pre-departure training, reading critical literature as documented in this chapter, etc.) may indeed facilitate a deep critique and reflection, thus getting much closer to achieving what Erhichs (2002) terms a "counter-discourse" and improved personal consciousness of the ethical implications and potential contributions through LVA.

One of the highly thoughtful insights on the value of international volunteering for development arises from the work of Palacios (2010). In his work on volunteer tourism, he argues that

> the use of a volunteering – and therefore a helping – language in a global context of inequality and post-colonialism directly relates to a history of Western domination and draws public attention to questions of effectiveness, and even desirability, of IVS programs in developing countries. Leaving intact – if not reinforcing – the dominant position of the North.

(p. 864)

Critical development scholars from Escobar (1995) to Kothari (2005) have challenged the possibilities for 'new' practices such as LVA to alter these relations of inequality and exploitation. However, international volunteering is now a deeply entrenched strategy for promoting international development and Sustainable Development Goals and for the promotion of global change (Sherraden *et al.*, 2006; Palacios, 2010: 864). Thus, the structural limitations of neo-colonial practices remain important considerations and reminders of the need for improved development practice through LVA.

Summary

Returning to the analytical frameworks noted above, these deconstructive analyses are useful for thinking about the broader context in which decisions to host international volunteers as well as decisions to go abroad for volunteering are made. They offer important considerations regarding the systemic challenges through which people make decisions. However, the personal choices and experiences articulated in this study reinforce the need for thoughtful consideration of the values and desires expressed not just by volunteers but, more importantly, by host organizations. Despite a range of potentially harmful practices, inequality of opportunity, among other challenges, many positive sentiments and outcomes were expressed by the volunteers and host partners alike. A decolonization of the current research analysis is thus required to ensure that we are not reproducing colonialism by privileging (in our critique) the rationales for participation in volunteer abroad programmes provided by those from privileged positions and countries of greater opportunities.

While the limitations of helping must be explored in careful detail and used as strategies to prevent additional problems in volunteer abroad options, the prospects for broader forms of assistance in terms of solidarity movements, mutual assistance, shared responsibility, and improved cross-cultural relations can be valuable contributions to international development efforts.

However, these two sets of debates, I argue, create a simplistic dichotomy that does not accurately reflect the range of motivations, experiences, and realities of LVA programmes. Rather, as the interview participants in my study demonstrate, the desire to help and the experiences of 'helping' are complicated and contested notions. The Canadian participants in this study as well as those host country staff from seven countries in the Global South offer a highly nuanced and thoughtful engagement on the nature of 'helping' in LVA programmes. It is important to capture the agency and aspirations of those who participate in LVA4D programmes because these narratives provide rich insights into the perceived value of international volunteering outcomes in relation to 'helping', having an impact, or making a difference. However, the structural limitations (neo-colonialism, for example) identified in some of the scholarly literature, particularly pertaining to the perpetuation of neo-colonial discourses and practices as justified through international volunteering rationales of global justice and equality, reinforce a particular development aid discourse that is bound up in a neo-colonial paradigm.

The emphasis on the actions of 'helping' or 'having an impact' through volunteering serve to reinforce the sentiment of what the Global North can do for the Global South: a highly unidirectional and inequitable arrangement. Yet, the participants in this study emphasized more than the actions of doing development or delivering some tangible skill or outcome and also remarked on the value of cross-cultural learning with and from each other. Such an analysis opens up possibilities for reflecting on international volunteering options in ways that move away from neo-colonial development discourses, and into a new direction of praxis, improved reflectivity, and mutual learning. In the following chapter I continue this analysis with emphasis on mutual learning in LVA4D and global competency.

7

CONCLUSION

Understanding rationales and the possibilities for effective practices in volunteer abroad programmes

Introduction

Throughout this book, the focus has been on the motivations for participation in learning/volunteer abroad for development (LVA4D) programmes in the Global South. Research for this study included qualitative interviews with Canadian youth between the ages of 18 and 30 who travelled abroad on LVA4D programmes for approximately 3–6 months in duration (or medium-term placements) to a country in the Global South. Interviews were also carried out with host country staff members who receive international volunteers. Details of medium-term placements and the study sample are provided in Chapters 1 and 2. The book hinges on questions geared to understanding why volunteers and host organization staff and community members participate in these programmes. An important starting point for examining this question is reflections on privilege. Building on scholarly contributions to understanding white and male privilege, the introduction to this book examines a broader range of privileges such as time (for those who can take time off from work or school to travel); mobility (the freedom to travel and cross national borders, often without the need for a visa); affluence (the relative wealth enabling a select group of individuals to purchase passports, airline tickets, and often expensive volunteer abroad excursions or travel packages); and position (a particular status resulting from educational levels and work experience that enables young Northerners to travel abroad as 'development experts'). These privileges are examined throughout the chapters of this book in relation to the experiences of volunteers' and host partners' positive and critical assessments of volunteer abroad programmes.

Furthermore, the privileges highlighted above provide insights into some of the motivations or justifications for participation in volunteer abroad programmes. The privilege of time and mobility often translated into reflections on motivations for adventures and travel abroad for Canadian youth, for example. All the participants in this study (Canadian youth and host partners) were asked to reflect on why they chose to participate in volunteer abroad programmes. The Canadian youth summarized their motivations for participation using a ranking exercise (details provided in Chapter 2). The motivations identified as the most significant by the Canadian youth overlapped in a number of ways. Personal growth, for example, was articulated as a specific motivation. However, references to personal growth were identified in relation to other motivations such as cross-cultural understanding, skills development, and travel and adventure, discussed in each of the relevant chapters. Host country partners also identified their reasons for participating in volunteer abroad programmes, listing a variety of justifications from the personal value they found in getting to know people from other places, to pragmatic reasons such as the perceived credibility for donors or the status these placements may portray to host communities when hosting a foreigner in the organization. Chapters 3, 4, 5, and 6 deal with specific and distinct motivations identified by the Canadians and host partners. In each of these chapters, broader rationales for participation are also examined, ranging from rationales of solidarity or intercultural competence to egoistic rationales for social, cultural, or economic capital gains. The rationales articulated by the participants, and analysed in the context of international development debates, shed light on diverse and sometimes overlapping rationales for participation in volunteer abroad programmes. These rationales enable a deeper reflection on the scholarly debates in volunteer abroad literature. Many of the critical insights gained from postcolonial analyses were apparent in the participants' comments and the analyses that followed. These critical insights contribute to deep reflections on structural and systemic inequality, neo-colonial practices, neoliberalism, and paternalism, and serve as important reminders of the limitations of the current models of volunteering abroad (the North–South context).

Nonetheless, careful reading of the quotes and contributions of the study participants lends support for a deeper reflection and careful analysis of agency-oriented or empowerment possibilities. Normative frameworks such as the human capabilities approach offer additional lenses to consider the contributions of volunteers, particularly since the host partners' perspectives were very much focused on reciprocity, mutuality, solidarity, ethics, and social justice. In other words, while the host organization staff articulated many structural and systemic challenges that exist in volunteer abroad models, they also highlighted many agency-oriented analyses of the potential for global engagement, mutual understanding, and interpersonal relations. Both the Canadian and the host country participants considered volunteer abroad programmes important for promoting cosmopolitan values and global citizenship identities. However, the range of identities around global citizenship must be considered.

Scholarly literature on international volunteering includes analyses of the potential for 'thick' or 'thin' global citizenship (Cameron, 2014) resulting from volunteer abroad opportunities. Throughout the interviews with Canadian and host country participants, many references to global citizenship were made. Aspirations of global citizenship – or cosmopolitan – identity thus served as an important rationale for participation in LVA4D. In Chapter 3 there are some considerations of global citizenship as an important rationale underpinning the motivation of cross-cultural understanding. Here, I return briefly to a discussion of global citizenship and its potential for contributing to more effective practices in volunteer abroad programmes.

What stood out most from the study participant comments is the desire for a connection across cultures and aspirations of *learning* from each other. These rationales emerged in the Canadian youth ranking of their perceived 'most important motivation' for taking part in LVA4D, and this motivation was also frequently mentioned in the interview transcripts from host country participants. Other motivations such as skills development, personal growth, and career advancement are rationalized by both the Canadian and host country participants in relation to the benefits they bring to individuals and organizations alike. Chapter 4 explores these overlapping and complex rationales in greater detail. Travel and adventure were also rationalized as necessary and significant motivations for participation in LVA4D, as outlined in Chapter 5, and while Canadian youth may be motivated by desires to see the world in ways that require more careful attention to ethical issues and debates, the host country staff appreciate the value of seeing all that a country has to offer, a country's geographical beauty, and the diverse people who inhabit it, so long as the priorities of the development projects and the organization come before travel plans. In Chapter 6 the motivations of making a difference, having an impact, and helping were examined in relation to broader rationales of 'helping imperatives' (Heron, 2007) and the colonial continuities that contribute to perceptions of white privilege. While these critiques have resonance and are valuable analyses of the structural and systemic global inequalities, the reflections provided – especially by the host country participants – added an additional dimension that helps make sense of the rationales for participation in LVA4D programmes, such as agency-oriented claims of the value (real and perceived) that international volunteers bring to the host organizations and the nature of 'helping' or 'impacts' experienced. The primary goals, motivations, and rationales for participation in LVA4D, therefore pertain to cross-cultural understanding, which can lead to global citizenship identity formation.

Global citizenship identity and cosmopolitan values

Global citizenship is being increasingly defined in relation to social processes in which individuals and groups negotiate, claim, and practice rights, responsibilities, and duties (Isin and Wood, 1999; Sassen, 2002). The notion of global citizenship puts a more contemporary stamp on cosmopolitanism. However, generally speaking, literature on global citizenship is highly optimistic of the potential for improved global engagement and participation. Criticisms of global citizenship have led authors such as Vanessa Andreotti (2006) and John Cameron (2014) to reflect on different modes of operationalizing global citizenship which enable us to think more reflectively on the impact of cosmopolitan values on changing individual attitudes and behaviours. Cameron (2014) employs a framework of thick versus thin global citizenship identity in part to address the conceptual ambiguity of the term and also to differentiate between thin or thick forms of global citizenship. Thin global citizenship, Cameron argues, can include "charity-based, and neocolonial approaches to issues of global social and environmental justices" (Cameron, 2014: 37–38), building on compassion-oriented rationales for helping vulnerable individuals (Dobson, 2006). Global citizenship as 'thick cosmopolitanism' is constructed in relation to obligations stemming from our complicity in global inequality and the "chains of causal responsibility" (Cameron, 2014: 30). Thick forms of global citizenship are characterized by efforts to alter the structural conditions that produce vulnerability and inequality, and our moral responsibility to do so.

Within the discourse of global citizenship, the individual sees himself or herself as an important player on a global level. Individuals can develop a sense of empowerment and meaning from their global citizenship identity. The fluidity and flexibility of the global citizenship discourse makes it a convenient language for organizations and individuals constructing the identity they wish to project. Nonetheless, volunteer abroad discourses rely heavily on the conceptual vagueness of global citizenship as it is used to represent many different and often contradictory ideas (Cameron, 2014; Tiessen, 2012). Cameron, building on the ideas of Dobson (2006), distinguishes between the range of global citizenship identities. This division serves as a useful framework for reflecting on the nature of current global citizenship identity for LVA4D and how we wish to shape it in the future. It is also very likely that effort to foster thick cosmopolitanism through volunteer abroad programmes can be disruptive as it aligns with highly politicized activities that question and seek to dismantle the status quo. As I explore further in the next section, learning/volunteer abroad (LVA) programmes that seek to foster thick forms of global citizenship will presumably aim *not* to produce "little developers" but rather to encourage the acquisition of attitudes and skills related to political struggles for global, social, and environmental justice (Cameron, 2014).

A survey of the now broad body of literature on global citizenship and some of the material from which global citizenship emerges (such as cosmopolitanism) provides important insights into the shifting discourse among those who have increasingly picked up the language (and at times, the identity) of the global citizen. While some global citizenship identity may be 'thin' in orientation for many of the Canadian youth (emphasis on Canadians' travel rather than development/social justice impacts), host country staff members and the Canadian youth saw intercultural exposure as a long-term project that has the potential to translate into 'thick' practices. Thus, the rationales for participation in LVA4D examined in the chapters in this book offer a nuanced analysis of the limitations and potential for meaningful engagement and thick global citizenship, drawing on insights into the perspectives of Canadian youth who travel abroad and the host country partners who receive them.

The centrality of learning in cross-cultural encounters

One of the prominent features of the motivations for cross-cultural understanding, getting to know people from other nations, and global citizenship identity formation is the emphasis on *learning*. The learning-oriented commitments that form a core part of the LVA4D work require time spent with people in intercultural and cross-cultural contexts. Thus the commitment of 3–6 months for placements abroad is integral to the building of global competency and for fostering the learning required for it. Host country participants frequently noted the importance of 'getting to know the person', with less emphasis on what that person could bring (in terms of resources or skills). The majority of host country staff also agreed that longer-term placements of approximately six months or more must be the minimum amount of time for effective LVA4D or volunteer abroad programmes. Other attributes are also important for effective LVA4D programmes, such as cultural immersion; in particular, one-on-one cross-cultural experiences that allow the participants to immerse themselves more fully in the local, cultural context. The interviews conducted for this study also highlight the role that technology and social media play in creating opportunities for sustained and deepened relationships over time, since many LVA4D participants talked about maintaining contact with their host country counterparts long after returning to Canada.

Host country staff members also remarked on the importance of sustained engagement after the volunteers leave the host country, noting that many volunteers continue to collaborate with them after they return home. Sometimes the connections are specific to staying in touch and maintaining friendships. Other times, the host country participants noted the commitments former volunteers make to continue to fundraise for their host organizations upon their return to Canada. Some of the volunteers returned or expressed a commitment to return to the host country to continue work and mutual learning efforts. Many Canadian participants and host staff members said they stayed in regular contact with each other through email communication or Facebook. As such, the official volunteering component has ended but the learning and engagement continues through communication via social media or email for many of the participants in LVA4D. I return to these important reflections on sustained impact and global competency in LVA4D later in this chapter as these notions have been captured, partially and inconsistently, in global citizenship rhetoric. I first turn to an analysis of motivations for – and reflections on – global citizenship identity in LVA4D.

In order to be more effective global citizens, the participants who travel abroad to the Global South must

> unpack their culturally and subjectively based assumptions about their role in the globalized world. Deconstructing … global identity and examining inequality, race, privilege, and difference are just as critical to pre-departure preparation as general packing concerns … students will first need to problematize, confront, and change their own attitudes and behaviours.
> *(Zemach-Bersin, 2009: 318)*

Other possibilities include the need to "raise awareness of the social environment and provide the tools to address problems" and

> teaching students to reason, to consider ethical claims, and to understand and work with such fundamental ideas as human rights, human diversity and interdependence and … instil in the content of our educational efforts a new emphasis on ethical values and on public debate and democracy.
>
> *(Skelly, 2009: 28)*

Skelly goes on to note:

> consumerist sensibilities that have begun to pervade education both at home and abroad … to move away from 'relentless commodification' (Said, 1993, p. 387) of education in order to help students understand the manner in which the consumerist sensibilities to which they have been socialized distort their understanding of other cultures and peoples.
>
> *(Skelly, 2009:28)*

The desire for adventure and travel, for cross-cultural understanding and personal growth, for career advancement or to test a career/academic choice, and also to 'make a difference' or help are all prevailing motivations that were articulated at times in egoistic and individualistic terms. The experience of volunteering abroad for Canadian youth has value in the form of cultural, social, and economic capital. Yet many of these motivations were also linked to the aspiration of global citizenship identity formation. Canadian youth aspire to an identity that links them to the global world we live in: an identity that reflects a generosity of spirit and concern, a sense of community, and connectivity. The diverse interview responses from Canadian youth remind us that there is a large and growing cohort of individuals who are dedicated to making the world a better and more equitable place. Yet structural challenges and neo-colonial practices continue in some instances, limiting the possibilities for effecting the change these youth may wish to see. Volunteer abroad participants must also be mindful that the representation of the experiences abroad, when presented in problematic ways, can reinforce the problems they seek to address and perpetuate negative stereotypes of the Global South. The images and discourses surrounding the volunteer abroad programmes are rife with messages of conquest and adventure (such as climbing a mountain), simplistic or charity-oriented ways of providing help (by holding babies), or egoistic career-oriented outcomes (building a better CV). These messages are indeed problematic and host organization staff from the Global South articulated their concerns regarding the perpetuation of such messages. As Precious (from Zambia) argued, after listening to a presentation of a returned volunteer back in Canada who was presenting stereotypical images of helplessness: "I didn't recognize the Zambia she was describing." However, the critical analysis of such problematic practices was often accompanied by optimism that improved training and better facilitation of learning during and after the volunteer placement can address such issues.

With the cautions noted above for the challenges of reinforcing stereotypes and inequality in public presentations post-placement, youth need to find ways to not only deconstruct their experiences but also to find sustainable strategies for building on their experiences; making continued connections and relations with host communities (Tiessen, 2012); and finding ways to meet the expectations of host country staff who may require long-term commitments of the volunteers in fundraising efforts or finding ways to support the initiatives of the Global South.

From the perspective of learning and education, Cook (2008) employs the construct of 'critical literacy' in order to "listen (rather than preach) to others, [and] to learn from them what their lives are like and what they need, what has not worked in the past and why, who are the people to initiate change" (Cook, 2008: 24–25). There are many opportunities for global citizenship identity formation when critical literacy is taken seriously, and I turn to those possibilities in the section below.

Possibilities for effective practices in volunteer abroad programmes

This concluding section examines the prospects for effective practices that emerged in the analysis of the research findings presented in this book. Keeping in mind the structural and global inequalities and diverse challenges identified throughout, the following discussion offers an analysis of the possibilities for improved global/community development impacts. As such, several windows of opportunity were identified by both the volunteers and the host organizations for improving volunteer abroad programmes and for maximizing the positive impacts on all participants.

Several themes are examined in this section, including the importance of keeping 'learning' at the centre of LVA programmes, or LVA4D more specifically. Subsequent themes addressed here encompass more practical suggestions for improving the volunteer abroad experience for all concerned.

The main point of departure guiding the analysis of the findings is the role that 'learning' plays in framing and rationalizing the LVA4D approach as distinct from other international volunteering and voluntourism initiatives. I argue that learning is integral to LVA4D and offers an important dimension building on intercultural capacity, cross-cultural engagement, and global competency. The notion of 'learning' came up frequently in the interviews and is significantly linked to cross-cultural understanding and global citizenship identities for both the Canadians and the host country partners. Learning-based outcomes are best captured in considerations of mutual exchange of knowledge. To improve learning-based outcomes in volunteer abroad programmes, increased efforts are needed prior to the departure of the volunteers, throughout the placement period and also in the post-placement period.

Several universities have taken up this challenge and have developed curricula to aid in the deconstruction of the discourse and to facilitate a deeper, more reflexive analysis of the motivations for – and impact of – LVA. Offering an academic seminar and a reading list for students pre-departure is a good starting point (see Tiessen and Kumar, 2013). A growing body of literature is now available to help reflect on the LVA experience in greater depth. Several scholars have documented the value of the reflexivity (see MacDonald, 2014; Desrosiers and Thomson, 2014; Langdon and Agyeyomah, 2014) for a range of considerations: personal and individual motivations and expected outcomes as well as global considerations of solidarity and/or mutual benefit. However, critical reflection on the motivations for participation in volunteer abroad programmes needs to take place before the decision to go abroad has been made and before tickets are booked. For some prospective international volunteers, critical reflection may result in decisions to not go abroad. Many young Canadians who identify as global citizens have made explicit decisions to not volunteer abroad on short- or medium-term volunteer programmes (Heron, 2013). The possibility for international volunteering remains for these individuals, but they have, at least, carefully considered the prospects for improved impact in light of their commitment to the time required to do the volunteer work well, and the skills they may have to offer at that time.

To ensure youth are able to make informed decisions about when, where, and how to volunteer abroad, it is necessary for potential volunteers to have access to readings and/or facilitated reflection opportunities that can inform them of the benefits and challenges of volunteer abroad options. For some students in social science programmes, courses may be available that prepare young people to reflect more critically on their decisions to go abroad. However, even these courses tend to be offered to students who are already enrolled in international internships or LVA programmes. Students who seek out pre-departure preparation – or have been advised to do so – often have already invested financially in a programme and/or have committed to the project.

Since it is difficult to capture students and youth before they lock-in their decisions to go abroad, the next best option is to provide solid and critically informed pre-departure preparation (see Tiessen and Kumar, 2013). Information that can be useful in preparing yourself or others for LVA4D can be found in an online resource, www.globalcitizenshipedu.weebly.com, where modules help prepare volunteers for the range of considerations and issues they may encounter. The modules cover topics that introduce global citizenship literature, motivations, critical analysis, ethical issues, discourse and images of international volunteering, and ways to make the most of the experience abroad. Videos, discussion questions, and activities accompany each of the modules, making it a user-friendly resource guide.

Transformative learning through LVA programmes can start with an awareness of the ethical impacts of international experiential learning (see Tiessen and Huish, 2014). Transformative learning is grounded in the struggles for equality and justice (Langdon and Agyeyomah, 2014). A result of this transformative approach is the creation of "authentic allies" (Thomas and Chandrasekera, 2014). If global citizenship is the goal and/or motivation for LVA programmes, then a better understanding of how global citizenship is articulated and expressed by individuals and the volunteer-sending organizations is also important. Returning to Dobson's (2006) and Cameron's (2014) examination of global citizenship in relation to thin and thick conceptions, it is clear that thin global citizenship reflects individualistic and egoistic motivations (Tiessen, 2012): a process in which international volunteers may engage in 'othering'. Approaches to thin global citizenship initiatives are more likely, then, to lead to the solidification of asymmetries of power and wealth. An approach that involves thick conceptions of global citizenship can alter the structural conditions faced by people living in disadvantaged positions (Dobson, 2006) and challenge the voluntouristic, charity-based, and neo-colonial approaches to issues of global, social, and environmental injustice (Cameron, 2014). Such possibilities exist, according to Langdon and Agyeyomah (2014), for LVA programmes that challenge the status quo and foster awareness among youth. Several core lessons can be gleaned from the analysis of quotes included throughout this book. These lessons offer insights into what host communities want through collaborations with volunteer-sending organizations and/or the learners/volunteers who travel abroad. I elaborate on some of these core themes below, including: (1) a shared understanding of the appropriate amount of time to spend abroad; (2) reciprocity of opportunity and lasting relationships; (3) skill-sharing and development; and (4) ethical preparation. There are other lessons to take away from this study as highlighted by the diverse perspectives shared in this book. However, the most fundamental strategy in moving forward begins with communication with the host organization such that the desires, expectations, and requirements are explained before the start of the LVA4D programme.

Deciding on the right amount of time

According to the host staff, international volunteers from the Global North need to spend a realistic amount of time in the host country in order to ensure the impact they wish to have. For the majority of the host organization staff (70 per cent), six months in the host country was considered an important minimum requirement for the necessary cross-cultural engagement. However, there may be significant variation on perspectives of effective volunteering across a range of time frames, depending on the specific skills required and sustainability of the project. Nonetheless, the cross-cultural and interpersonal motivations expressed by host organization staff in terms of "emotional connections" and "getting to know the person" demonstrate the immense desire to build friendships and collaborations through international volunteering initiatives. Other considerations in relation to length of time must factor in the economic rationales that organizations may have for hosting international volunteers. Smedley's research in Costa Rica, for example, documented the preference for short-term volunteers because the volunteers paid more per night when they came for shorter periods of time than the long-term volunteers (defined here as stays of longer than four months). The economic rationale in this study must be considered in relation to other benefits identified for those volunteers or students who stay for longer periods, including improved language facility and increased benefit to the host communities (Smedley, 2015). Other studies have documented a preference among host communities for longer-term commitments on the part of international volunteers and students. MacDonald and Vorstermans (2015) note the desire among hosts for longer-term connections with students since there is a significant desire from hosts "for cultural exchange and future relationships as integral to how we can move forward in an ethical way" (p. 138).

Reciprocity of opportunity and lasting relationships

Reciprocity of opportunity is essential to a fully developed global citizenship model. The current, largely one-directional nature of Northern volunteers travelling to the Global South for experiences that promote personal growth and career and academic advancement, among other perks, is clearly an unequal system. Funding mechanisms are required to ensure that an exchange of opportunity is made available. Third, a sustained commitment to the host community is important for the meaningful exchange of assistance. Young Canadians often reflect on how much more they got out of the experience than they were able to give back to the host communities. However, the experience in the host country need not be the end of the exchange. Rather, host communities and host organization staff often count on ongoing commitments; fundraising upon return to Canada; or even just the personal connection of long-term communication and engagement.

E-volunteering and ongoing support can thus further accommodate the needs of host country participants and offers a strategy for improving a system of inequality that facilitates the travel of 'privileged' individuals who take part in LVA4D. Emphasis on how to build lasting and ongoing commitments post-return can inform the pre-departure training with examples of ongoing e-volunteering and long-distance support over an extended time frame.

Considering skills-sharing and development

A second challenge identified by host participants is lack of skills and language proficiency of some of the international volunteers, particularly for travel to Spanish-speaking countries. Pre-departure orientation is not the place for requiring improved language abilities (this must be done in the selection process), but pre-departure orientations may offer spaces for additional reflection on the value of language immersion in the host country as part of the training leading up to the application to the programme. Feedback from the host country participants points to the limited value-added of excessive community-based work where the Canadian volunteer is unable to speak the local language and may require resources of translation that the organization may not easily have to share. It is important to remind participants in LVA4D, however, that there are many skills valued by the host organizations, including the fresh perspectives, new insights, and enthusiasm for the development work carried out. More specifically, skills including English language proficiency, writing skills, and a willingness to take risks in preparing project applications are also highly valued by the host partners.

Ethical preparation

There remain important ethical considerations to impart to participants in LVA programmes. These ethical considerations include the reflections identified through this book, particularly in relation to privilege, inequality of opportunity, and structural inequalities that facilitate the benefits (perceived or real) of hosting an international volunteer as status and credibility for the organization. The identification of these privileged-oriented insights is the first step in understanding systems of inequality and building solidarity-oriented strategies to dismantle the disparities between international volunteers and host country recipients. Ethics-oriented training and preparation requires that the international volunteers consider ethical issues they may encounter while working in different contexts, as well as the ethical implications of privilege and inequality of opportunity for which the Canadian volunteers benefit. Chances to provide reciprocal opportunities for host organization staff to visit Canada offer one way of changing the unidirectional flow of travel and exchange of expertise.

Establishing effective practice

The critiques and challenges identified in this book offer depth and nuance to the issues surrounding ethical practice in LVA4D. Other scholars have offered strategies for improving international volunteer practice through 'fair trade learning', or 'standards of practice'. Hartman (2015), for example, explains fair trade learning in relation to standards adhering to nine principles:

1) Explicit dual purposes in our work, serving community and serving students simultaneously, and explicitly not privileging students over community
2) Community voice and direction—at every step in the process
3) Institutional commitment and partnership sustainability—and supporting multidirectional exchange
4) Transparency, specifically in respect to economic relationships and transactions
5) Environmental sustainability and footprint reduction
6) Economic sustainability in terms of effort to manage funding incursions in the receiving community and fund development at the university in a manner that takes a long view of the relationships involved
7) Deliberate diversity, intercultural contact, and reflection to systematically encourage intercultural learning and development among participants and community partners
8) Global community building—in the sense that we keep one eye always on the question of how this work pushes us into better relationships around the world; how our civil society networks grow into community; how our efforts abroad should inform our actions at home
9) Proactive protection of the most vulnerable populations.

(p. 224)

All of these principles of practice are important. However, the ones that relate most closely to the arguments and issues raised in this book challenge us to facilitate greater control of the process on the part of the host communities' community members to ensure the host organization staff or host communities have great involvement in the selection of international volunteers, the amount of time they spend in the host country, the longer-term commitments to the initiatives, as well as the nature and content of the work they will be doing in this collaboration. More information about this work can be found at www.globalsl.com.

A second example of effective practices can be found in the work of the Better Volunteering, Better Care organization, which has raised the profile of the issues and challenges created through orphan tourism or international volunteering that involves work with children in orphanages. Information about their efforts, including a university pledge to stop orphan voluntourism, can be found here: www. bettercarenetwork.org/bcn-in-action/better-volunteering-better-care.

Students are often looking for safe, reliable, and reputable organizations for LVA4D opportunities. However, it can be difficult to discern such information from webpages. Gonzalo Duarte has developed a 'standards of practice' set of guidelines that can be used to consider volunteer-sending organizations. Duarte (2015: 246) summarizes the core standards as: (1) organizational alignment of the mission with capacity and collaboration; (2) sustainable and ethical organizational management; (3) integrated design, preparation, and implementation; (4) responsible marketing materials; (5) protection of children, vulnerable populations, and environment; and (6) monitoring and evaluation. These six standards are elaborated on his website: http://companeros.ca/globalxchange.html.

Many of these standards of practice, fair trade learning principles, and coordinated efforts facilitate accountability and improved understanding for host organizations, prospective volunteers, and the intermediaries who facilitate LVA4D. The data presented in this book provide the context and evidence to further support the need for addressing principled practice. In addition to these very practical guides and opportunities, this chapter explores some of the learning objectives and deeper conceptual issues that must also (first) be considered in order to ensure these practical strategies of 'fair trade learning' are considered a priority. In other words, this book provides a foundation for reconciling why standards of practice are important, but, more importantly, how the practice of international volunteering and LVA4D are rationalized by Canadian learners/volunteers and host organization staff.

Building on successes and meeting host country expectations

The host country participants highlighted many benefits of hosting international volunteers, including international volunteers who come for medium-term placements of 3–6 months. The pre-departure training for LVA4D participants could include some discussion of these benefits and use these discussions as opportunities to build on successes, and to expand positive experiences. In particular, focusing on the value associated with fresh ideas, new insights, positive energy, flexibility, creativity, and optimism could be examined. Training for international volunteers may benefit from examining how to sustain these positive attributes in light of some of the challenges that hosts and volunteers alike may experience during the placements.

Rethinking how we talk about cultural adaptation

A more careful reflection on the language of 'culture shock' and its employment as a means to explain the kind of experience international volunteers will have is also necessary. 'Culture shock' was generally considered an offensive term by host country participants. Volunteers can be reminded that specific practices, modes of dress, habits, and activities can be perceived as offensive to host communities as well. Furthermore, the employment of this lens sets the international volunteers up for a particular kind of experience that may not resonate with the participants. The host organizations suggested the shift in language from 'culture shock' to 'challenges of integration' or 'cross-cultural challenges'. This change in language not only removes the notion of 'shock', but also depicts the dynamics specific to the interaction between individuals in cross-cultural scenarios.

"It's about getting to know the person": relationship formation

Finally, LVA4D participants would benefit from being reminded of the importance of the human connection and the value placed on the cross-cultural experience. Over and over, the host country participants referred to the value of "getting to know the person" irrespective of the skills volunteers contributed, resources brought, or the amount of time spent in-country. While there is a general preference for medium- to long-term placements (six months or longer abroad), the depth of the relationship developed between the host and the volunteer was highly valued by the host partners. This is a relationship that could be sustained over a much longer period of time through ongoing social media and email correspondence, as noted above. Ultimately, the value of hosting international volunteers falls more squarely in line with the interpersonal relationship and exchange, and less with the value associated with Global North volunteers solving Global South problems, 'helping', or skills transfer.

Considering diversity of programme options

When considering possibilities for improved volunteer abroad experiences for both the volunteers and the hosts, it is important to keep in mind that the success of the programmes depend, in part, on the nature of the placements. There are many diverse opportunities for learning and volunteering in volunteer abroad programmes. The range of options includes directional variations of volunteers travelling between regions and countries such as South–South, South–North, North–North, and North–South as part of international volunteering programmes. Volunteer abroad programmes also include a range of options from short-term to medium-term or long-term placements. Some of the differences between these lengths of stay are addressed in Chapter 2. Furthermore, there is a vast spectrum of thematic options for volunteer abroad participants, including wildlife conservation, orphan care (which is widely challenged as appropriate volunteer abroad work), infrastructure development (such as building a school), community development, etc. Making any meaningful analyses of such a wide set of volunteer options is challenging, at best, and drawing useful conclusions from such a wide set of practices is indeed problematic. Thus, in an effort to examine more carefully a particular sub-group of volunteer abroad programmes, this book has focused explicitly on North–South international volunteering programmes specifically defined as medium-term (3–6 month) LVA programmes concentrating on development outcomes. The Canadian participants in these LVA4D programmes were university and college students and recent graduates, many of whom are interested in careers in international development contexts, whether in international development project work or other professions such as nursing, engineering, etc. LVA4D, as a particular kind of volunteer abroad option, must be understood in relation to its own opportunities and limitations, but distinct from volunteer tourism or voluntourism.

The recommendations for improved pre-departure training and reflection can be summarized from the reflections above as:

1   Consideration of LVA placements as one part of the placement – combined with longer-term commitments through e-support and developing connections in home communities through fundraising or development education initiatives. Opportunities for reciprocity of opportunity may arise from these sustained relationships such as opportunities to bring host community staff to Canada.

2   Coming prepared with the right skills combined with realistic expectations of contributions within the organization and the community. Language skills and other specific skill-sets may be in great demand for the host staff. Learning the language through intense language immersion before travelling or immediately upon arrival is one strategy. Another consideration is careful reflection on demands made by volunteers to visit areas where language translation is required – and the resource constraints this may put on the organization.

3   More opportunities for reflection on the ethical issues and ethics-based scenarios the learners/volunteers and hosts/partners may encounter. These reflections need to be facilitated by experienced trainers; ethics-related discussions could be facilitated at several points of the internship.

4   Building on successes and identification of what is valued or needed. Knowing the host country priorities and what they value is a starting point for moving forward with improved LVA4D. Beyond understanding host country priorities and desires, we must also find ways to act on this knowledge – a consideration aptly captured by Reynolds and Gasparini's work "Saying it doesn't make it so: Do we listen and act when the host community tells us what they want?".

5   Avoiding problematic language such as 'culture shock' and shifting the focus to the dynamics of intercultural competency between individuals.
6   Understanding the value associated with interpersonal relationships, with a reduced focus on Northern volunteers setting out to solve problems in the Global South.

All of these recommendations facilitate an improved agency-oriented focus in analysing the LVA4D experiences of hosts and volunteers alike.

Throughout this book there are substantial critiques and words of caution regarding some of the ethical and development-related challenges of effective volunteering programmes. The critiques include the analyses developed in the writing of this book, but also in the evaluations offered by both the learners/volunteers and the host country staff. As other scholars have concluded, research with host communities and host organization staff include "(often muted) suggestions, both explicit and implicit, that the impacts were not all positive" (O'Sullivan and Smaller, 2015: 62). Several considerations pertaining to motivations and rationales point to individualist or egoistic frames for participating in LVA. Employing a postcolonial lens also helps make sense of the structures and systems of inequality that perpetuate the predominate one-directional nature of international volunteer options, inequality of power and privilege, as well as potential for reproducing tropes or stereotypes of the other. Global citizens engaged in volunteer abroad development work (or development workers) "undertake personally challenging reflexive work" (Cook, 2008: 24). However, this reflexive work takes place within the "processes and histories that have already predetermined what needs Others have" (Cook, 2008: 24).

Nonetheless, these critical analyses do not fully explain the broad range of rationales and motivations for participation, particularly from the host country participants who express their agency, capability, and stated desires to continue to work with international volunteers. Nonetheless, the host community staff members do highlight some challenges relating to volunteer abroad practice and these challenges serve as important starting points for improving and enhancing pre-departure training sessions for participants taking part in LVA4D. Among the challenges identified by the host staff include the reciprocity of opportunity – to which pre-departure training can do little. This systematic challenge fits well in the context of the postcolonial critiques examined throughout the book. However, there is scope for encouraging longer-term relationships between volunteers and host partners. Host staff reflected often on the value of staying in contact with volunteers after they returned home. Ongoing support from the volunteers and their respective communities can also provide some elements of a more meaningful engagement, and with fundraising effort, possibilities for reciprocity (for host community members to visit the volunteers in their home country) are possible.

Structural limitations remain pertinent to the broader context in which challenges remain, such as structures of inequality of opportunity, colonial language, stereotyping, or trope-confirmation. Furthermore, skills have value but the skills needed by host country staff may be different than the skills imagined. The desired skills are often linked to interpersonal ones in which relationships are formed and a meaningful exchange of ideas and friendship emerges. The depth of relationship formation does hinge on the kind of placements that ensure the international volunteers are able to break free from the bubbles of Western culture and enclaves, and to 'leave the verandah'. As such, deep cultural immersion is ultimately the quality that stands out from the research findings; this, along with the value that is associated with international volunteering more broadly as a process of – and contribution to – solidarity building are essential agency-oriented elements of the experience. In other words, LVA programmes can provide opportunities for better understanding ourselves and the people we meet in our cross-cultural encounters (Benham Rennick and Desjardins, 2013).

Conclusion

If cross-cultural exposure is one of the most important motivations for the Canadian youth, as this study has highlighted, then the ongoing interaction with individuals across cultures could easily be sustained through modern technology that provides inexpensive means of communication. In fact, many references to ongoing support and communication between volunteers and host country staff were noted throughout the interviews. Global citizenship identity is bound by a commitment to cross-cultural understanding and acting on the knowledge gained through these exposures. It is an exciting time for actualizing these commitments to global citizenship, but they do require deeper and more nuanced conceptions of global citizenship matched with actions that are aimed at building solidarity and fighting for equality of opportunity. There has been substantial growth in the number of programmes and opportunities available for youth from the Global North to take part in LVA programmes (as I documented in Chapter 2), and it is likely that these trends will continue in the long term with a growing number of young people, among other groups such as mid-career professionals and retired individuals, aspiring to travel to the Global South to learn/volunteer and/or 'help'. While many 'difficulties' of hosting international volunteers were identified throughout this book, host country participants offered an overall positive experience of LVA4D participation in terms of cross-cultural engagement, skills-sharing, and broader notions of helping or providing assistance for larger development goals. If the host communities say overwhelmingly that they find value in these LVA4D experiences, then we need to build on the benefits of participation in LVA4D and begin to minimize some of the weaknesses or difficulties. However, these changes require more than technical or superficial changes to volunteer abroad programmes; rather, they require a concerted effort to ensure that learning and cross-cultural communication for solidarity and social justice purposes remain at the core of the rationales for participation in LVA4D. In making this case, I echo, in part, the conclusions offered by Palacios (2010), who noted that "cultural contact represents real value and long-term support for the host organization, not in the form of 'one way' aid, but in the form of reciprocal relations of mutual learning; reciprocity and mutuality are the real sources of production" (p. 874). While these goals reflect the value associated with LVA programmes identified by many of the participants in this study, they also lend support for an alternative, people-centred and agency-oriented sustainable development paradigm. Larsen (2015) examines a similar phenomenon in the context of post-critical practice in ISL. She points to local epistemologies as a starting point for avoiding ethnocentrism such as Ubuntu (the value of communal context over individualism), which can foster new foundation-building for relationships that can be nourished and sustained by embracing different ways of learning, doing, and being (p. 259).

In doing so, we honour the perceived value of the host community participants who place extraordinary weight on 'getting to know the person' and create the opportunities for an improved understanding of international development challenges as part of a global context, and in line with solidaristic values and mutually shared responsibilities for addressing global inequalities.

The Sustainable Development Goals – or Global Goals as they are commonly referred to – provide scope for shifting the narrative away from Global North 'solutions' to Global South 'problems' by centring the responsibility for change and action on all actors in all regions. This rhetorical shift is an important framework to guide volunteer abroad programmes. The challenge is to ensure that the rhetoric translates into practice such that LVA4D or any volunteer abroad programmes in the Global South shift the focus *away from* volunteers offering solutions to Global South problems *towards* mutual learning, shared benefits, reduced inequalities, global competency, cross-cultural understanding, and solidarity in our combined efforts to enable opportunities for positive change.

BIBLIOGRAPHY

Adler, P. S. (1998). Beyond cultural identity: Reflections on multiculturalism. In M. J. Bennett (ed.), *Basic Concepts of Intercultural Communication: Selected Readings* (pp. 225–245). London: Nicholas Brealey Publishing.

Adler, P. S. (2002). Beyond cultural identity: Reflections on multiculturalism. Originally published in 1977 in *Culture Learning*, East-West Center Press (pp. 24–41). Retrieved November 14, 2016 from www.mediate.com/articles/adler3.cfm.

Al Jazeera. (2012, June 27). Cambodia's orphan business. Retrieved June 16, 2014 from www. aljazeera.com/programmes/peopleandpower/2012/05/201252243030438171.html.

Anderson, L. E. (1994). A new look at an old construct: Cross-cultural adaptation. *International Journal of Intercultural Relations, 18*(3), 293–328.

Andreotti, V. (2006). Soft versus critical global citizenship education. *Policy and Practice: A Development Education Review, 3*. Retrieved June 13, 2014 from www.development educationreview.com/issue3-focus4.

Anheier, H. K., & Salamon, L. M. (1999). Volunteering in cross-national perspective: Initial comparisons. *Law and Contemporary Problems, 65*(4), 43–65.

Barnhart, E. L. (2012). Engaging global service: Organizational motivations for and perceived benefits of hosting international volunteers. Portland State University Dissertations and Theses. Retrieved November 14, 2016 from http://pdxscholar.library.pdx.edu/cgi/viewcontent.cgi?article=1371&context=open_access_etds.

Beezer, A. (1995). Women and 'adventure travel' tourism. *New Horizons, 21*, 19–130.

Benham Rennick, J., & M. Desjardins. (2013). *The World is Your Classroom: International Learning and Canadian Higher Education*, Toronto, ON: University of Toronto Press.

Boyle, D. P., & C. Barranti (1999). A model for international continuing education: Cross-cultural experiential professional development. *Professional Development: The International Journal of Continuing Social Work Education, 2*(2), 57–62.

Boyle, D. P., Nackerud, L., & Kilpatrick, A. (1999). The road less traveled: Cross-cultural, international experiential learning. *Journal of International Social Work, 42*(2), 201–214.

Bringle, R. G., & Hatcher, J. A. (2011). International service learning. In R. G. Bringle, J. A. Hatcher, & S. G. Jones (eds), *International Service Learning: Conceptual Frameworks and Research* (pp. 3–28). Herndon, VA: Stylus Publishing.

Brown, L. (2005, January 22). Students at home in the world. *Toronto Star*, 1–26.

Cameron, J. (2014). Grounding experiential learning in thick conceptions of global citizenship. In R. Tiessen & R. Huish (eds), *Globetrotting or Global Citizenship? Perils and Potentials of International Experiential Learning* (pp. 21–42). Toronto, ON: University of Toronto Press.

Campbell, A., Gurin, G., & Miller, W. E. (1954). *The Voter Decides*. Evanston, IL: Row, Peterson.

Canadian Council for International Co-operation. (1997). Appendix 2: Global citizenship – new way forward. In D. Gillies (ed.), *Strategies of Public Engagement: Shaping a Canadian Agenda for International Co-Operation* (pp. 201–219). Montreal, QC: McGill-Queen's University Press.

Carlson, J., et al. (1991). *Study Abroad: The Experience of American Undergraduates in Western Europe and the United States (Abridged Version)*. New York: Council on International Education Exchange.

CASID & NSI. (2003). *'White paper' on International Development Studies in Canada*. Ottawa: CASID and NSI.

CBC (Canadian Broadcasting Corporation) (2015). Volunteering Do's and Don'ts. Retrieved from www.cbc.ca/doczone/features/voluntouring-dos-and-donts.

CBIE. (2012). A world of learning: Canada's performance and potential in international education. Retrieved on July 7 from: www.cbie-bcei.ca/wp-content/uploads/2012/11/flagship-report-exec-summary-E-v4.pdf.

CCIC (Canadian Council for International Cooperation). (1997). Global citizenship: A new way forward, report from the CCIC Task Force on Building Public Support for Sustainable Human Development. Retrieved June 13, 2014 from www.ccic.ca/_files/en/what_we_do/002_public_a_new_way_forward.pdf.

CIDA. (2004). CIDA's global citizenship in action. Retrieved from www.acdi-cida.gc.ca/Cida_Ind.nsf/5b0ca220d5f25fee8525677e00725c7a/09898567.

CIDA. (2005). Journal library. Retrieved May 12, 2005, from www.acdi-cida.gc.ca/cida_ind.nsf/AllDocIds/616BD2AD8315A4A085256F390048B8DF?OpenDocument.

CIDA. (2007a). *Sustainable Development Policy 2007–2009*. Gatineau, QC: CIDA.

CIDA. (2007b). Evaluation of Netcorps Canada International Program (NCI). Prepared by the Evaluation Division Performance and Knowledge Measurement Branch. Retrieved November 14, 2016 from www.acdi-cida.gc.ca/inet/images.nsf/vLUImages/Evaluations/$file/NETCORPS-Final-Evaluation-Report-Eng-5-nov-07.pdf.

Clost, E. (2014). Visual representation and Canadian government-funded volunteer abroad programs: Picturing the Canadian global citizen. In R. Tiessen & R. Huish (eds), *Globetrotting or Global Citizenship? Perils and Potentials of International Experiential Learning* (pp. 230–257). Toronto, ON: University of Toronto Press.

Cohen, E. (1988). Authenticity and commoditization in tourism. *Annals of Tourism Research*, 15(3), 371–386.

Cook, N. (2007). *Gender, Identity, and Imperialism: Women Development Workers in Pakistan*. New York: Palgrave Macmillan.

Cook, N. (2008). Shifting the focus of development: Turning 'helping' into self-reflexive learning. *Critical Literacy: Theories and Practices*, 2(1), 1–26.

Crabtree, R. D. (1998) Mutual empowerment in cross-cultural participatory development and service learning: Lessons in communication and social justice from projects in El Salvador and Nicaragua. *Journal of Applied Communication Research*, 26(2), 182–209.

Crabtree, R. (2008). Theoretical foundations for international service-learning. *Michigan Journal of Community Service Learning*, 15(1), 18–36.

Cross Continental (n.d.). Being welcomed as a volunteer abroad (the experience of a lifetime). Video. Retrieved from: www.youtube.com/watch?v=39Ln3Xim4tY&feature=c4-overview&list=UUUDaiwmovQUFJ8IDkoxnZFQ.

Crosscultural Solutions (n.d). Volunteer abroad in Ghana for 1–12 weeks with CCS. Retrieved from www.goabroad.com/providers/cross-cultural-solutions/programs/volunteer-abroad-in-ghana-for-1-12-weeks-with-ccs-10248.

Crosscultural Solutions (2014). Our approach. Retrieved June 16, 2014 from www.crossculturalsolutions.org/learn-about-ccs-difference#our-approach.

CUSO (2007). *The Overseas Experience: A Passport to Improved Volunteerism. A Research Report prepared by Sean Kelly and Robert Case.* Toronto: Imagine Canada. Retrieved June 16, 2014 from http://cusointernational.org/sites/default/files/CUSO_OverseasExperience070111_E_tcm77-20672.pdf.

Desforges, L. (1998). 'Checking out the planet': Global representations/local identities. In T. Skelton & G. Valentine (eds), *Cool Places: Geographies of Youth Culture* (pp. 175–192). New York: Routledge.

Desrosiers, M., & Thomson, S. (2014). Experiential learning in challenging settings: Lessons from post-genocide Rwanda. In R. Tiessen & R. Huish (eds), *Globetrotting or Global Citizenship? Perils and Potentials of International Experiential Learning* (pp.140–160). Toronto, ON: University of Toronto Press.

Devereux, P. (2008). International volunteering for development and sustainability: Outdated paternalism or a radical response to globalisation? *Development in Practice, 18*(3), 357–370.

DfID (Department for International Development) (2011). Final mid term review evaluation of DfID's International Citizen Service (ICS) pilot stage. Retrieved November 14, 2016 from www.gov.uk/government/uploads/system/uploads/attachment_data/file/67460/eval-int-citz-serv-ics-pilot-stg.pdf.

Dobson, A. (2006). Thick cosmopolitanism. *Political Studies, 54*(1), 165–184.

Duarte, G. (2015). Mi Casa Es Tu Casa: A framework for reciprocal public benefit. In M. A. Larsen (ed.), *International Service Learning: Engaging Host Communities* (pp. 235–252). New York: Routledge.

Ehrichs, L. (2002). Volunteering in development: A post-modern view. Retrieved from www.iyv2001.org/iyv_eng/research/articles/articles.htm.

Epprecht, M. (2004). Work-study abroad courses in international development studies: Some ethical and pedagogical issues. *Canadian Journal of Development Studies, 25*(4), 687–706.

Erikson-Baaz, M. (2005). *The Paternalism of Partnership: A Postcolonial Reading of Identity in Development Aid.* London: Zed Books.

Escobar, A. (1995). *Encountering Development: The Making and Unmaking of the Third World.* Princeton, NJ: Princeton University Press.

Fizzell, K., & Epprecht, M. (2014). Secondary school experiential learning programs in the Global South: Critical reflections from an Ontario study. In R. Tiessen and R. Huish (eds), *Globetrotting or Global Citizenship: Perils and Potential of International Experiential Learning* (pp. 112–140). Toronto, ON: University of Toronto Press.

Foroughi, B., Langdon, J., & Abdou, N. (2014). The onion effect: Exploration of the impacts of multiple experiential service learning experiences in St. Francis Xavier Development Studies Program. Paper presented at the Canadian Association for Study of International Development (CASID) conference, St. Catharine's, ON, Brock University, May 30.

Fuchs, L. H. (1967). *Those Peculiar Americans: The Peace Corps and American National Character.* New York: Meredith Press.

Garrison, K. (1961). Worldminded attitudes of college students in a southern university. *Journal of Social Psychology, 54*, 147–153.

Georgeou, N., & Engel, S. (2011). The impact of neoliberalism and new managerialism on development volunteering: An Australian case study. *Australian Journal of Political Science, 45*(2), 297–311.

Global Volunteer Network. (2014). Volunteer abroad. Retrieved June 16, 2014 from www.goabroad.com/volunteer-abroad.

Goudge, P. (2003). *The Whiteness of Power: Racism in Third World Development and Aid.* London: Lawrence and Wishart.

Government of Canada. (2014). 'Coping with culture shock'. Retrieved July 7, 2014 from http://travel.gc.ca/travelling/living-abroad/culture-shock.

Graham, L., Mazembo Mavungu, E., Perold, H., with Cronin, K., Muchemwa, L., & Lough, B. (2011). International volunteers and development of host organisations in Africa: Lessons from Tanzania and Mozambique. Volunteer and Service Enquiry Southern Africa (VOSESA). Retrieved July 7, 2014 from www.vosesa.org.za/sadcconference/papers/6.pdf.

Grusky, S. (2000). International service learning. *The American Behavioral Scientists, 43*(5), 858–867.

Guiney, T., & Mostafanezhad, M. (2014). The political economy of orphan tourism in Cambodia. *Tourist Studies, 15*(2), 1–24.

Hartman, E. (2015). Fair Trade learning: A framework for ethical global partnerships. In M. A. Larsen (ed.), *International Service Learning: Engaging Host Communities* (pp. 215–234). New York: Routledge.

Heron, B. A. (2005a). Changes and challenges: Preparing social work students for practicums in today's sub-Saharan African context. *Journal of International Social Work, 48*(6), 782–793.

Heron, B. A. (2005b). Self-reflection in critical social work practice: Subjectivity and the possibilities of resistance. *Journal of Reflective Practice, 6*(3), 341–351.

Heron, B. A. (2007). *Desire for Development: The Education of White Women as Development Workers.* Waterloo, ON: Wilfrid Laurier Press.

Heron, B. A. (2011). Challenging indifference to extreme poverty: Considering southern perspectives on global citizenship and change. *Revue Éthique et Économique/Ethics and Economics, 8*(1), 109–119.

Heron, B. A. (2013). To go or not to go: Global citizenship through education vs. experience. Canadian Association for the Study of International Development (CASID) Conference Paper presented in Victor, BC, June 6, 2013.

Heron, B. A. (2015). Southern perspectives on ISL volunteers: Reframing the neo-colonial encounter. In M. A. Larsen (ed.), *International Service Learning: Engaging Host Communities.* New York: Routledge.

Hudson, S., & Inkson, K. (2006). Volunteer overseas development workers: The hero's adventure and personal transformation. *Career Development International, 11*(4), 304–320.

Hutchings, M., & Smart, S. (2007). *Evaluation of the Impact on UK Schools of the VSO/NAHT Pilot Scheme: International Extended Placements for School Leaders.* Retrieved from www.vso.org.uk/Images/VSO-NAHT-evaluation-report_tcm8–11965.pdf.

Illich, I. (1968). To hell with good intentions. An address given at the InterAmerican Student Projects in Cuernavaca, Mexico, April 20, 1968. Retrieved November 14, 2016 from www.swaraj.org/illich_hell.htm.

Illich, I., & Rahnema, M. (1997). Twenty-six years later: Ivan Illich in conversation with Rahnema. In M. Rahnema & V. Bawtree (eds), *The Development Reader.* London: Zed Books.

Independent, The. (2013). Brangelinas need not apply: A Cambodian orphanage is leading the march against 'voluntourism'. Retrieved June 16, 2014 from www.independent.co.uk/news/world/asia/brangelinas-need-not-apply-a-cambodian-orphanage-is-leading-the-march-against-voluntourism-8444762.html.

International Student Volunteers. (2014). Volunteer abroad. Retrieved June 16, 2014 from www.goabroad.com/volunteer-abroad.

Isin, E., & Wood, P. (1999). *Citizenship and Identity.* London: Sage.

Jones, A. (2011). Theorising international youth volunteering: Training for global (corporate) work? *Transactions of the Institute of British Geographers, 36*(4), 530–544.

Jorgenson, S., & Shultz, L. (2012). Global citizenship education (GCE) in post-secondary institutions: What is protected and what is hidden under the umbrella of GCE? *Journal of Global Citizenship and Equity Education, 2*(1). Retrieved January 7, 2015 from http:// journals.sfu.ca/jgcee/index.php/jgcee/article/view%0BArticle/52/26.

Kapoor, I. (2013). *Celebrity Humanitarianism: The Ideology of Global Charity*. New York: Routledge.

Kauffmann, N. L., Martin, J. N., & Weaver, H. D. (1992). *Students Abroad, Strangers at Home: Education for a Global Society*. Yarmouth, ME: Intercultural Press.

Kelly, J. R., & Freysinger, V. J. (2000). *21st Century Leisure: Current Issues*. Toronto, ON: Allyn and Bacon.

Kelly, R. J., & Godbey, G. (1992). *The Sociology of Leisure*. State College, PA: Venture Publishing Inc.

Korten, D. (1990). *Getting to the 21st Century: Voluntary Action and the Global Agenda*. Boulder, CO: Kumarian Press.

Kothari, U. (ed.) (2005). *A Radical History of Development Studies: Individuals, Institutions and Ideologies*. London: Zed Books.

Langdon, J., & Agyeyomah, C. (2014). Critical hyper-reflexivity and challenging power: Pushing past the dichotomy of employability and good global citizenship in development studies experiential learning contexts. In R. Tiessen & R. Huish (eds), *Globetrotting or Global Citizenship? Perils and Potentials of International Experiential Learning* (pp. 43–70). Toronto, ON: University of Toronto Press.

Larkin, A. (2015). I am because we are: Rethinking service learning and the possibility of learning from Ubuntu. In M. A. Larsen (ed.), *International Service Learning: Engaging Host Communities*. New York: Routledge.

Larsen, M. A. (2015). International service learning: Engaging host communities – introduction. In M.A. Larsen (ed.), *International Service Learning: Engaging Host Communities*. New York and London.

Lewin, R. (ed.) (2009). *Handbook of Practice and Research in Study Abroad: Higher Education and the Quest for Global Citizenship*. New York: Routledge.

Li, P. S., & Bolaria, B. S. (1993). *Sociology: Critical Perspectives*, Toronto: Copp Clark Pitman.

Lockhart, J. (2012, February 19). International volunteering: State of the nation. *Verge Magazine: Volunteer Abroad*. Retrieved June 23, 2014 from www.vergemagazine.com/articles/ volunteer-abroad/international-volunteering-state-of-the-nation.html.

Lough, B. (2008). International volunteerism in the United States, 2008. In *Centre for Social Development Research Brief, March 2010*. St. Louis, MO: Center for Social Development.

Lough, B. J. (2011). International volunteerism in the United States, 2008. *Center for Social Development, 10*(11). Retrieved from www.scribd.com/doc/33744391/ International-Volunteering-from-the-United-States.

Lough, B. J. (2012a). *International Volunteerism from the United States, 2004–2010*. St Louis, MO: Center for Social Development, Washington University.

Lough, B. J. (2012b). *Participatory Research on the Contributions of International Volunteerism in Kenya: Provisional Results*. Strasbourg: International Forum for Volunteering in Development.

Lough, B. J. (2013a). International volunteer service. *Encyclopedia of Social Work, Edition, 20th*. Retrieved November 14, 2016 from www.researchgate.net/publication/ 243963532_International_Volunteer_Service.

Lough, B. J. (2013b). *Measuring and Conveying the Added Value of International Volunteering*. Strasbourg: International Forum for Volunteering in Development.

Lough, B. J. (2016). *Global Partners for Sustainable Development: The Added Value of Singapore International Foundation Volunteers*. Singapore: Singapore International Foundation.

Lough, B., McBride, A. M., & Sherraden, M. (2009). *Perceived Effects of International Volunteering: Reports From Alumni, CSD Research Report 09–10.* St. Louis, MI: Center for Social Development, Washington University.

Lough, B. J., McBride, A. M., Sherraden, M., & O'Hara, K. (2011). Capacity building contributions of short-term international volunteers. *Journal of Community Practice, 19,* 120–137.

Lutzker, D. (1960). Internationalism as a predictor of cooperative behavior. *Journal of Conflict Resolution, 4*(4), 426–430.

Lyons, K. D., & Wearing, S. (eds) (2008). *Journeys of Discovery in Volunteer Tourism: International Case Study Perspectives.* Wallingford: CABI.

MacCannell, D. (1976). *The Tourist: A New Theory of the Leisure Class.* Berkeley, CA: University of California Press.

MacDonald, K. (2014). (De)colonizing pedagogies: An exploration of learning with students volunteering abroad. In R. Tiessen & R. Huish (eds), *Globetrotting or Global Citizenship? Perils and Potentials of International Experiential Learning* (pp. 209–229). Toronto, ON: University of Toronto Press.

MacDonald, K., & Vorstermans, J. (2015). Struggles for mutuality: Conceptualizing hosts as participants in international service learning in Ghana. In M. A. Larsen (ed.), *International Service Learning: Engaging Host Communities.* New York: Routledge.

McBride, A. M., & Sherraden, M. (eds). (2007). Civic Service Worldwide: Impacts and Inquiry. New Newk: M.E. Sharpe.

McBride, A. M., Benítez, C., & Sherraden, M. (2003). *The Forms and Nature of Civic Service: A Global Assessment.* St. Louis, MI: Center for Social Development, Washington University.

McBride, A. M., Sherraden, M., Lombe, L., & Tang, F. (2007). Building knowledge on civic service worldwide. In A. M. McBride & M. Sherraden (eds), *Civic Service Worldwide: Impacts and Inquiry,* Armonk, NY: M.E. Sharpe.

McBride, A. M., Lough, B. J., & Sherraden, M. S. (2012). International service and the perceived impacts on volunteers. *Nonprofit and Voluntary Sector Quarterly, 41*(6), 969–990.

McGloin, C., & Georgeou, N. (2015). 'Looks good on your CV': The sociology of voluntourism recruitment in higher education. *Journal of Sociology, 52*(2), 1–15.

McIntosh, P. (1989). White privilege: Unpacking the invisible knapsack. *Peace and Freedom Magazine,* 10–12. Retrieved January 6, 2015 from http://nationalseedproject.org/white-privilege-unpacking-the-invisible-knapsack.

Mostafanezhad, M. (2013). 'Getting in touch with your inner Angelina': Celebrity humanitarianism and the cultural politics of gendered generosity in volunteer tourism. *Third World Quarterly, 34*(3), 485–499.

Norris, E. M., & Gillespie, J. (2009). How study abroad shapes global careers: Evidence from the United States. *Journal of Studies in International Education, 13*(3), 382–397.

Noy, C. (2004). This trip really changed me: Backpackers' narratives of self-change. *Annals of Tourism Research, 31*(1), 78–102.

Nussbaum, M. (2011). *Creating Capabilities: The Human Development Approach.* Cambridge, MA: Harvard University Press.

O'Sullivan, M., & Smaller, H. (2015). Solidarity or neo-colonialism? The challenge of understanding the impact of ISL on Nicaraguan host communities. In M. A. Larsen (ed.), *International Service Learning: Engaging Host Communities.* New York: Routledge.

Ogden, A. (2008). The view from the verandah: Understanding today's colonial student. *Frontiers: The Interdisciplinary Journal of Study Abroad, 15,* 35–55.

Otoo, F. E. (2013). Motivations of American volunteer tourists in Ghana. *African Journal of Hospitality, Tourism and Leisure, 4*(2), 1–12.

Palacios, C. M. (2010). Volunteer tourism, development and education in a postcolonial world: Conceiving global connections beyond aid. *Journal of Sustainable Tourism, 18*(7), 861–878.

Peace Corps. (2007). *Peace Corps Congressional Budget Justification Fiscal Year 2008: Reaching Around the Globe One Community at a Time.* Washington, DC: Peace Corps.

Perold, H., Graham, L., Mavungu, E., Cronin, K., Muchemwa, L., & Lough, B. (2012). The colonial legacy of international voluntary service. *Community Development Journal, 48*(9), 179–196.

Pires, M. (2000). Study-abroad and cultural exchange programs to Africa: America's image of a continent. *African Issues, 28*(1/2), 39–45.

Plewes, B., & Stuart, R. (2007). Opportunities and challenges for international volunteer co-operation. Paper presented at the IVCO Conference, Montreal, QC.

Powell, S., & Bratović, E. (2006). *The Impact of Long-Term Youth Voluntary Service in Europe: A Review of Published and Unpublished Research Studies.* Brussels: AVSO and ProMENTE.

Raymond, E. M., & Hall, C. M. (2008). The development of cross-cultural (mis)understanding through volunteer tourism. *Journal of Sustainable Tourism, 16*(5), 530–543.

Reas, P. J. (2013). 'Boy, have we got a vacation for you': Orphanage tourism in Cambodia and the commodification and objectification of the orphaned child, *Thammasat Review, 16*, 121–139.

Rehberg, W. (2005). Altruistic individualists: Motivations for international volunteering among adults in Switzerland. *Voluntas: International Journal of Voluntary and Non-profit Organizations, 16*(2), 109–122.

Reynolds, N. P., & Gasparini, J. C. (2015). Saying it doesn't make it so: Do we listen and act when the host community tells us what they want? In M. A. Larsen (ed.), *International Service Learning: Engaging Host Communities.* New York: Routledge.

Roddick, M. (2014). Volunteer stories about international development: Challenges of public engagement campaigns in youth NGOs. In R. Tiessen & R. Huish (eds), *Globetrotting or Global Citizenship? Perils and Potentials of International Experiential Learning* (pp. 258–279). Toronto, ON: University of Toronto Press.

Rundstrom Williams, T. (2005). Exploring the impact of study abroad on students' intercultural communication skills: Adaptability and sensitivity. *Journal of Studies in International Education, 4*(9), 356–371.

Said, E. (1993). The politics of knowledge. In C. McCarthy & W. Crichlow (eds), *Race, Identity and Representation in Education* (pp. 306–314). New York: Routledge.

Sampson, D., & Smith, H. (1957). A scale to measure world-minded attitudes. *Journal of Social Psychology, 45*, 99–106.

Sassen, S. (2002). The repositioning of citizenship: Emergent subjects and spaces for politics. *Berkeley Journal of Sociology, 46*, 4–26.

Schech, S., Mundkur, A., Skelton, T., & Kothari, U. (2015). New spaces of development partnership: Rethinking international volunteering. *Progress in Development Studies, 15*(4), 358–370.

Sen, A. (1999). *Development as Freedom.* Oxford: Oxford University Press.

Sherraden, M. S., Stringham, J., Sow, S. C., & McBride, A. M. (2006). The forms and structure of international voluntary service. *Voluntas: International Journal of Voluntary and Nonprofit Organizations, 17*, 163–180.

Sherraden, M. S., Lough, B., & McBride, A. M. (2008). Effects of international volunteering and service: Individual and institutional predictors. *Voluntas: International Journal of Voluntary and Nonprofit Organizations, 19*(4), 395–421.

Shiratori, S. (2015). What motivates Japan's international volunteers? Categorizing Japan overseas cooperation volunteers (JOCVs). Paper presented at the International Volunteer Cooperation Conference (IVCO), Tokyo, Japan, October 4–7.

Simpson, K. (2004). 'Doing development': The gap year, volunteer-tourists and a popular practice of development. *Journal of International Development, 16*, 681–692.

Simpson, K. (2005). Dropping out or signing up? The professionalization of youth travel. *Antipode, 37*(3), 447–469.

Skelly, J. (2009). Fostering engagement: The role of international education in the development of a global civil society. In R. Lewin (ed.), *The Handbook of Practice and Research in Study Abroad: Higher Education and the Quest for Global Citizenship* (pp. 21–32). New York: Routledge.

Smedley, C. T. (2015). The economic circle: Impacts of volunteerism and service learning on three rural communities in Costa Rica. In M. A. Larsen (ed.), *International Service Learning: Engaging Host Communities.* New York: Routledge.

Sørensen, A. (2003). Backpacker ethnography. *Annals of Tourism Research, 30*(4), 847–867.

Stebbins, R. A., & Graham, R. T. (2004). *Volunteering as Leisure/Leisure as Volunteering.* Wallingford: CABI.

Stukas, A. A. Jr., Clary, E. G., & Snyder, M. (1999). Service learning: Who benefits and why. *Social Policy Report: Society for Research in Child Development, 23*(4), 1–20.

The Onion. (2014, January 28). 6-Day visit to rural African village completed changes woman's Facebook profile picture. *The Onion, 50*(4). Retrieved October 31, 2015 from www.theonion.com/article/6-day-visit-to-rural-african-village-completely-ch-35083.

Thomas, G. (2001). *Human Traffic: Skills, Employers and International Volunteers.* London: Demos:, Retrieved from www.demos.co.uk/files/humantraffic.pdf.

Thomas, L., & Chandrasekera, U. (2014). Uncovering what lies beneath: An examination of power, privilege and racialization in international social work. In R. Tiessen & R. Huish (eds), *Globetrotting or Global Citizenship? Perils and Potentials of International Experiential Learning* (pp. 90–111). Toronto, ON: University of Toronto Press.

Tiessen, R. (2010). Youth ambassadors abroad? Canadian foreign policy and public diplomacy in the developing world. In J. M. Beier & L. Wylie (eds), *Canadian Foreign Policy in Critical Perspective* (chapter 11). Toronto: Oxford University Press.

Tiessen, R. (2011). Global subjects or objects of globalisation? The promotion of global citizenship in organisations offering sport for development and/or peace programmes. *Third World Quarterly, 32*(3), 571–587.

Tiessen, R. (2012). Motivations for learning/volunteer abroad programs: Research with Canadian youth. *Journal of Global Citizenship and Equity Education 2*(1),1–21 [Special Edition].

Tiessen, R. (2014). Career aspirations and experiential learning abroad: Perspectives from Canadian youth on short-term placements. In R. Tiessen & R. Huish (eds), *Globetrotting or Global Citizenship: Perils and Potential of International Experiential Learning* (pp. 77–90). Toronto, ON: University of Toronto Press.

Tiessen, R., & Heron, B. (2012a). Volunteering in the developing world: Perceived impacts of Canadian youth. *Development in Practice, 22*(1), 44–56.

Tiessen, R., & Heron, B. (2012b). Creating global citizens? The impact of learning/volunteer abroad programs. IDRC Final Report.

Tiessen, R., & Huish, R. (2014). International experiential learning and global citizenship. In R. Tiessen & R. Huish (eds), *Globetrotting or Global Citizenship? Perils and Potentials of International Experiential Learning* (pp. 1–20). Toronto, ON: University of Toronto Press.

Tiessen, R., & Kumar, P. (2013). Ethical challenges encountered on learning/volunteer abroad programs for students in International Development Studies: Youth perspectives and educator insights. *Canadian Journal of Development Studies, 34*(3), 416–430.

Tiessen, R., Lough, B., & Cheung, S. (Forthcoming). Agency and the role of partner organizations in the Global South: A theoretical and methodological case for North–South volunteering research collaborations, *Voluntaris: Journal of Volunteer Service.*

Travelanthropist. (2009). Industry snapshot: Volunteer travel abroad – where is it headed? Retrieved from http://travelanthropist.com/2009/02/market-snapshot-volunteer-travel-aboard.html.

UNDP. (2003, October 12). *Volunteerism and Development. Essentials: UNDP Practice Area – Cross Cutting Synthesis of Lessons Learned.* Geneva: United Nations.

Unstead-Joss, R. (2008). An analysis of volunteer motivation: Implications for international development. *Voluntary Action: The Journal of the Institute for Volunteering Research, 9*(1), 12–24.

UNV. (2011). State of the world's volunteerism report 2011: Universal values for global well-being. United Nations Volunteers. Retrieved July 7, 2014 from www.unv.org/swvr2011

UNV (2014). *UN Volunteers: Inspiration in Volunteer Action.* Bonn: UNV. Retrieved from www.unv.org/annual-report-2014.

Urry, J. (1990). *The Tourism Gaze.* London: Sage.

Verge Magazine. (n.d.). Cross-Cultural Solutions: Volunteer or intern abroad. Retrieved from www.vergemagazine.com/program-search/volunteer/cross-cultural-solutions-volunteer-or-intern-abroad.html.

Vodopivec, B., & Jaffe, R. (2012). Save the world in a week: Volunteer tourism, development and difference. *The European Journal of Development Research, 23*(1), 111–128.

Volunteertourismviews. (2013). What is the size of the voluntourism market? Retrieved June 23, 2014 from http://volunteertourismviews.wordpress.com.

VSO (2006). *Raising Awareness.* London: VSO.

VSO (2015). *Valuing Volunteering.* London: VSO.

Wearing, S. (2001). *Volunteer Tourism: Experiences That Make a Difference.* New York: CABI.

Weinmann, S. (1983). *Cultural Encounters of the Stimulating Kind: Personal Development through Culture Shock.* Washington, DC: ERIC Clearing House.

Zemach-Bersin, T. (2007). Global citizenship and study abroad: It's all about U.S. *Critical Literacy: Theories and Practices, 1*(2), 16–28.

Zemach-Bersin, T. (2009). Selling the world: Study abroad marketing and the privatization of global citizenship. In R. Lewin (ed.), *The Handbook of Practice and Research in Study Abroad: Higher Education and the Quest for Global Citizenship* (pp. 303–320). New York: Routledge.

INDEX